TOP SPOTS

Spot the Elusive Quetzal

EVEN NEOPHYTE BIRD WATCHERS CAN'T RESIST THE QUEST FOR THE RESPLENDENT QUETZAL, with its iridescent emerald and sapphire tail feathers twirling in a flirtatious dance.

The Maya, who apparently never made it from Mexico and Guatemala to Costa Rica, considered the quetzal the most sacred of all birds. The quetzal is Guatemala's national bird and the name of its currency, yet you would be hard put to spot the bird's crimson belly in that country's forests or around any Mayan temples, save perhaps those in Honduras at Copán.

Alexander Skutch, birder extraordinaire, calls the resplendent quetzal "the most magnificent of all the trogons… both lovely and irreproachably peaceful." I can vouch for its elusive nature, having listened to its cackling and sometimes melodious call numerous times without catching a glimpse of its precious plumes.

As is typical in the avian world, male quetzals wear the more alluring feathers and use them in elaborate swooping performances to attract mating females. No shrinking violets themselves, the females puff up their ruby-red bellies while inspecting nests made by the males high in deep holes in laurel trees. The male can swirl his tail all he wants, but the female won't settle her wings in his nest unless it's fit for her two blue eggs.

The mating ritual of the quetzal is one of those natural wonders that captivates even jaded wildlife watchers. Come March through June, *pajareros* (bird watchers) of all levels of interest flock to **Monteverde**'s cloud forest, craning their necks to spot a green or blue flash.

Gradually emerging as key quetzal watching spots are the equally mystical cloud forests around the **Cerro de la Muerte**, where a few dedicated souls have protected and nurtured forests of laurels, whose avocado-like fruit is the bird's favorite meal.

Bird watching in general is one of Costa Rica's biggest draws, and persistent travelers are sure to spot toucans, parrots and macaws. But nothing equals the mystique of the resplendent quetzal.

OPPOSITE: Waterfalls fed by constant rain cascade down the sides of mountains and volcanoes.
ABOVE: Birders search the thick rain forest canopy for a glimpse of the elusive quetzal.

Sample the Scenery

SUNDAY AFTERNOONS ARE SACRED TO TICOS, WHO DRESS IN THEIR BEST CASUAL STYLE AND PLAY IN THE PLAZAS, FLOCK TO THE BEACH OR CRUISE THE COUNTRYSIDE. Along the way, they stop for a midday meal that lasts until dusk, sharing bocas, piles of lobster and dishes of homemade cheese.

Naturally, a fair number of cervezas and shots of tequila accompany the meals, and kids play on lawns, in gardens and down mountainside trails while the grownups gossip. The restaurants hosting these celebrations are typically tucked in rural neighborhoods. But my favorite spot happens to be right on the Interamericana Sur, north of San Isidro. Orchids fill the greenhouse garden in front of **Mirador Vista del Valle** (see WHERE TO EAT under SAN ISIDRO DE EL GENERAL, page 199), where the Calderón Vega family have created a rustic family-style dining room that seats 50 persons at most. The glassed-in main room is filled with the tools of farm life and fragile rare orchids. The yards-long counter on the back porch is set against treetops with views into and over the verdant Valle de el General. The aromas of hearty *olla de carne*, *pozol*, *chicharrones* and trout broth are enough to keep hunger pangs sharp through several courses, and the hummingbirds buzzing from flowers to feeders can mesmerize you for hours.

Some of the best Sunday dinner spots are so hidden you're not likely to chance upon them unless invited by a friend. I spent a deliciously extended Sunday afternoon under such fortuitous circumstances at **Rancho Tipico La Finca Chifrijo**, a family ranch at the end of a maze of rugged back roads in Santo Domingo de Heredia. A thatched roof covers the open-air dining room, where parents watch their children playing soccer on a wide grassy field. A long table of young men had accumulated a good collection of Imperial beer bottles by the time we arrived; three hours (and at least one bottle of tequila) later we were posing together for snapshots and joking about book royalties. Jaya, who had worked with a friend in Washington, D.C., gave me one of my first courses in Tico life; now, when I see a parking lot packed with Costa Rican license plates on a Sunday afternoon, I can't help but lose sight of my errand and stop.

Which is how another friend, Joe, discovered **Restaurante Ehecatl** in the far northwest overlooking Bahía Salinas on the Nicaraguan border. The Range Rovers and Jeep Cherokees in the lot were from both sides of the border, and the tables under heaviest demand edged the second-floor balcony atop a 300-m (1,000-ft)-high escarpment looking out to the sea. Joe swears he had the best lobster of his stay in the country at Ehecatl ("God of the Wind" in the Chorotega Indian language), while sharing a few brews with a friend.

Savor Tropical Fruits

GUANÁBANA, MANGO, PAPAYA, BREADFRUIT. ZAPOTE, SAPODILLA AND CAS. Orange, yellow, purple and red mounds of tropical fruits tempt travelers to halt at roadside stands and ponder sidewalk carts in the city.

OPPOSITE: The rolling hills and picturesque landscape of Lake Arenal. ABOVE: Pineapple plantations are common in the warm, dry Guanacaste climate.

Rudy Zamora, a naturalist guide who spends weeks at a time in the rain forest, nearly swoons at the thought of fragrant guanábana ice cream; tropical fruit farmer Peter Aspinall boasts of eating a 11-kg (25-lb) breadfruit (with help, of course). Costa Ricans are justifiably proud of their tropical crops. Their papayas are sweet and smooth; pineapples drip with juice. Fruits are so special to them, Ticos even import glossy red apples from Washington State as Christmas gifts.

I always order a fruit plate at breakfast, or at least a large glass of mixed-flavor juice — orange and papaya, watermelon and mango, guava and blackberry. *Frescas* of ice, water and tamarind paste are the perfect pickup when I'm hot and thirsty. Granted, I've tasted some mighty bitter fruits while experimenting; like most gringos I hope never to be near a nasty-smelling *nance* again. As one New Yorker said repeatedly while sampling dozens of flavors during a tropical fruit farm walk, "It might taste good mixed with vodka."

Like the monkeys swinging in the trees, we humans learn by sampling. Wander through the *mercado* (market) in San José or Cartago and you'll find plenty of educational materials. Buy one of everything that looks interesting, pull out your Swiss army knife and have at it, peeling and slicing and tossing discards to the birds. Keep a lookout for roadside

stands in the country, especially in Orotina, Orosí and the San Isidro valley. The best ones display piles of whatever is in season along with homemade guava jams, jars of *palmitos* (palm hearts) and bags of salty banana chips. An Indian woman in Puerto Viejo once sold me a bag of *pejibayes* boiled in salt water. They didn't do much for me, but these small orange balls that grow on palm trees are considered a delicacy. The most wonderful gift I received while visiting the country was a plate of exotic seasonal fruits, a still-life of waxy yellow ridges of star fruit against the coarse red hairs of a rambutan.

Awaken in the Wilderness

MORNING BEGINS WITH THE MOURNFUL GROANS OF HOWLER MONKEYS STRETCHING IN THE FOREST CANOPY. Branches shuffle as spider monkeys swing through the trees. Toucans croak, parrots shriek, motmots chatter and even slumbering sloths have a hard time staying asleep.

You can't resist greeting the day with a smile when a keel-billed toucan flashes his candy-colored beak beside your shower or a baby monkey overextends his reach and tumbles through the trees. Mornings in the wilderness bring out the best in most folks (unless they've slept uneasily in the land of scorpions and other creepy beings). Fortunately, several wilderness lodges provide mosquito nets, screens, strong coffee and comfortable settings for observing nature's awakening. **Tiskita Lodge** on the far southern Burica Peninsula offers white hawks soaring over tropical fruit trees; **Lapa Ríos** presents scarlet macaws screeching across the Osa Peninsula toward the shimmering sea. Throughout the countryside, beside national parks, in private preserves and along beaches and mountain peaks, hardy hoteliers have created winsome lodgings.

Comfort is a matter of personal preference, of course, and tents lit by oil lamps might not be your perfect perch. But I wouldn't trade sleeping to the patter of rainfall and the endless cicada chant at

Almonds and Corals on the Caribbean Coast for anything — even a hot-water shower. I dream of trying not to toss and turn on a canopy-high platform at **Corcovado Tent Camp** next to the national park of the same name, and will always remember flying clouds of white egrets over the pink-hued lagoon at **Aviarios del Caribe** on the Caribbean.

Howler monkeys are the crowing roosters of Costa Rica; their grumpy barks and hoots awaken guests at the classy **Meliá Conchal** resort in Nicoya, the rain-drenched lodges in Tortuguero and the windswept beaches of the Zona Sur. Coatamundis scratch through the dirt in Monteverde, while hummingbirds buzz through the flowers and bellbirds whistle and bong. Expect to awaken by five most mornings no matter where you sleep. Grab your binoculars and coffee and get set for the show.

OPPOSITE: White-faced capuchin monkeys stop off at local eateries for snacks in Manuel Antonio.
ABOVE: The Reserva Biológica Carara near Jacó is immensely popular with day trippers from San José and cruise ship passengers from Puntarenas.

Cruise the Coast

EXPLORERS HAVE BEEN APPROACHING COSTA RICA BY SEA SINCE WELL BEFORE SPANISH GALLEONS ARRIVED IN 1502. Ecuadorian Indians may have paddled their dugout canoes to the Nicoya Peninsula 1,000 years earlier; pirates and pioneers have been arriving at its ports ever since.

Cruise ships passing through the Panama Canal often use Puerto Caldera on the Pacific or Puerto Moín on the Caribbean as their Central American port of call. But passengers see little of the country. Better by far is a week-long cruise on the *Temptress*, an adventure-oriented ship cruising the Pacific Coast. Each morning the ship docks in a quiet bay, and passengers assemble for hikes before the animals have begun awakening. Birders head off with their scopes and life lists, pursuing motmots, trogons and macaws. Botanists lather up with repellent and debate the names of trees and leaves. Amateur naturalists go for the fun of it, learning to walk slowly and silently while peering upward for crashing branches and fluttering vines —

the signs of monkeys and sloths in the trees. Afternoons are spent on the beach or in the water kayaking, swimming, body surfing, snoozing and hiking to secluded gardens and inns.

The boat has enviable access to blissful, secluded spots, where roads have yet to carve their way through rain forests, around rivers and over canals. Highlights? Golden dawns, lightning-streaked night skies, a walk through town at Bahía Drake. The beach at Manuel Antonio *sans* crowds, and a constant stream of information couched in Tico humor and myths. The opportunity to visit four national parks while unpacking just once, and having the crew dry the mud off your shoes. The chance to meet guides from Tortuguero, waiters from Puntarenas, and crew from all parts of the country. The *Temptress* is Tico-owned and staffed, and passengers gather innumerable insights into the country and its people while sipping gin and tonics at the bar. *Temptress* devotees are a mixed lot of alumni and naturalist groups, seniors on tour, curious independent travelers and entire families. The cruise line offers specialized family sailing, but children seem to enjoy the ride no matter what age their playmates.

Following in the wake of the *Temptress*, Windstar is slated to start offering luxury cruises along the Pacific Coast, and many cruise lines have expanded their Costa Rica itineraries. World Explorer hangs around for an overnight at Limón, and passengers from a dozen or so lines pack Reserva Biológica Carara while at Puntarenas. Cruising appears to be a rising trend. Catch it before the bays get overcrowded.

Ride the Rivers

WHITE WATER FOAMS OVER BOULDERS AND FALLEN TREES IN THE RÍO REVENTAZÓN, ONE OF SEVERAL MIGHTY RIVERS RUSHING DOWN MOUNTAIN PEAKS AND VOLCANIC SLOPES.

River rafting can be as tranquil or terrifying as your heart can handle. For me, the ultimate challenge is the Reventazón, where fully helmeted and swaddled in a life jacket I fell three times into crashing freshwater waves, bouncing off rocks and branches. Braver (and more experienced) rafters get their thrills during the rainy season in the highest reaches of the river. More timid types glide between the forested banks of the Río Pacuare or past howler monkeys and herons on the Corobicí. While Costa Rica's rapids don't compare with those of the Amazon or Zambize, its rivers are accessible and exciting.

Rivers were the original roadways throughout the country, and remain the main thoroughfares to settlements in the northern Caribbean and the south Pacific. The ride through dark canals reminiscent of scenes in the *African Queen* is a rush for birders and naturalists, and entire sections of the coast lie between rivers, mangrove swamps and lagoons. Many forms of watercrafts glide under 30-m (100-ft)-high ajillo trees, used by local inhabitants for constructing canoes. Egrets, ibises, herons, jacunas and kingfishers alight from palo verde trees, cattails and water hyacinths; lizards slither through fallen tree trunks. The best river rides for scenery include the Moín to Tortuguero route and sections of the Corobicí, Savegre and Taracoles.

Mane Attraction: Horseback Riding in the Wilderness

HORSEBACK RIDING IS ONE OF COSTA RICA'S MOST SUBLIME PLEASURES, A CHANCE TO COMMUNE WITH BOTH NATURE AND BEAST.

Horses have been an integral part of the rural landscape for nearly four centuries and are perhaps the best way to experience the Costa Rica of bygone days and the splendid terrain that lies off the beaten path.

As a land of ranches and hardy *sabaneros* (cowboys), the country offers a multitude of equestrian adventures from a one-hour jaunt along a river or beach, to overnight treks into the jungle and across the cordillera. In most cases the rides are conducted by real cowboys who have plenty of other chores besides showing tourists around the hacienda. They're glad to demonstrate how they groom and feed the horses, and their saddle skill is often phenomenal, the

OPPOSITE: The *Temptress* LEFT anchors off Parque Nacional Corcovado. ABOVE: Personable nature guides enhance wilderness experiences all over the country.

kind of riding and roping talent that captures blue ribbons at local rodeos.

The advent of tourist haciendas, especially in Guanacaste province, has vastly increased horseback riding options. Each property offers its own unique trails and equine specialties, and at several ranches its possible to bunk with the sabaneros. **Los Inocentes** near La Cruz offers trips along the boundary of Guanacaste National Park, a dry tropical forest environment where wildlife viewing is often excellent. **Buena Vista Lodge** and **Rincón de La Vieja Mountain Lodge** near Liberia tender horseback trips to the local mud baths or into the wilds of Rincón National Park. **La Pacífica**, a historic hacienda on the highway between Cañas and Liberia, has equestrian trails along the Rio Corobicí and across the open savanna.

However, riding is not limited to ranch country. Several outfitters in Monteverde offer equestrian trips through the cloud forest, including a two-day adventure over the mountains to Arenal Lake and back. In the deep south, you can ride through pristine rain forest or along the empty beaches of the Osa Peninsula and Parque Nacional Corcovado.

A Mountain with an Attitude: Volcán Arenal

COSTA RICA'S MOST SPECTACULAR NATURE SHOW IS THE INCESSANT ERUPTION OF THE VOLCÁN ARENAL, LOCATED ABOUT A THREE-HOUR DRIVE NORTHWEST OF SAN JOSÉ. Nearly every hour the cone-shaped mountain spews forth volcanic ash, rocks, lava and poisonous gas. The pyrotechnics are especially dramatic at night when the red-hot magma gleams like liquid neon flowing down the mountainside.

But it hasn't always been that way. Arenal was dormant for hundreds of years, a jungle-shrouded peak with a tranquil crater that was popular for camping. The surrounding countryside was home to sugar cane plantations, cattle pastures and peaceful villages. Then on July 29, 1968, Arenal erupted with all the fury of a nuclear explosion. The geological chaos lasted for three days, demolishing Pueblo Nuevo and Tabacón villages and killing 78 people, mostly from toxic gases that inundated the slopes after the initial explosion. Things would never be the same again.

Arenal has been erupting ever since, although some periods are more violent than others. Activity in the early 1990s created a second cone at the summit and a massive lava field on the mountain's western flank. Geologists have classified three distinct types of Arenal eruptions based on their sound: "chug" is a series of rhythmic gas emissions from lava fountains; "whoosh" is a minor blast of ash and lava that sounds like a jet plane; "kaboom" is a short but powerful discharge that feels like an earthquake and sounds like a bomb exploding.

Despite its fame (it has appeared in several Hollywood films including Michael Crichton's *Congo*), Arenal is Costa Rica's youngest major volcano. It was formed a mere 3,700 years ago, about the same time as the Egyptians were building their great pyramids and the Olmec civilization was thriving in Mexico. Currently the best place to view Arenal's fire and smoke show is the north flank, especially at Tabacón Hot Springs, and anywhere along the road between Fortuna and Lago Arenal. A trail leads from the national park headquarters and Arenal Observatory Lodge across the 1992 lava field, which still smolders in places.

Mud in Your Eye (and Between Your Toes)

MUD BATHS ARE A NATURAL SPIN-OFF OF COSTA RICA'S INTENSE VOLCANIC ACTIVITY, especially in Parque Nacional Rincón de la Vieja, in the northwest, where access to these thermal wonders is easier (and safer) than at other volcanic zones.

Bubbling hot mud pools inside the park are for eyes (and cameras) only — a sprawling "hot zone" called **Las Pailas** (The Cauldrons) near the ranger station and campground. The smell of rotten eggs, a mix of sulfur dioxide and hydrogen sulfide, fills your nostrils as your move from pool to pool. The mud varies in hue from dark gray to pastel yellow and is alleged to possess amazing healing qualities.

For close encounters of the muddy kind, try the rustic **Buena Vista Lodge** on the park's western flank (access via Cañas Dulces). You can hike, bike or drive (four-wheel drive only) to the local hot springs and mud pools. But the best way to get there is in the saddle of a hacienda horse. Ranch employees scoop scalding hot volcanic mud into buckets and let it cool — but not too much, because one of the most unique sensations of a "mud bath" is the warmth on your skin. You're free to decide how much of your body you want smothered in mud. But locals say you don't get the full medicinal and cosmetic effect unless you cover your entire body, including hair and face. Once the gooey stuff is firmly in place, the next step is letting it dry in the sun until it reaches the consistency of ash or powder. The final phase is slipping into the hot springs or the nearby ice-cold stream. Once the mud is washed away, your skin feels tingly and clean, your muscles feel as if they've been massaged by a professional, and your aching bones are revitalized for the gallop back to the hacienda.

OPPOSITE: Volcán Arenal spews ash and fire hourly, though the pyrotechnics must compete with low-lying clouds and fog. ABOVE: Mud baths revive weary travelers at Buena Vista Lodge, Parque Nacional Rincón de la Vieja.

**YOUR
CHOICE**

The Great Outdoors

Earthquakes, fire-spitting volcanoes, exorbitant rainfall and hurricanes — Costa Rica has them all. Trails and back roads etch the topography up mountains, down rivers, through cloud forests and along the sands of two seas. Visiting the country without getting involved in nature is virtually impossible. Parakeets, hummingbirds, butterflies and moths invade the most urban quarters, and even a walk in a city park reveals sights seldom seen. Every type of adventurer finds challenges worth pursuing, from climbing through cloud forest to the peak of Cerro el Chirripó to diving with whale sharks off Cocos Island. Every level of skill is accommodated as well. First-time river rafters find suitable rapids for moderate thrills; amateur bird watchers get easily hooked.

Hiking is inevitable and completely rewarding; some of the shortest walks bring white-faced monkeys, toucans, giant iguanas and scarlet macaws into easy view. Wildlife-spotting can be as easy as staring for hours at sweet-faced sloths hanging beside your cabin, or as difficult as slogging through pounding rain and slipping down red clay hills for a view of the elusive quetzal. Costa Rica's many national parks, along with a slew of private reserves, offer a range of hiking options you won't find anywhere else outside Africa or the Amazon.

The **National Parks Office** (257-0922 FAX 223-6963 HOTLINE IN COSTA RICA (192, publishes a number of valuable books and maps. Most ranger stations, called *puestos*, have trail maps and printed information. I find it invaluable to hike with a naturalist guide well versed in the local wildlife scene. Many of the best guides work for top-notch adventure companies such as Costa Rica Expeditions, Horizontes and Sun Tours. Returning travelers often arrange their guides personally, choosing ones they've found particularly knowledgeable and amenable. Internet websites have become immensely valuable in learning about the background and training of individual guides (see TRAVEL AGENCIES in TRAVELERS' TIPS, page 242).

Bird watching goes hand in hand with hiking; both activities will find you spending much of your time with neck craned, searching for streaks of color. *Pajareros,* as bird watchers are called, are easily spotted with their gangly tripods, scopes, binoculars and weighty copies of *A Guide to the Birds of Costa Rica,* by Stiles and Skutch, which lists some 70 prime birding spots. Monteverde, Cerro de la Muerte, Tortuguero, Corcovado and Palo Verde are among the favorites, as is Skutch's home base in the San Isidro area. Tortuguero and much of the Caribbean Coast, along with Playa Grande on the Pacific are best for **turtle watching.**

Volcán Arenal explodes over a rain forest waterfall.

Green, ridley and leatherback turtles visit these beaches during certain months to lay their eggs, sometimes arriving by the thousands in *arribadas* (mass arrivals).

Cerro el Chirripó is the best site for **mountain climbing**, with trails leading through lowlands and forests to the peak at 3,819 m (12,526 ft). Chirripó can be climbed in a day in clement weather; rustic accommodations are available near the summit. **Spelunking** is best at Parque Nacional Barra Honda, where a few operators provide gear and guides.

Sporting Spree

The narrow, shoulderless roads make bicycling in Costa Rica difficult, although Ticos in the countryside bike frequently between home and work. You're likely to come across local bike races while traveling back roads on weekends, but only the hardiest traveler would attempt to tour the country on a road bike. **Mountain bicycling**, however, is becoming more popular with adventure tour companies and local lodges, some of which now rent equipment. Lago Arenal and the Volcán Arenal are among the best spots for cruising past waterfalls, forests and birds, and rentals are available. Dirt roads etch the foothills of Cerro de la Muerte and into the rain forest behind Bahía Drake. If you're serious about bicycling, check into the availability of good bikes, helmets and trail maps before your travels. Most beach resorts have bicycle rentals for cruising from cafés to surfing spots.

With all the rivers, lakes, lagoons and two seas beckoning boaters, it's difficult to stay off the water. **Rafting** was one of the first major attractions for travelers to Costa Rica, and it continues to draw in more participants than any other sport. Diehard, death-defying river rafters may not count the country's rivers among the world's best, but there are still plenty of thrills on the Reventazón, Pacuare and Sarapiquí rivers. Hydroelectric dams have harnessed and diminished these rivers'

great force, but rapids of all classes are still available, depending on the season. The Naranjo and Savegre rivers are better suited to those who prefer a bit of a splash along with their scenery, as they are of moderate difficulty. The Río Corobicí is usually calm and excellent for bird and animal watching.

Rafting experts abound, and most lodging providers near the rivers can arrange trips. A good source for general information, and one of the country's leading rafting companies, is **Ríos Tropicales** (233-6455 FAX 255-4354, #130 at Avenida 2, Calle 32, in the big red house one block south of Kentucky Fried Chicken on Paseo Colon, San José; IN THE U.S. P.O. Box 025240, Miami, FL 33122. Other resources are **Aventuras Naturales** (224-0899 or 225-3939, Apdo 812, San José 2050, located between Calles 33 and 35 and Avenida Central, **Sarapiquí**

OPPOSITE: A suspension bridge swings above a fern-filled ravine in the rain forest reserve, Parque Nacional Braulio Carrillo. ABOVE: When they are not dammed to provide electricity, the waters of the Río Corobicí provide more tranquil rafting than the Reventazón or Pacuare rapids.

Aguas Bravas (292-2072 or national and international adventure travel companies (see TRAVEL AGENCIES in TRAVELERS' TIPS, page 242).

Waterways are the main roads in some parts of the country. **Motorboats, canoes and kayaks** glide through the canals in the northern Caribbean and southern Pacific regions, ferrying guests to remote lodgings, and carrying wildlife watchers past herons, egrets, monkeys, turtles and innumerable other creatures and plants. Canoe and kayak rental agencies are not as prevalent as you might hope. The best availability is in Tortuguero, Bahía Drake, Manuel Antonio, the Río Sarapiquí region and Lago Arenal.

Marlin, sailfish, dorado, tarpon, snook, trout and other estimable catches have long attracted serious anglers to great **sport fishing** spots on both coasts and in the interior. Richard Krug, sport fishing columnist for the *Tico Times* and owner of the sport fishing desk in San José's Hotel del Rey (223-4331 FAX 221-0096, is a great source for fishing tips, and can arrange a boat, captain and lodging at prime fishing grounds. Deep sea anglers get most excited about the big ones around Playa Cocos, Tamarindo and Flamingo on the northern Pacific Coast and Manuel Antonio and Dominical to the south. Tarpon and snook are the quarry in the northern Caribbean, where remote lodges exist strictly for their pursuers.

Surfing is legendary as well. Australian and American surfers with sun-bleached hair and bronzed bodies follow the wave action to Jacó, Dominical and secluded beaches in the southern Pacific Coast, Tamarindo and Playa Grande in the north, and Cahuita and Puerto Viejo on the Caribbean Coast. The mother of all surf spots is Playa Pavones, home to one of the longest waves in the world. There is also a good break at the mouth of the river between Playa Grande and Tamarindo.

Windsurfing is best at Lago Arenal, though most big hotels at beach resorts rent equipment as well. SCUBA **diving** off islas Murciélago, Catalina and Caño in the Pacific can be sublimely rewarding when whale sharks, manta rays and tropical fish make a showing; playas Cocos and Ocotal have the best dive shops in the north, while Manuel Antonio and Bahía Drake are good bases in the south. But the best spot by far is Isla del Coco, 300 miles off the southern tip of Costa Rica, where hammerhead, white-tipped and whale sharks are common.

The *Okeanos Aggressor* TOLL-FREE IN THE U.S. ((800) 348-2628 is the best (and frequently the only) transport to Isla del Coco. Operators along both coasts offer SCUBA diving and snorkeling trips to a variety of other destinations.

Guanacaste is the province of *sabaneros* and *vaqueros*, true cowboys who work the cattle ranches on typical criollo horses. **Horseback riding** is available throughout the northwest region; the best places to ride are at the ecolodges in remodeled haciendas such as Los Inocentes, Buena Vista and La Pacífica. Other great rides include those around Lago Arenal and Monteverde cloud forest, as well as Turrialba in the Meseta Central. Horses are available at many beach areas, where sturdy mounts carry their riders past waterfalls, through rain forests and down steep trails to gallop along secluded beaches.

Refined sports such as **golf** are beginning to take hold around the resort areas, and future plans include a number of golf resorts. San José has long had its 18-hole Cariari course, and the Meliá

Conchal in the Pacific northwest opened an 18-hole course designed by Robert Trent Jones in 1997. **Ballooning** over the Volcán Arenal provides an extreme, nearly mystical rush; **Serendipity** (225-6055 can take you.

Soccer is the leading spectator sport, and it is of nearly religious importance in Costa Rica. Every small town has its soccer field, and games between major teams practically shut down the country on Sunday afternoons. Flags billowing outside rural homes are hung in honor of winning provincial teams; the best players go on to contribute to the national team which fares well in international competitions. **Bullfighting** is enormously popular at local fiestas. Given the peaceful nature of the country, the bulls are never slaughtered or even hurt to any bloodletting degree.

OPPOSITE: Divers exploring the waters of Isla de Caño discover their camera has a new attachment. ABOVE: Poles, paddles and motors power ferries along Playa de Coco, Nicoya Peninsula.

The Open Road

Driving can be easily the most thrilling way to see Costa Rica, and often the most dangerous. Road conditions are abysmal, but the scenery is utterly spectacular and worth every pothole and rut. Standard sedans can handle some of the prettiest drives in the Meseta Central, and though I've wandered afar and found every road a worthwhile experience, some of the best drives have been close to San José.

Josefinos are masters of the Sunday drive. At times it seems the entire city has emptied onto roads in every cardinal direction. On the most popular routes there's usually a restaurant or two famed for its country-style Sunday afternoon congregations, and endless variations of scenery, temperature and produce at roadside stands. Highly memorable among my wanderings is a long afternoon's cruise around the Orosí Valley: bougainvillea entwined with pines; rivers splashing building-sized boulders; the **Casa el Soñador**, the Dreamer's House covered in woodcarvings; a young girl shaded under broad coffee leaves. The southern route along Cerro de la Muerte is equally rewarding with its ascent of the Cordillera Talamanca foothills and descent into the agricultural valley of San Isidro de el General. I'd gladly do this drive just for lunch at Mirador Vista del Valle (see SAMPLE THE SCENERY in TOP SPOTS, page 13). City dwellers eagerly drive east towards Orotina, where roadside stands display homegrown cashews, dried papaya, homemade *cajeta* candies and local coffee.

My favorite day trips are the spooky, surreal climbs through fog and mist to the Poás and Irazú volcanoes. I'm on the road by 7 AM, rapidly leaving the city behind as I cruise past small towns and settlements. The roads to both volcanoes begin with a gradual ascent past cattle ranches and farms, twisting and turning past staggering vistas of checkerboard valleys and wisps of smoke from distant chimneys. The temperature drops and wisps of cloud and fog descend toward the treetops. Near the end of the ascent the landscape grows ever more eerie, stripped of greenery by lava flows and ash. If my timing is right, the parking lots at the edge of the volcanoes are empty, and I walk in solitude toward smoldering craters. With luck, I've beaten the fog that descends with unpredictable frequency upon the volcanoes, and am able to clearly see the vast expanses of barren landscape while shuffling through fields of ash. The air is heavy with the smell of sulfur, and a few hardy birds chirp in the background. More often than not a fog begins to settle over the landscape as I'm wandering, adding an edgy uneasiness to the experience as I wonder if I'll ever find my car. Then the descent begins, through raindrops and clouds back to the sunny valley.

Longer road trips are even more rewarding, but a four-wheel drive is essential for true road warriors. With sturdy tires and high suspension to support your wanderings, drivers can master rutted dirt and mud, slippery bridges and shallow river crossings leading into the wilderness. Among the best long drives are the route through the Parque Nacional Braulio Carrillo to the Caribbean Coast, and the Pan-American Highway north through the vast cattle ranges in Guanacaste. Potholes, sandy roads and terrifying one-lane bridges greet those meandering along the Pacific Coast from the Nicoya to Osa peninsulas. All these drives require patience, fortitude and flexibility and are best approached as adventures unto themselves rather than simply a means for getting from point A to point B.

Backpacking/Budget Travel

Costa Rica has a higher standard of living than its bordering countries, and is a far more expensive vacation destination overall. Yet there are ways to curb expenses, as budget travelers hanging on for months here can attest.

The first rule for saving money is to avoid travel in peak seasons and on holidays. Travelers on extended stays typically hole up in low-cost regions and wait out the hordes at more popular spots. The best time of year for all

travelers is just before or after the dry season, which typically lasts from November to April. The rainy season, called the "green season" in Costa Rica, has definite drawbacks the longer the rains last. But you may experience dry days and even weeks in May, June and October and be able to take advantage of lower room rates.

Certain areas, especially along the beaches, are established budget destinations with a fervent following. Cahuita and Puerto Viejo on the Caribbean Coast are the epitome of backpacker havens, offering space in cheap cabinas and private homes. Montezuma and Brasilito are the magnets in the North Pacific, while Jacó and small towns south of Dominical draw their share of hangers-on. Surfers and beach dwellers with plenty of time head far south to playas Zancudo and Pavones, close to the Panama border. All of these areas have upscale accommodations as well, but specialize in inexpensive and moderate options. For lodging slightly above the rock-bottom range you can get cold-water showers, sturdy window screens and mosquito netting, dependable locks and clean sheets. Youth hostels are not as common here as in Europe or the United States. (For information on availability see YOUTH HOSTELS in TRAVELER'S TIPS, page 247.)

At many budget destinations, food is half the price of what you find in Manuel Antonio, San José or the resort towns. But your choices can be severely limited. Stick with rice, beans, chicken and fish on the coast and you'll stretch your dining dollars farthest.

Despite the prevalence of parks and reserves, camping isn't as easy as you might think. Inclement weather is a serious drawback, and tents are a must for any length of stay. Many of the national parks have at least rustic facilities and welcome a certain number of campers; for easiest access, arrange permits in advance

A San José-bound bus bumps and jiggles its way along a country road.

through the **National Park Office** (283-8004 or 283-8094 FAX 283-7118 or 283-7343 HOTLINE IN COSTA RICA (192. You may also be able to sleep and eat at the park ranger stations, especially during low season.

The parks and reserves of Monteverde, Rincón de la Vieja and Corcovado are particularly popular with experienced backpackers. Getting around by bus is cheap and not terribly difficult, at least between major destinations. It is, however, time consuming. Just as those with the colones to rent cars must deal with horrid road conditions, bus passengers must adjust to flat tires, breakdowns and accidents. As a rule the first-class buses are comfortable, relatively clean and safe. Travel off the beaten path, however, and you deal with old rattletrap contraptions of the ancient school bus genre. The beds of pickup trucks serve as local transport in some rural areas, and hitching a ride from passersby is common in these areas. When hitching, remember that drivers are more likely to stop for travelers who look sane and pleasant. Costa Ricans despise confrontation and avoid potentially unpleasant situations. Practice your Spanish manners liberally, thanking drivers and showing consideration to fellow passengers.

Air transport to remote regions is worth considering even if you're on a slim budget, especially if your time is limited. Small planes commute between the cities and wildly remote areas, and the fares are quite reasonable. You may end up on a puddle jumper landing by beaches, lagoons and even cemeteries en route to your final destination, but it's great fun to see civilization yield to wilderness from above.

Boats of all sorts ferry passengers to bays, towns and settlements along rivers and lagoons. Most travelers reach Tortuguero via river ferry from Moín, spotting herons, Cayman and Jesus Christ lizards along the route. Several wilderness camps near remote national parks are best accessed by boat, though some have private airstrips.

Living It Up

EXCEPTIONAL HOTELS
Big, lavish resorts are not Costa Rica's style, though they are starting to shape the environment of picturesque bays in Guanacaste and Nicoya. Small, one-of-a-kind hotels are more common and run the gamut from truly luxurious architectural gems to quirky wilderness hideaways.

San José has dozens of unique inns with less than 40 rooms, many former mansions and handsome residences. The **Grano de Oro** is the standard bearer for interior detail, amiable service and fantastic food. **La Casa Verde de Amón** harks back to the coffee baron era with its European antiques and sun porches, while **L'Ambience** has long been the city's most elegant mansion. Several deluxe inns dot the countryside in the Meseta Central, many of them near enough the airport to make convenient bases. **El Cafetal** and **Finca Rosa Blanca** combine exceptional architecture with generous service.

Casa Turire near Turrialba is Costa Rica's best country inn, while **Sapo Dorado** beats out the competition in Monteverde. The tendency toward intimate elegance is reflected throughout the Pacific Coast, at **Escaleras Inn** in Dominical, classy **Capitán Suizo** in Tamarindo and **Lapa Ríos** on the Osa Peninsula. Manuel Antonio has a half-dozen sublime inns, including **Makanda by the Sea**, and a plethora of less-expensive places tucked into the forest; I'm particularly fond of **Villas Nicolas**.

Though often not particularly luxurious by urban standards, wilderness lodges are often the best and most comfortable escapes from normality. **Tiskita Lodge** in the Zona Sur, **Buena Vista Lodge** in Guanacaste and the **Arenal Observatory Lodge** are all exceptional. When it comes to coastal resorts, nothing touches the classy **Meliá Conchal**.

EXCEPTIONAL RESTAURANTS
Stumbling upon truly outstanding dining experiences is a challenge in Costa Rica, often well rewarded. One of my favorite

top-quality restaurants is found off a sandy road at a backwater Caribbean beach in Cahuita. **Casa Creole's** candlelight and crystal ambiance befits its outstanding cuisine, which uses the freshest lobster, cheeses and homemade patés to woo diners from faraway cities. Many of the more innovative restaurants are located in hotels, from the **Sapo Dorado** in Monteverde to **El Velero** in Playa Hermosa and **Karoles and Plinio's** in Manuel Antonio. San José has the best selection of international restaurants — try the continental cuisine at **Grano de Oro**, and the Peruvian ceviche at **Machu Picchu**.

Family Fun

Children find multiple distractions no matter where they travel in Costa Rica. How can they resist toucans, monkeys, snakes and butterflies? The Serpentarium in San José offers a great introduction to poisonous snakes, scorpions and other hazardous creatures for which kids love to be on the lookout. Animal refuges give everybody a chance to get close to boas, sloths, toucans and even jaguars; some small inns have menageries of animals saved from poachers, road accidents and cruelty.

Adventures are endless, and any child with an imagination will keep *Jurassic Park* in mind. Michael Crichton based his believable dinosaur theme park in Costa Rica; some scenes in the movie were filmed from above Isla del Coco and the Pacific Coast. Depending on age and ability, kids have a great time on nature hikes and boat rides. They can saddle up with real *vaqueros* on cattle ranches in Guanacaste, fantasize at length while watching Volcán Arenal spew fire and rocks, and acquire a healthy, knowledgeable respect for rain forests, cloud forests, rivers and wildlife. Parents: bring plenty of film and quick-dry shorts and socks; encourage both caution and curiosity; carry sunscreen and insect repellent everywhere; and watch your kids grow.

Cultural Kicks

Costa Rica has few of the cultural aspects that typically draw travelers to Central America; however, San José has several galleries and museums worth visiting. The **Museo Nacional** presents a good overview of Costa Rica's history and indigenous peoples. The **Museo de Oro** and **Marco Fidel Tristan Museo de Jade** both showcase pre-Columbian treasures. The **Museo de Arte Costarricense** is housed in San José's original airport terminal in Parque Sábana, and offers the best overview of traditional murals, religious paintings and contemporary art. A blocks-deep brick and golden stucco brewery in one of the city's prettiest neighborhoods houses the **Centro Nacional de la Cultura**.

Small regional museums are beginning to organize throughout the countryside, though most are poorly staffed and have erratic hours. A must for history buffs is the **La Casona Hacienda** at Parque Nacional Santa Rosa in Guanacaste.

A monument marks a battleground at Parque Nacional Santa Rosa.

The restored nineteenth century hacienda houses a museum explaining Costa Rica's most important war, the battle against American intruder William Walker and his band of mercenaries. A monument behind the museum commemorates the battle against Walker and the skirmish against the Somoza regime from Nicaragua.

The most significant archeological site in the country is **Guayabo** near Turrialba in the Meseta Central. Sprawling *calzados* (roads), well-engineered aqueducts, stone carvings and a few small structures are the visible remains of a city archeologists believe was begun around 1400 BC.

Architectural highlights include the restored coffee baron mansions of San José, the handsome **Teatro Nacional**, restored haciendas in Guanacaste and some of the designs used for new country inns and hotels. Many of the dreamers who have created one-of-a-kind hostelries have used imaginative techniques to maximize wilderness viewing and the use of local tropical hardwoods.

Shop till You Drop

Handpainted miniature *carretas* (ox carts) are Costa Rica's souvenir cliché, followed by mountain-grown coffee and tropical wood boxes, plates, bowls, picture frames and furniture. Both folk and fine arts are receiving unprecedented attention, and the selection of memorable items has grown considerably. San José has the best selection of shops and galleries, including **Atmósfera** and the art and wood sculpture galleries near Parque Morazán. Some of the best quality can be found at hotel gift shops: Anne Marie's in the Hotel Don Carlos is a traditional favorite for bits of everything; the Grano de Oro displays unusual paintings, enamel ware, banana-paper stationery and a few masks; the Meliá Cariari has a modest array of sleek wooden boxes and puzzles by master craftsmen.

Woodcrafts in general are the best buy in Costa Rica. Artists including Barry Biesanz (who has a workshop in Escazú and a shop in San José) and Jay Morris have perfected woodcraft and turned it into an art form; their rounded, beveled and highly polished boxes are gorgeous. The hardwoods themselves are so lovely that some shops sell charts of wood samples, with small, slick squares of rosewood, mahogany, teak and purpleheart wood. Given the endangered status of many precious tropical forest trees, much of the woodcraft is done from trees felled by nature or wood salvaged from old buildings.

Regional crafts and traditional folk arts are also gaining attention. The Chorotega peoples of the Guanacaste region have long produced terra-cotta pottery with fascinating animal and human motifs. The water jars, pots and figurines are fired in outdoor ovens and burnished with river stones which give a gleam unlike any glazed finish. Guaitíl, a small village near Santa Cruz on the Nicoya Peninsula, is the center for this pottery. You'll see stands set up along the highway between Santa Cruz and Liberia, where hammocks hang in front of the pottery displays. The Boruca peoples of the Zona Sur make fanciful and sometimes frightening balsa wood masks, which are used during the Fiesta de los Diablitos in December. They are also noted weavers, creating textiles from cotton dyed with plants, mud and mollusk shells. Their work can be found at The Drake Bay Wilderness Camp, Tiskita and the Mirador del Valle restaurant near San Isidro. Caribbean Bribrí and KéköLdi groups weave baskets and mats from natural fibers; women from the groups visit Cahuita and Puerto Viejo to sell their wares at local shops and street stands.

Savvy shoppers keep an eye out for exceptional folk art collections displayed in various lodges and restaurants. Among the best displays are those at Toad Hall by Lago Arenal, Cassem Gallery in Monteverde and Buena Nota in Manuel Antonio.

Elaborately painted *carretas*, ox carts — a specialty of the highland craft village of Sarchí — are displayed in parades and exhibitions in provinces throughout the country.

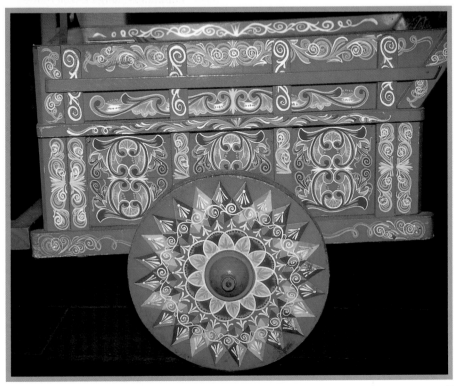

Sarchí in the Meseta Central is the crafts hub of the country, with rows of warehouse-sized shops selling miniature ox carts, wood and leather furniture and all sorts of souvenirs.

Short Breaks

San José is the perfect base for day trips to several of Costa Rica's biggest attractions. Day trippers can easily fill a week with tours to the Poás and Irazú volcanoes, white-water rafting on the Pacuare or Reventazón rivers, mountain biking around Lago Arenal, or riding in a sky-high tram over the Braulio Carrillo forest canopy. Visitors hopping about the country typically drop in and out of the city several times during their stays, turning in their rental cars, catching short flights to outlying areas, or meeting up with travel companions.

Travel on regional airlines makes it possible to visit beach areas on quick jaunts; Quepos and Parque Nacional Manuel Antonio make a good combination for hotels, restaurants, beaches and wildlife hiking.

The Meseta Central is filled with parks and small villages and can be seen in two days or more. In fact, I once covered most of the country's highlights in an exhausting 10-day drive, though I don't recommend this approach for vacationers. Better to pick an interest (hiking, bird watching, surfing, fishing) and fly or drive to one or two of the best spots.

Festive Flings

Though Costa Ricans are not, as a rule, fervently religious, they make great use of Catholic holidays and saint's feast days for celebrations. **Christmas**, the highlight of the year, starts early. Decorations fill San José's shops by early November, while ornament and gift salesmen trod door to door in rural areas with their glittering temptations. December 15 marks the beginning of **Las Posadas**, recreating the search for a birthplace for the Baby Jesus. Candlelit processions, fireworks and partying surround the Christmas season, which culminates in San José's largest parade and fiestas during the week after Christmas and a big bash and dance in the Parque Central on **New Year's Day**.

The most important religious event of the year is the **Fiesta de la Virgen de los Angeles** at the basilica in Cartago on August 2. Pilgrims arrive from throughout the country, walking on their knees down the long cement plaza in front of the church to honor the country's patron saint.

Ash Wednesday and **Semana Santa** (the week before Easter) are marked by religious processions, as are the feast days of patron saints in small towns.

Limón's **Carnaval** is the biggest bash in the country, and has nothing to do with Lent or Easter. Instead, it is celebrated in October, around Columbus Day, and consists of a riotous week-long celebration in the streets. Puntarenas also celebrates Carnaval; it's usually scheduled in November while the schoolchildren are on holiday.

El Día de la Independencia on September 15 is the most important national holiday, with **Día de los Trajabadores** (Labor Day) on May 1 running a close second. There are

17 official holidays, or *días feriados* in Costa Rica when banks, shops and businesses shut down and everyone takes to the countryside or beach.

Guanacaste is one of the best areas for regional celebrations. Most fiestas include bloodless bullfights, rodeos, folk dancing and parades. The best parties are held during the **Fiesta de Cristo Negro de Esquipulas** in Santa Cruz on January 15, and throughout the province (especially in Liberia) on the anniversary of Guanacaste's annexation on July 25.

OPPOSITE: The aerial tramway at Parque Nacional Braulio Carrillo gives day trippers an overview of the rain forest. ABOVE: A team of oxen pulls a workaday *carreta*. RIGHT: An Easter procession leads to more boisterous celebrations in Nicoya.

In the Meseta Central, **Día del Boyero** (Ox Cart Drivers' Day) is celebrated on the second Sunday of March in Escazú, where the streets are filled with brightly painted carts with designs representing the various provinces of the country. **Juan Santamaría**, Costa Rica's national hero, is honored with a parade in Alajuela on April 11. The **Fiesta de los Diablitos** is one of the few indigenous celebrations and can be witnessed in the Buenos Aires region in the Zona Sur during February.

Galloping Gourmet

Costa Rica is not known for brilliant cuisine; it takes some time to get acquainted with the most flavorful selections and find the best cooks. *Gallo pinto* (black beans and rice) is the ubiquitous national dish, served alone, with eggs or cheese at breakfast or with meat and fried plantains for lunch and dinner. The next step up is the one-dish mix of beans, rice and meat, fish or vegetables called *el casado* (the married one). Tropical fruits abound, and restaurants are serving more export-quality seafood and beef. Seasonings are used sparsely; you won't find fiery hot *jalapeño* or *habanero* chilies here. Instead, the daily diet is rather bland — and healthy, except for the fondness for frying nearly everything.

APPETIZERS OR *BOCAS*

Some of the best treats are the snacks and side dishes served in neighborhood restaurants and bars. *Patacones,* refried plantain patties, are great when cooked fresh, salted and topped with sour cream, which also garnishes corn pancakes called *chorreadas*. Deep fried pork skins, or *chicharrones*, inspire thirst and rising cholesterol, as do salty banana chips. Sandwiches are called *arreglados; empenadas,* turnovers filled with beans, potatoes, cheese or meat are a better choice.

FRUITS

Tropical fruits are varied, abundant and delicious: pineapple, watermelon, bananas and papayas frequently appear on *platos de frutas* (fresh fruit plates), which you can order any time of day. Costa Ricans mark the seasons by what's ripe at the time — mangoes in March, *jocotes* (also called mombins or hogfruit) in September, apples imported from Washington State at Christmas. Fruits are used in *frescas*, fruit drinks with water and sugar, ice creams, and sauces for fish and meat.

VEGETABLES

Oh, what one wouldn't give for a huge tossed salad after a few weeks in Costa Rica. Vegetables are nonentities here, unless you count the shredded cabbage and pale tomatoes served with nearly every dish. The ubiquitous *plátanos* (plantains), related to the banana, are actually a vegetable but they become sweet as they ripen and cook. Yucca and chayote, both bland roots, are also common.

The great exception is *palmitos* or hearts of palm, each of which comes from the heart, or trunk, of a small tree. Palmitos are peeled and cooked, then served chilled as salads; they are not cheap, but they do satisfy the craving for something at least pale green. Canned and bottled *palmitos* make good souvenirs.

Don't get excited if you see pasta primavera or steamed veggies on a menu — they're usually made with carrots, cabbage and perhaps a bit of cauliflower. Some restaurants have their own vegetable and herb gardens or buy from small organic farms — if you find such a place eat all you can handle.

SEAFOOD
Though Costa Rica has two coasts, seafood is surprisingly scarce and often unimaginatively prepared. Highland restaurants tend to favor *corvina* (sea bass) served with *casados*. Far better is *ceviche,* fresh fish marinated with lime juice and spices. Since the fish is essentially raw, be careful where you eat it — stick to places on the coast or exceptional San José restaurants. Sport fishing is big on the Pacific Coast; if you're staying in a fishing lodge you're sure to sample dorado, wahoo, marlin and the occasional swordfish. Whole fried fish is common on both coasts. Shrimp and lobster are available but cost dearly — most are exported.

MEAT
Much of Costa Rica's rain forest was destroyed for cattle grazing in the early 1900s, and Costa Rican beef is excellent if you can get the export-quality cuts served in more expensive hotels and restaurants. Here you'll find thick, tender fillets cooked to order. In Costa Rica, meat ordered *rojo,* or rare, is barely cooked; though I prefer rare meat, I usually order mine *medio* (medium) and get what I want. The beef served in *sodas* is usually thin, tough and not worth eating. My favorite beef dish is *bisteck* or *lomito encebollado,* a tender beefsteak marinated with Lizano sauce (see SAUCES below) and grilled or sautéed with sliced onions.

In Costa Rican homes and typical restaurants, meat is usually used as an ingredient in stew including the satisfying *olla de carne* (simmered beef and vegetables) and *chiprio,* a mix of chicharrones, onions and beans.

Chicken roasted over a wood fire (*pollo de la leña)* is fragrant and filled with juices; *arroz con pollo* is a filling mix of rice, carrots, celery, onion and chicken slivers.

SAUCES
The key to typical daily Costa Rican dishes is Lizano sauce, a bottled marinade of vegetables and spices. Ask for it as you would salsa or soy sauce and sprinkle it liberally on nearly everything. Pepper sauce is also common; for a spicy kick ask for *chilero,* a marinade of onions, peppers and vinegar. There are also some wonderful bottled sauces made from papaya, mango and lime, though most restaurants shun them. The tomato, onion and chili salsa common in other Latin American countries is nonexistent here, except in Mexican restaurants.

CHEESES
With so much cattle grazing about the countryside, it's no surprise that Costa Rica has great cheese. Many of the best cheddars and *queso blanco,* a low-fat white cheese with the consistency of tofu, come from the Monteverde Quaker's and the Italian communities in San Vito. *Natilla* is sour cream of a thin consistency.

RICE AND BREAD
Rice is to Costa Rica what pasta is to Italy — an absolute essential for any meal and the base for regional dishes. Most menus list rice with chicken, palm hearts, pork or fish, called *arroz con pollo, arroz con palmito, arroz con cancho* or *arroz con pescado.* Beans are usually served on the side rather than blended with the rice mix as they would be in *gallo pinto.* Rice is also used in *arroz con piña,* a refreshing drink of blended rice and pineapple.

Tortillas are not the staple item you might expect, but small corn tortillas are served with some dishes. Sliced white bread is used for sandwiches and toast; cross your fingers and ask for *pan integral* if you want whole wheat.

DESSERTS, SWEETS AND PASTRIES
Costa Ricans love their sweets, and every town has at least one *panaderia* or bakery selling cookies, Danish-like sweet rolls (called *pan dulce)* and fancy cakes (called

Colorful and friendly toucans appear in the most unlikely spots — such as right outside your shower.

queques). *Tres leches*, or three-milk cake, is rich, moist and sweet. Though coconut is the typical ingredient in *flans* (custards), some places also serve wonderful flans made with mangoes, papaya or blackberries.

Candies shaped like Christmas trees, hearts, dolls and animals are made of *cajeta*, a sticky sweet paste of condensed milk and sugar. Nougat bars with almonds or macadamias are great treats and travel well.

The local ice creams are exceptional, especially those made with tropical fruits. Don't miss the *guanábana*, *coco*, or *mango* blends.

BEER, WINE AND LIQUOR
Imperial and Bavaria beer (*cerveza*) seem to be the national drink, though more hard core imbibers prefer *guaro*, the local firewater made from fermented sugar cane. Café Rica, a coffee liqueur similar to Kahlua is served alone or with milk. Local wines are to be avoided; stick with the more inspired, imported Chilean and Argentinean wines.

JUICES AND DRINKS
Costa Rica's abundant tropical fruits make extraordinary fresh juices. Try guava, mora or pineapple, or ask to have a tropical flavor blended with fresh orange juice. *Refrescos*, or simply *frescos* are made of fruit blended with water or milk — nothing tastes better after a hot hike. Carbonated sodas are called *gaseosas*.

COFFEE
The *grano de oro*, coffee, is Costa Rica's great pride and a major export crop. Few travelers leave the country without several kilos packed in their bags. The coffee served in hotels and restaurants may not be the best, however. Export coffee fetches a much higher price than that made from rejected beans. *Café con leche* is served with hot milk; ask for *sin leche* or *negro* if you want it black. Some places serve coffee ground with sugar; when purchasing bags to take home make sure they don't say *con azúcar* unless you like sweet coffee.

Café Britt is the leading label and has become so synonymous with vacationing shoppers that the company even runs daily tours of its plantations and processing plants. Café Britt coffeehouses are springing up around San José and serve cappuccino, espresso and flavored coffee. Though I typically carry a few bags of Britt home (it's the only good decaffeinated brand), I like to experiment with the numerous labels now appearing on grocery store shelves. Sunburst, though far more expensive than the rest, is truly wonderful; Café Zeus, one of the least-expensive, is among my favorites and comes in small bags that make great gifts.

Special Interests

Travelers typically have some form of education on their minds when visiting Costa Rica. Birders are intent on expanding their life lists, and surfers count on mastering a north break. Botanists go wild over rare orchids; biologists go bats over butterflies. Students abound. At least one-quarter of Costa Rica's guests attend universities or language schools. There is no shortage of special interests to pursue.

LANGUAGE CLASSES
Spanish language schools abound in San José and around the country, especially at Monteverde, the cultural center of the northwest. The quality of education varies; it helps to talk with other students before committing to a course. Most offer the opportunity for students to live with Costa Rican families for full immersion, and most tailor their classes to your level of ability. **UCEEPE (Union of Spanish Language Centers)** (225-2495 FAX 225-4665, Apdo 1001, San Pedro 2050, has a list of schools for foreign students. The following schools have been recommended by students:

Academia Tica (234-0622 FAX 233-9393, Apdo 1294, Guadalupe, San José 2100, offers language and culture courses that can be extended indefinitely, and is

popular with German-speaking visitors.
**Central American Institute for
International Affairs** (255-0859 FAX 221-
5238, C/o Educators, Apdo 10302, San
José; IN THE U.S. ((714) 527-2918 FAX (714)
826-8752, P.O. Box 5095, Anaheim,
CA 92814, mixes culture, including
dance lessons, with language study.

Centro Panamericano de Idiomas (265-
6866 FAX 265-6213 E-MAIL *cpi@huracan.cr*,
Apdo 161, San Joaquin de Flores, Heredia
3007, IN THE U.S. ((409) 693-8950 TOLL-FREE
(800) 347-8087, has group and private
classes and a one-day "survival course"
for tourists. The **Instituto Británico**
(234-9054 FAX 253-1894, Apdo 8184, San
José 1000, adds field trips to museums,
archaeological sites and conservation
projects. The **Instituto de Español Para
Extranjeros** (225-5878 FAX 225-2907,
Apdo 1380, San José 1000, has intensive
courses through the Universidad
Autónoma de Centroamérica. **Pura Vida**
(237-0387 FAX 237-0387, Apdo 890,
Heredia 3000; IN THE U.S. ((714) 534-0125
FAX (714) 534-1201, P.O. Box 730, Garden
Grove, CA 92642, offers intensive
language classes with cultural instruction,
classes for children and a three-day
"survival course" for beginners.

BIRDING
Scarlet macaws, quetzals, trogons and
toucans lure bird watchers to Costa Rica's
rain forests and isolated beaches. At least
850 species of birds have been spotted
within the country's borders, and birders
gripping their life lists and binoculars are
common sights on most hikes. Serious
bird watchers are best off having a tour
company prepare an individual itinerary
with a driver and a specialist guide
through Horizontes, Costa Rica
Expeditions or Costa Rica Sun Tours
(see TRAVEL AGENCIES in TRAVELERS' TIPS,
page 242). Birding is included on most
country tours, but not all address the
subject with a high level of expertise.
Ask in advance about the availability
of specialist guides when signing up for
a tour. There is usually a birding guide
on board the *Temptress* cruise ship, and
lodges in prime birding spots such a

Monteverde, Cerro de la Muerte and the
Corcovado National Park can arrange
guided hikes.

BUTTERFLIES
The dazzling blue morpho is but one of
about 3,000 species of butterflies found
in Costa Rica. Net-covered butterfly
gardens and farms filled with
flowering tropical plants are beginning
to appear alongside hotels and parks
throughout the country. The best
gardens include educational displays
on the emergence of butterflies from
their larvae and chrysalis, and plenty
of varieties of fluttering adults. Several
butterfly farms are located close
enough to San José to be included on
day trips; check out the **Spirogyra**
butterfly farm near the Villa Tournon
Hotel or the **Butterfly Farm** in La
Guácima de Alajuela. Among the best
butterfly exhibits in outlying areas
are **Selva Verde** in Chilmate in the
Sarapiquí region, the **Butterfly Garden**
in Monteverde and the garden at **Villas
Lapas** near Jacó on the Pacific Coast.

MOTORCYCLING
Diehard bikers eye Costa Rica's roads
longingly, imagining the thrills involved
in guiding a motorcycle along tortuous
paths. **Tour Harley** (/FAX 253-3451 offers

Torch ginger catches and holds the eye in Parque
Nacional la Amistad.

guided Harley tours to outlying areas; they don't rent bikes without a guide.

SURFING

Surfers tend to head out on their own for legendary surf spots on the Caribbean and Pacific coasts, piling their boards atop rented four-wheel drives. The North Pacific Coast and Nicoya Peninsula have the greatest number of surf spots within close proximity to each other, and you're sure to see wave riders around playas Naranjo, Tamarindo and Nosara. South of Puntarenas surfers head for the camaraderie and breakers at playas Jacó and Hermosa and at Dominical. True fanatics continue south past Golfito to Playa Pavones, a lonely outpost with an extraordinary left break. On the Caribbean surfers shoot the curl at several points between Cahuita and Manzanillo, making sure to ride the big ones at Salsa Brava.

GARDEN VISITS

Orchids, heliconia, bromeliads and an abundance of tropical plants thrive in Costa Rica's climate. The most famous of all the nation's gardens is the **Wilson Botanical Gardens** at the **Las Cruces Biological Station** south of San Vito (see SAN VITO in THE ZONA SUR, page 200). The 10-hectare (25-acre) gardens were created by Robert and Catherine Wilson with the help of Brazilian landscape designer Roberto Burle-Marx. Over 7,000 species of tropical plants, including 700 species of palms, create a gorgeous setting attracting hummingbirds, tanagers, toucans, trogons and a bounty of butterflies. **Jardín Botánico Lankaster** near San José has 10.5 hectares (26 acres) of landscaped gardens including a miniature bamboo forest, a cactus and succulent garden, several palm groves and vivid clusters of heliconia. Over 800 species of orchids are showcased in greenhouses and along paths through the gardens; the best time to see them in bloom is from February to May. Many of the hotels, lodges, restaurants and private reserves throughout the country are landscaped with impressive gardens; of particular interest are the acres of tropical fruit tree orchards at **Tiskita Lodge** in the

Zona Sur, the heliconia collections at **Tortuga Lodge** and **Laguna Lodge** in Tortuguero and the orchids at **Casa Orquideas** near Golfito. Plant lovers won't want to miss the fanciful topiaries in **Zarcero** and the overview of the forest canopy from the **Teléferico del Bosque Lluvioso** (Rainforest Aerial Tram).

VOLUNTEERING

Nearly every worldwide conservation agency is active in Costa Rica. Many rely on volunteers to keep projects running. Some count migrating sea turtles in Tortuguero; others keep an eye on scarlet macaws above the Osa Peninsula. Students from all over the world pursue volunteering opportunities in marine biology, botany and dozens of fields related to nature. Many programs are affiliated with colleges and universities. Agencies that work with volunteers include:

The **Organization for Tropical Studies** (OTS) (240-6696 FAX 240-6783 E-MAIL oet@cro.ots.ac.cr, Apdo 676-2050, San Pedro, San José, is a nonprofit consortium of more than 50 universities and research institutes. OTS oversees three prime biological stations with research facilities: La Selva in the Sarapiquí region; Palo Verde in Guanacaste; and Las Cruces, which includes the Wilson Botanical Gardens, in the southern zone.

The **Caribbean Conservation Corporation** (CCC) ((904) 373-6441 TOLL-FREE (800) 678-7853 E-MAIL ccc@cccturtle. org, P.O. Box 2866, Gainesville, FL 32602, enlists paying volunteers, students and researchers to assist with conservation efforts, such as tagging sea turtles.

Earthwatch TOLL-FREE (800) 776-0188 FAX (617) 926-8532 E-MAIL info@ earthwatch.org, has several ongoing projects in the country.

Many private nature reserves and ecolodges welcome (and depend upon) volunteer help with clearing trails, watching out for poachers and cataloging wildlife in the area. Ask about opportunities to live in the wild in exchange for your labors at **Genesis II** in the Cerro de la Muerte area, **Lapa Rios** on the Osa Peninsula, and **Finca Brian y Milena** in Dominical.

Taking A Tour

Guided tours abound, and there are several excellent international and Costa Rican companies covering a broad variety interests.

ADVENTURE
Tours combining mountain biking, whitewater rafting, hiking, kayaking and other activities are becoming more popular, and are offered by: **Costa Rica Connection** ((805) 543-8823 TOLL-FREE (800) 345-7422 FAX (805) 543-3626; **Remarkable Journeys** ((713)721-2517 TOLL-FREE (800) 856-1993 FAX (713) 728-8334; **Holbrook Travel** TOLL-FREE (800) 451-7111 FAX (352) 371-3710; **Mariah Wilderness Expeditions** ((510) 233-2303 TOLL-FREE (800) 4-MARIAH FAX (510) 233-0956; and **Overseas Adventure Travel** TOLL-FREE (800) 221-0814.

INDEPENDENT TRAVEL
Many visitors to Costa Rica, especially those on their second or third trip, prefer to rent a car and follow their interests. Arranging such an expedition can be time consuming and costly, however, and it often pays to work with an agency adept at juggling all the details. **Euro-Global** ((213) 525-3232 TOLL-FREE (800) 235-5222 FAX (213) 525-3234 offers a fly-drive-hotel voucher program that allows you to design your own itinerary as you travel, using vouchers for a selection of accommodations in your price range. Other agencies adept at working with independent travelers include Costa Rica Connection (see above), Horizontes, and Costa Rica Expeditions (see TRAVEL AGENCIES in TRAVELERS' TIPS, page 242).

NATURAL HISTORY
Total immersion in the natural habitats, wildlife and topography of Costa Rica is available on specially-designed tours that incorporate visits to several nature reserves, volcanoes, rivers and beaches. Among the most comprehensive are those designed by Holbrook Travel and Remarkable Journeys (see above); **Costa**

Rica Expeditions (257-0766 FAX 257-1665; **Destination Costa Rica** (223-0744 or 233-4758 FAX 222-9747 TOLL-FREE (800) 835-1223 and **Costa Rica Sun Tours** (255-3418 FAX 255-4410.

CRUISING
Several major cruise lines include Costa Rica in their ports of call on Panama Canal itineraries, but passengers see little of the country. More satisfying are the week-long cruises to national parks along the pacific on the *Temptress* TOLL-FREE (800) 336-8423.

Windstar TOLL-FREE (800)258-7245 offers upscale nature-oriented cruises of the Pacific Coast of Costa Rica and Panama.

An enduringly popular day trip from San José is a cruise on the *Calypso* (256-2727 FAX 256-6767 in the Golfo de Nicoya; the trip includes transportation to and from Puntarenas and a cruise past isolated islands and beaches with time for feasting, drinking, sunbathing and swimming.

WOMEN'S TRIPS
Tours reserved for women's groups are run by **Remarkable Journeys** ((713) 721-2517 TOLL-FREE (800) 856-1993 FAX (713) 728-8334 and **Holbrook Travel** TOLL-FREE (800) 451-7111 FAX (352) 371-3710.

Cowboys herd cattle, compete in rodeos and follow a lifestyle pioneered by European settlers and indigenous peoples in the Guanacaste range lands.

Welcome to Costa Rica

OVERWHELMINGLY GREEN AND MOIST, smelling of river mud and the salty sea, Costa Rica is Earth's national park. Cupping the Mar Caribe, the skinny country curves snake-like from Lago Nicaragua to the isthmus of Panama in the tropical belt. Nearly impassable mountains, *cordilleras*, bisect rain forests, cloud forests, lowland forests and savannas, trapping valleys and settlements against Pacific and Caribbean coasts. Mammals, birds, reptiles and insects fare far better than humans in this country comparable in size to Nova Scotia, Holland or West Virginia. Orchids flourish, passion flowers twine between *ajillo* trees, ferns wave beside sky-high cecropia hiding monkeys and sloths.

Nearly one third of Costa Rica's land mass is protected by international, national or private preserves. Environmental organizations from the Nature Conservancy to the World Wildlife Fund have stakes in the land and sea. I sometimes envision howler monkeys, jaguars, quetzals and whale sharks swarming across invisible borders to this gentler wilderness.

Costa Rican poet Yolanda Oreamundi describes her homeland in *El Espíritu de Mi Tierra*:

I have seen sunny afternoons on the high plains of my land.

But if I had seen only trees moored eternally by their umbilical cord to the land's womb, if I had seen only carts writing songs on the road, if I had seen only roofs of the little houses and the campesinos in their Sunday best wandering idly in the ditches along the road, I would not have seen the meaning of my land.

If I had seen only that, I would have seen nothing.

Perhaps what Oreamundi was getting at is the country's *Costarricense*, which makes it such an unusual presence in Central America. Costa Rica sits below Guatemala, Honduras, El Salvador, Belize and Nicaragua, and above Panama and the Colombian Coast of South America. Surrounded by revolutions, spies, internal intervention and human cruelties, the country of some three million residents has been internally peaceful since 1949. Costa Ricans call themselves Ticos, a diminutive

endearment that camouflages their power. The Costarricense approach to conflict is based on negotiation and a certain finesse in conversation. Ex-president Oscar Arias used his native skill with utmost advantage to win the Nobel Peace Prize in 1987 when he brokered a signed accord between the chaotic governments of Central America.

Nature conspires to protect Costa Rica from outside intervention. Ticos tend toward isolationism and fierce national pride. Mountains, rivers, volcanoes and endless

forests separate communities within the country as well, and regional blood runs strong. Ticos can typically identify the region other Costa Ricans are from, and are intensely proud of the cities, villages and provinces of their youth. Guanacaste residents boast of broad savannas, cattle ranges, skillful *vaqueros* and a pioneer spirit.

PRECEEDING PAGES: Horseback riders LEFT have endless landscapes to explore, from the fires of Volcán Arenal to the coffee and sugar cane plantations of Turrialba and the beaches of Dominical. RIGHT *Cocos helados* (cold coconuts) provide refreshing sweet milk straight from the source. OPPOSITE: Manuel Antonio may be the most popular beach in Costa Rica, but you can still find solitary hideaways. ABOVE: Imperial beer and Derby cigarettes are staples in neighborhood bars from Nicoya to Tortuguero.

Alajueans are proud to have raised the country's only national military hero. Flags hanging outside rural homes support provincial soccer teams, and *boyeros* (ox cart drivers) claim that the wheels of a cart sing differently in Heredia than they do in Escazú.

In a prescient and practical approach to husbanding natural resources, Costa Rican governments have long protected critical watersheds in the mountains, creating informal refuges for hawks, marguays, anteaters and sloths. The official national park

movement began in the 1960s, and by the mid 1980s foreigners were trampling through rain forests and forcing wildlife to respond to human intrusion. In only three decades Costa Rica has created at least 15 national parks and a dozen natural reserves supervised by the national government. Countless other private reserves, ranches, farms and indigenous settlements protect lands around the parks, creating corridors of forest canopy.

Visitors tend to get caught up in the environmental spirit when hiking across rivers, up volcanoes, and deep in primary rain forest — an ever-shrinking resource. Like most Ticos and many travelers, I think of Costa Rica as a place to be protected and

cherished as a living natural history exhibit to be explored for centuries. But, all those who are attuned to the country's marvelous natural attributes sense damage in the air. Perhaps this comes from learning about so many endangered animals rescued from poachers, loggers and car accidents, or from the sight of unstoppable hydroelectric dams straddling once-raging rivers.

Costa Rica feels as if it is balancing between nature's longevity and the short-term payoffs of industry and tourism. When giant tour buses clog park entrances

and spider monkeys swing by happy hour haunts for treats, Costa Rica feels more like an amusement park than a natural sanctuary.

Progress is inevitable. All one can hope is that it travels in accord with the natural realm.

ABOVE: Bright awnings LEFT decorate jungle boats on the Río Tempisque in Palo Verde. RIGHT: Chunks of hardened lava tumble down the sides of Volcán Arenal. OPPOSITE: A pleasure boat finds snug harbor along Playa Espadilla, Parque Nacional Manuel Antonio.

Welcome to Costa Rica

The Country and Its People

COSTA RICA IS CENTRAL AMERICA'S ANOMALY. It lacks the conflict, culture and controversy of El Salvador, Nicaragua, Panama or Guatemala, and seems most akin to former British Honduras (now called Belize) in terms of European influences. It's the third smallest nation in a cluster of countries as inter- and independent as the British Isles or Scandinavia, squeezed between the massive powers of North and South America.

PRE-COLUMBIAN YEARS

Unlike it neighbors north and south, Costa Rica lacks evidence of huge pre-Columbian cities or civilizations. Its earliest inhabitants appear to have lived in several isolated and distinct groups. Little is known about the residents of Guayabo, the country's largest archaeological site, near the modern city of Turrialba. The ancient city, with burial mounds, sophisticated irrigation systems, stone monoliths, petroglyphs, and cobblestoned streets called *calzadas,* is believe to have been inhabited as early as 1000–1400 BC, and deserted by 1400 AD. Archaeologists call the residents of this city — which at its height may have held about 500 people with thousands living in the surrounding region — the Guayabo peoples, and have little knowledge of their daily lives or connection to the other early peoples of Costa Rica.

The Nicoya Peninsula on the Pacific Coast is believed to have been a port of call for early marine traders, perhaps from Ecuador. They brought precious metals and stones, jewelry and pottery between Mexico and South America and traded with the people of the Nicoya region who were known as the Chorotega, or "fleeing people." Perhaps the most advanced of the groups in this region, the Chorotega seem to have been influenced by the Olmec and other groups from the north and developed towns and agricultural systems. They produced highly detailed pottery, which today is still produced by their descendants in this region.

The names now used for the various groups spread sparsely throughout the country were created by the Spaniards, who used the region or name of the chief in power at the time to distinguish groups. The Caribes, Bribrí and KéköLdi were located on the Caribbean, while the Borucas and Diquis were located in the southwest. They were all semi-nomadic hunters and fishermen who raised yucca, squash, *pejibaye* (bright orange palm fruits), and tubers.

Intricate jade and gold figurines and jewelry, along with painted pottery, indicating sophisticated artistry, have been found at several archaeological sites in the coun-

try. The jade, in particular, is puzzling, since it is not native to this region. The figurines may have been used for trading. Gold, on the other hand, was mined in isolated regions of the country, and hundreds of pieces have been found and displayed at San José's Museo de Oro.

The most arresting archaeological presence is that of lithic spheres — huge, nearly perfectly round stone balls that

PRECEEDING PAGES: Work and play continue into evening hours on Playa Hermosa LEFT, Nicoya Peninsula. Vivid angels RIGHT adorn an Easter procession. OPPOSITE: A lone fisherman explores the waters of Barra del Colorado near the Nicaraguan border. ABOVE: Traditional pottery from Guaitil is one of Costa Rica's most highly-desired folk art purchases.

weigh several tons. The spheres have been found in the south and northwest, often grouped in formations that appear to relate to the constellations. Whether the rocks were made by nature or man is still under dispute, but their perfection is indeed astounding.

THE CONQUEST

On September 8, 1502, Christopher Columbus arrived on the east coast of Costa Rica, anchoring between Isla de Uvita and today's Puerto Limón. It was his fourth journey to the New World, and yet another attempt to find passage to the Pacific Ocean. His vessels damaged by storms, Columbus held anchor in the area for 18 days, and was much impressed with the amount of gold worn by the peoples who met his ships. His soldiers made excursions into the country with the Indians and reported an abundance of wildlife, fertile countryside and more gold. He later named the place La Huerta, "the Garden." Columbus reported his findings, believing he had indeed found a treasure land that would greatly add to Spain's holdings in Nueva España.

In 1506, King Ferdinand of Spain dispatched Governor Diego de Nicuesa and a group of settlers to establish a colony in La Huerta. The group ran aground in Panama, and were nearly decimated by tropical diseases, Indian resistance and lack of food on their trek north into Costa Rica. By 1513, Vasco Nuñez de Balboa had discovered the Pacific Ocean, and future expeditions concentrated on the Pacific Coast, which was believed to have more gold and better ports for further explorations. In 1522, Captain Gil González led an expedition to the Pacific. Soldiers hiked much of the Costa Rican Pacific Coast into Nicaragua, baptizing Indians along the way and collecting as much gold as they could carry. The Indians, while curious about the Spaniards and their horses, were not interested in being conquered and assimilated, and they rebelled in short spurts of battle; they were quickly repelled. The Spaniards left the region once again in search of riches elsewhere on the continent, leaving behind the seeds of destruction — smallpox and other diseases that rapidly decreased the Indian population.

Subsequent expeditions proved frustrating and futile. The Spaniards, always intent on finding the source of the gold that adorned the Indians, were directed south to the rivers of the Osa Peninsula, where all they found was placer gold (found on stream beds and not in mines) and not the vast amounts they were seeking. They never found the legendary gold mines of southern Costa Rica, and had to be content with what they could loot from the Indians, a paltry amount by the greedy standards of those seeking the wealth of the New World.

Attempts to conquer Costa Rica continued, though there was little to be conquered. This section of Central America held none of the mighty cities and thousands of potential slaves that existed in Mexico or Guatemala. The indigenous groups were small, nomadic and little impressed with the attempts of their conquerors, who were thwarted by endless mountain ranges, impenetrable jungle, tropical heat, diseases and a resistant populace. Having better luck in Panama and Nicaragua, the Spaniards established settlements there and in 1539 deemed the area between the two countries to be called Costa Rica.

Phillip II of Spain insisted that Costa Rica be colonized, and in 1561 a well-equipped expedition led by Juan de Cavallón achieved what Columbus had started decades earlier. Leading his troops inland, Cavallón established the settlement of Garcimuñoz, named after his place of birth. Juan Vásquez de Coronado arrived the following year, moved Garcimuñoz to what is now Cartago and renamed it El Guarco.

Coronado was Costa Rica's first true leader. He traveled throughout the country, visiting Spanish settlers barely eking out an existence and Indian leaders resistant to being conquered. The indigenous groups had their own battles going, which Coronado helped mediate and resolve, all the while approaching the Indians in a peaceful, friendly manner. Battles still took place between the indigenous residents and the settlers, but there was little of the overwhelming bloodshed so common in other conquered lands.

Still, the Spanish settlers found Costa Rica to be nearly uninhabitable. Without slaves they were unable to build colonial cities and churches or establish vast agricultural fields. They continued moving inland to the more fertile volcanic lands, cultivating their own property with the few Indians they could press into service. In 1569, the struggling settlers demanded

marginal, subsistence levels. Feuds between landowners were few, since there were no real class distinctions and little to fight over. The Catholic Church, so influential in New Spain, was of little importance here. The bishop was located in Nicaragua and rarely made the trip of several months to reach his flock in Costa Rica. The country grew slowly over the next century, largely uninfluenced by events taking place in the outside world, developing its own system of peaceful negotiation, democracy and independence.

that Coronado's successor allow enslavement, but few Indians were left to be conquered. Those who hadn't fled to the hills or jungles had been killed by disease, and Costa Rica became the province of the Spanish settlers willing to shape a new country.

THE COLONIAL PERIOD

By 1573 Cartago (El Guarco) contained about 50 families and smaller settlements had grown within the Meseta Central and the Nicoya Peninsula. Lacking gold or other precious metals for trade, these settlers used what they could raise on the land: corn, cacao, tobacco — and lived at

As Spanish settlements took hold in the interior during the 1700s, a few of the more established *criollos* (Spaniards born outside their country) began planting cacao on the Caribbean Coast and importing African slaves to tend the crops. But British pirates allied with the Moskitos, a band of African slaves who had intermarried with the Indians in Nicaragua and Honduras, found the plantations easy conquests and plundered the coast. The *criollos* built Fort San Fernando in Matina, north of Limón, to protect their plantations. But they were easily outnumbered and overwhelmed by the British. At the same time, the Spaniards and *criollos*

This venerable Josefina said that she is 101.

continued attempting to enslave the Indians who had fled to the Caribbean Talamanca mountain range, where dense vegetation and the harsh tropical climate discouraged Spanish settlement.

The Meseta Central continued to grow with the establishment of Cubujugui (now called Heredia), Villa Nueva de la Boca del Monte (now San José) and Villa Hermosa, now Alajuela. Still seeking manpower, the Spanish government instituted the Indian Resettlement Policies of 1747 and hundreds of Indians were forcibly relocated to the

Meseta Central to provide a labor force. In 1779, Costa Ricans began paying tributes (or bribes as they might more accurately be called) to the pirates to protect their plantations, a practice that continued into the mid-1800s.

INDEPENDENCE

Isolated from the turmoil in Mexico and Central America, Costa Rica was little involved in its neighbors' fight for independence from Spain. As the story goes, a letter from the officials in Guatemala arrived on October 13, 1821 in Cartago, informing Costa Rica that Guatemala, head of the Federation of Central American States, had declared its independence — and that of its neighbors — from Spain. The leaders of the small country's main settlements — Cartago, Alajuela, Heredia and San José — were at a loss. They had felt Spain's influence only minimally, but were not united by a common identity with their Central American neighbors.

On December 1, 1821 the local leaders drafted their first constitution, the *Pacto de Concordia*. Some felt the country was too small and sparsely populated to stand independently, and favored unification with Guatemala or the Mexican Empire. Others opted for independence. On April 5, 1823, the debate ended with a short battle in which 20 men were killed. The *independencistas* won, taking control of Cartago. The *Ley de Ambulancia* (Law of Mobility) was established, rotating the capital between the major towns. In 1824 teacher Juan Morn Fernández was named the first head of the sovereign state of Costa Rica.

Fernández led the country for nine years, overseeing its first printing presses and newspapers and the beginning of the coffee plantations that would shape Costa Rica's future. As *cafeteros* (coffee growers) around San José began attaining some wealth and prestige, the need for a strong leader became evident. In 1835, lawyer Braulio Carrillo was named president; he later declared himself the benevolent dictator of Costa Rica and moved the capital to San José. Coffee continued to take hold as the leading crop in the countryside, and the infant government grew evermore factious. Francisco Morazán, a Honduran and leading power in the attempt to create a united Central America, was enlisted by the coffee barons to overthrow Carrillo in 1842; a year later, Morazán was overthrown and executed. A series of shaky governments ensued as Costa Rica abolished its military and all ties to a Central American federation.

A strange historical quirk fueled the national identity of Costa Rica in the mid-1850s. William Walker, an American character of bizarre influence in much of Mexico and Central America, had failed in his attempts to create a slave state in Mexico. With the backing of wealthy United States capitalists who hoped to open tradeways through Central America, Walker landed in Nicaragua in June, 1855. Walker's intentions were even more grandiose than those of his backers. He aimed to establish a union of the five Central American countries and rule the union as emperor. He was able to win over and conquer Nicaragua's leaders and became their president, but was less successful with Costa Rica. When Walker attempted to invade Costa Rica's northern border at Guanacaste, he met an army of some 9,000 peasants who routed the potential potentate and his band in a battle that lasted less than 15 minutes. The site of the battle, La Casona in Parque Nacional Santa Rosa, is now a museum. Juan Santamaría, a youth from Alajuela, became Costa Rica's sole military hero when he followed Walker back to Nicaragua and lost his life while setting fire to the invader's fort.

The coffee barons continued to accumulate money and power through the 1800s, cultivating huge swaths of land in the Central Meseta with the *grano de oro,* grain of gold. They began building mansions around San José and fought amongst themselves for control of the country. By the turn of the century Costa Rica had an established constitution, a controlled military and mandatory primary education for both sexes. A railroad to Puerto Limón was under construction for transporting exported coffee, and Costa Ricans began looking towards Europe for their sense of style and grandeur. In 1897 a coffee tax financed construction of the elegant Theatro Nacional in San José.

In 1889, those who were not female, Indian or black were allowed to vote in free elections.

THE TWENTIETH CENTURY

Although it is known today as a peaceful country, Costa Rica marked the first five decades of the twentieth century with a series of military takeovers, political and social reforms and a civil war. A series of political parties — conservative, reformist, Communist, Christian — took control while debating taxes, social justice and the country's future. Unable to remain isolated, Costa Rica was financially affected by World War I and the Great Depression, both of which reduced the international coffee market. Politics proved risky business: over its first 100 years Costa Rica saw presidents and ex-presidents executed or assassinated. In 1842 Francisco Morazán

was executed in San José; Braulio Carrillo was assassinated in El Salvador in 1844. Army chief Joaquín Tinico, brother of military dictator Federico Tinico, was gunned down in 1919.

As other Latin nations were struggling to define their political character, Costa Rica underwent a social revolution, of sorts, led by ex-Catholic priest Jorge Volio. Head of the Reformist Party, Volio served as vice-president during the 1920s, often rattling the elite power brokers with his demands for social justice. In 1931, Manuel Moras —

an intellectual concerned with the growing influence of not just the coffee barons but also the United Fruit Company and its vast banana plantations on the Caribbean Coast — formed the Communist Party.

From the first isolated indigenous groups, the country of Costa Rica grew into a collection of individualistic and relatively independent provinces, ultimately ruled by the coffee barons of the Meseta Central. By the 1930s, the United Fruit Company had become a measurable political and financial force, with its vast landholdings and banana plantations on the Caribbean Coast. Social and financial inequities were more visible than ever, and the educated populace resisted control by the elite. Moras and the Communist Party led a strike in the banana plantations in 1934; eventually, the largely black work

OPPOSITE: Rain forest villagers cruise in their wooden skiff off the Burica Peninsula near the border with Panama. ABOVE: Coffee beans, called the *grano de oro,* grain of gold, are among the country's leading exports.

force was granted wage guarantees and the right to unionize.

In 1939 Rafael Angel Calderón Guardia was elected president. Though supported by the coffee elite, Calderón proved himself to be a liberal leader, instituting the social security system, the right of workers to strike and other reforms. He also used his declaration of war against Nazi Germany during World War II as an excuse to confiscate the lands of powerful German coffee barons, which decreased his constituency considerably. Calderón gradually became allied with the Communist Party and the Catholic Church in an odd triumvirate that led to long-term partnerships. Calderón lost the 1944 election to his supporter, Teodoro Picado, in an election some said was filled with fraud. He lost again to Otillio Ulate Blanco in 1948, but both Calderón and Picado called the election a fraud. A brief, bloody civil war ensued on the streets of San José, with skirmishes throughout the country. Over 2,000 Costa Ricans are believed to have died during the 44-day war.

José Figueres, known as Pepe and eventually Don Pepe to his fellow countrymen, led the opposition forces in what he called "The War of National Liberation". Apparently backed by the United States and supplied with soldiers and arms from other Central American countries, Figueres won the war and leadership of Costa Rica for the next year. In that brief span of time he ensured passage of the Constitution of 1949, which abolished the military, gave citizenship to everyone born in Costa Rica, including the Afro-Caribeños of the Caribbean Coast, and granted women the right to vote. Figueres served nine years in intermittent presidential terms over the next two decades under the banner of the National Liberation Party (PLN).

The transfer of power has remained fairly orderly since Figueres moved in with his guerrilla band in 1948. Subsequent presidential elections have favored the Liberation Party, and power has been concentrated within a few politically elite families. The wave of revolutions in surrounding countries has tested, but not defeated Costa Rica's desire for peace. In the

country's greatest moment of international recognition, Costa Rican President Oscar Arias was granted the Nobel Peace Prize in 1987 for engineering peace in Central America.

TODAY'S COSTA RICA

The years since the Civil War of 1948 have been remarkably peaceful and largely prosperous for Central America's most stable country. The economy and living standards are among the highest in the region, and

citizens enjoy the benefits of free education and health care (paid for with taxes that some find exorbitant), generally sanitary and comfortable living conditions and an absence of armed conflict. Costa Rica has maintained a peaceful attitude towards its warring neighbors, managing to stay away from conflicts in El Salvador, Guatemala, Nicaragua and Panama through the past few decades of revolution, military intrigue and strife.

Granted, the tiny country of peace amidst revolution has not been allowed to be completely free of involvement. The United States, a long time ally of Costa Rica, unofficially installed military bases and training camps along Costa Rica's border with Nicaragua as part of its campaign to destabilize the Sandinista government during the Contra insurgency. In the 1980s the United States poured money into Costa Rica, constructing a massive embassy with over 200 employees and a second huge edifice to house the Agency for International Development (AID). Both buildings, set amidst the nouveau riche suburbs of San José, provide visible evidence of the United States presence and Costa Rica's growing dependence on United States investments. Between 1983 and 1990, Costa Rica received

credited with introducing peace to the region by bringing the five presidents of the Central American nations into a mutual accord.

Dependence on United States funds created a false economy in Costa Rica during the 1980s; with the end of armed conflict in Nicaragua and Panama, United States aid began drying up. Costa Rica was considered to be financially stable and able to control its future finances without such mighty intervention. The transition was less than comfortable.

over $1.1 billion from AID, creating what some Ticos called a "parallel state" intent on promoting the country's private sector economy.

Despite United States involvement, the Costa Rican government, led by President Oscar Arias, refused militarily involvement in its neighbor's conflicts. Reports of military training camps on the borders still occasionally surface, and the country was certainly a center of intrigue during the 10 years that United States supported the Nicaraguan Contras. But Arias remained firm in his commitment to peaceful negotiations over armed conflict, bringing the wrath of some United States politicians and the support of others. Arias is largely

The 1990s have been hard on Costa Rica's economy. Immigrants from all over Central America have put a heavy strain on the country's social services. Though the population increase within the country has been stabilized through successful birth control programs, the influx of new poverty-stricken residents is difficult to stem.

At the same time, however, Costa Rica has become extraordinarily attractive to international investors and retirees. Real estate prices in suburban and coastal areas have risen dramatically as expatriate communities have grown in clusters of villas, condominiums and entire neighborhoods

Mares and their colts are herded along a Nicoya Peninsula road.

of United States-style ranch houses. The population of North Americans living in Costa Rica has reached somewhere between 30,000 and 60,000, in a country of three million people. *Pensionados*, as these gringo retirees are called, must prove they have an independent monthly income, which the retirees find goes a lot farther in a third-world country. English is as common as Spanish in many parts of the country, where it seems all the landowners are expatriates.

Politically, Costa Rica remains stable, though the citizenry is highly vocal and critical of the government. The country's infrastructure is in need of a comprehensive overhaul — one need only drive the roads to perceive that — and middle-class workers are expressing their resentment over high taxes that hardly improve their daily lives. After Oscar Arias brokered peace among his neighbors, Costa Ricans elected the son of ex-president Rafael Angel Calderón to the presidency; in 1994 the son of Don Pepe Figueres, José María Figueres became president. Figueres has been much maligned by his countrymen, who have witnessed an unprecedented rise in corruption and crime in Costa Rica.

As Costa Rica enters the twenty-first century, it appears far better prepared for the future than its neighbors. Democracy seems to be firmly entrenched, and international companies look to this peaceful nation for expansion of high-tech industries. Outside the cities and burgeoning coastal resorts Costa Rica remains the same as it was in decades past, when *campesinos* tended their sugar cane, coffee and cows in relative tranquillity.

THE PEOPLE

Often overlooked in the turmoil that besets most Central American countries, Costa Rica is a relatively peaceful enclave boasting more teachers than policemen, more nature preserves than cities and an enviable absence of confrontation. Its character is subtle yet enduringly strong, able to resist the political influences of mightier governments and interference from its neighbors.

Europeans conquered Costa Rica in a far different manner than in more valuable lands such as Guatemala or Mexico. They settled in haciendas, stripped the land for cattle ranches and relied on their wits and skills to survive. The society that emerged during the region's next century emphasized independence from outside influences and interdependence within small communities. Geographically isolated between mountains, rivers, volcanoes and rain forests, Costa Rica's early communities developed distinctive characters based on nature's influences and the immigrant families shaping a new world.

Costa Rica's indigenous peoples — the Bribrí, Boruca, KéköLdi and Chorotega groups living in coastal outposts and verdant valleys when the Spaniards arrived — were gradually displaced during the seventeenth and eighteenth centuries. Today, their influence is nearly invisible to the casual eye, which makes this Central American nation rather disconcerting for fans of Guatemala, Mexico or Peru. Some tourists are shocked to discover the absence of important archaeological sites, indigenous communities, folk art and colorful clothing amidst the country's natural beauty. Less than three percent of Costa Rica's current population is made up of indigenous peoples. And these small indigenous communities live primarily in remote reserves.

The people of Costa Rica's major settlements reflect a polyglot heritage. Waves of immigrants from Europe and North and South America have been settling in the country's fertile agricultural valleys and ranch lands ever since Columbus and his men first arrived in 1502. In some places Italian is spoken as readily as Spanish; in others, German prevails. In the northern Caribbean region, you hear the lisping, melodic Spanish of Honduras; along the Pacific, you learn Nicaraguan slang. English is pervasive in the capital, but in the countryside Spanish prevails, filled with the clever *tiquismos* that make it worth learning the local accent.

Costa Ricans, or as the call themselves, *Ticos*, have avoided military action since the Civil War of 1948 — no mean feat when one thinks of the Nicaraguan Contras, Manuel Noriega and other characters fomenting turmoil in neighboring countries. The *Costarricense* approach to conflict is based on negotiation. The Costarricense manner is to use humor, charm or disappearing acts to avoid offending anyone. Ticos and Ticas are among the most pleasant people you'll ever meet, filled with sincere courtesies.

Yet racial and ethnic equality among the country's citizens is a fairly recent phenomenon. Afro-Caribeños first began settling on the Caribbean Coast and working at cacao and banana plantations in the mid-1800s, but were denied citizenship until 1949. Indigenous peoples of the Bribrí, Boruca, KéköLdi and Chorotega groups were given citizenship in 1992, and allowed to vote for the first time in the 1994 elections.

Nearly 30,000 out of the country's three million residents have *pensionado* status. In other words, they've proven their economic viability and emigrated from Calgary, Vancouver, Minnesota and California. Entire communities of North American pensianados have sprung up on the edges of towns throughout the country, escalating land values to the peak of any found in a Latin Third World country. Many of the finest hotels, restaurants, private nature preserves and beach resorts are owned by noncitizens.

These outside entrepreneurs are attracted by Costa Rica's independence from Central America's woes and its relatively stable financial and political climate. The military was abolished in 1949, and democracy bordering on nepotism has been the government of choice ever since. Nearly 90 percent of the registered citizens vote in national elections. Public education is mandatory through sixth grade.

Though Costa Rica is far more peaceful than its neighbors, crime is on the rise and people are learning to fear their neighbors. Private security officers patrol banks, public parks, homes and ecolodges, and guns are now part of the standard uniform. The public health system, free to all taxpayers, is decent but inefficient; the public education system is burdened by an onslaught of ille-

gal resident students. Though still in the Third World, Costa Rica is relatively advanced technologically, financially and socially, and has many of the modern problems of a First World nation.

But out in the provinces, beyond the city smog, Costa Rica remains a landscape of small towns and villages, each with a unique identity — from Guanacaste with its skillful *vaqueros* and cowboy spirit to Alajuela where the national hero Juan Santamaría was raised. Flags billow outside rural homes in support of provincial

soccer teams and *boyeros* (ox cart drivers) know they're nearing home when the wheels of their carretas sing a familiar tune.

Costa Rica feels like a country in transition, yet much tradition remains. Costa Ricans have juggled environmental, social and financial issues in a temporizing manner ever since declaring themselves independent of any Central American federation in 1823. In enduring Costarricense style they remain subtle, amiable and tenaciously proud of their homeland.

Children participate in ranch chores.

San José and the Meseta Central

SAN JOSÉ

A few years back San José was a pleasant Central American capital city, atypically peaceful and safe. Ringed by mountain peaks and cratered volcanoes, the city attracted culture-oriented travelers and along with hummingbirds, parrots and flocks of dull-brown hilgueros, the country's national bird. The markets, parks and neighborhoods felt safe to even the most obvious, bumbling tourist, and *Josefinos*, as

the city's residents are called, were amiable and relaxed.

Today, San José's potholed streets are jammed with bumper-to-bumper traffic, and pedestrians clutch their parcels and purses with obvious fear. Pollution often obliterates the beauty of the countryside encircling the city, which sprawls over the Meseta Central 1,220 m (4,000 ft) above sea level.

Not that many people fall in love with San José, but myself, I truly enjoy strolling along the side streets of the city's older neighborhoods on a clear Sunday afternoon. Couples nuzzle on benches in a half-dozen green and fertile parks. Men in berets study the news under violet halos of jacaranda blossoms in the Parque España, while sidewalk vendors display feathers covered with delicate paintings at the Plaza de la Democracia. Cars cruise the streets around the Catedral Nacional and the Parque Central, where political dissidents are likely to be lecturing the crowd.

On weekdays, downtown San José is something of a battle ground, a challenge to travelers seeking tour guides, rental cars and supplies. At such times you're inclined to agree with Josefinos who dread trips to (or through) the city center. Most are embarrassed by what they face — handsome buildings crumbling in disrepair backed by bureaucratic towers of gray cement, and masses of buses, taxis, cars and pedestrians.

A growing tourist industry and booming population growth have had their impact on San José's fragile infrastructure. Despite the country's ecological stance, its capital city is polluted and overpopulated. Buses belch noxious fumes night and day, and the heart of the city looks like it's been hit by a disastrous earthquake. Gangs of street thieves called *chapulines* (grasshoppers) race through crowded plazas at set times of day, snatching purses, cameras and jewelry with impunity. Prostitution (a traditional tourist attraction) has expanded from the tolerated Red Light District into much of downtown, leading city leaders to fear San José's emergence as a leading destination for sex.

All in all, San José is growing into a typical Latin American metropolis, though it will never be as imposing as many Guatemalan or Mexican cities. Although over 300,000 residents live in the city, slums are still the exception rather than the rule. Costa Ricans are too proud to let their capital, with its historical mansions, museums and seats of government, disintegrate much farther.

San José is famous for one of the best climates in the world, with average daily temperatures in the 70s. Rain falls in sudden showers from May through October, cleaning the air and streets. But even then the air is crisp rather than chilly, an invigorating change from the sweltering heat at the beach.

PRECEEDING PAGES: A sulfurous lake of emerald green LEFT has formed in one of Irazú's craters. RIGHT: Statues of European conquerors and national heroes overlook most plazas in San José. OPPOSITE: The Teatro Nacional, built in the late 1800s with funds from coffee taxes, has become Costa Rica's enduring architectural and cultural landmark. ABOVE: Downtown San José's streets are a nightmare even for local drivers.

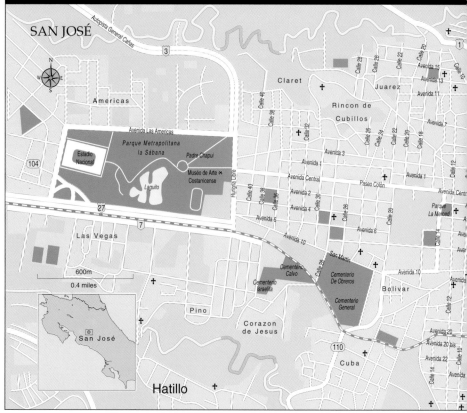

San José is the undisputed hub of Costa Rica's tourism industry, and the inevitable home base for most travelers. You can easily fill a week's stay in San José with day excursions either on guided tours or in a rental car. Popular trips include the Café Britt Coffee Plantation Tour, the Braulio Carrillo Rainforest Tram, the artisans' shops at Sarchí, Volcán Arenal when it's spouting sparks at night and Lago Arenal by day.

First-time visitors to San José tend to find lodging downtown; returning travelers opt for the quieter urban or suburban neighborhoods. Tourists on tight schedules stick to the modern resorts by the airport, zipping away as soon as possible. Sooner or later everyone wanders down Avenida Central to the pedestrian zone by the Plaza de la Cultura, sampling San José's shops, churches, museums and landmark sidewalk cafés. It's a good idea to get to know San José if you think you'll be back to Costa Rica. You just might find neighborhoods,

hotels, restaurants and shops that you wouldn't dream of leaving the country without visiting the next time around.

BACKGROUND

When the Spaniards first settled in Costa Rica in the sixteenth century, they chose Cartago, 20 km (12.4 miles) south of San José as their capital. Until 1737, Villa Nueva de la Boca del Monte del Valle de Abra (as San José was then awkwardly named) was nothing more than a few muddy streets and ramshackle buildings. Then the Catholic Church and the Spanish government declared it to be the focal point for villages and farms scattered through the valley. When much of Central America gained independence from Spain in 1821, various factions in Costa Rica fought for power. In 1823 a short civil war gave control of the country to the *independencistas* of Alajuela and San José, who favored the country's independence over

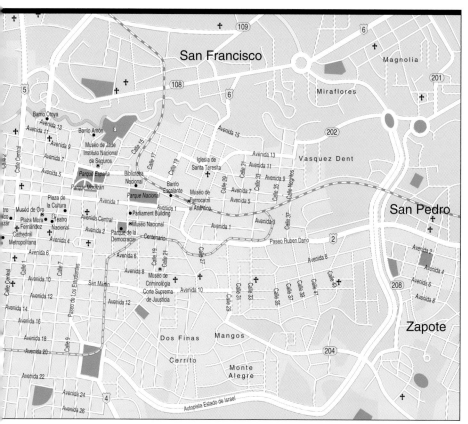

control by a larger nation such as Mexico or Guatemala. The winning faction conquered Cartago and made San José the capital city.

San José was attacked by opposing forces in 1837, but stood strong and has remained the tiny country's capital ever since. Traveling in 1841, the explorer John Lloyd Stephens described the burgeoning city:

"San José is, I believe, the only city that has grown up or even improved since the independence of Central America… The buildings in San José are all Republican; not one is of any grandeur or architectural beauty, and the churches are inferior to many erected by the Spaniards in the smallest villages. Nevertheless, it exhibited a development of resources and an appearance of business unusual in this lethargic country."

Little did Stephens know how much the city would change in the next few decades. By the mid 1800s San José was attracting tobacco and coffee barons and an intelli-

gentsia seeking a cultural center. Civic leaders looked to both France and Italy for their monuments and mansions.

The Teatro Nacional, built in 1897, firmly emphasized European influences with its imported artists, designers and craftsmen. Public electric lighting brightened the streets and electric trolleys ran through downtown around the turn of the century. In the early 1900s San José was a cosmopolitan city with a strong cultural and financial base, often compared to New Orleans.

An influx of foreign money in the 1960s and 1970s caused the city to boom. Several foreign governments established embassies and consulates in Barrio Amón, Escazú and Rohrmoser, which created a demand for high-class housing, services and cuisine. Tourism to the city increased, and émigrés from the United States, Canada and Europe settled in various neighborhoods. The 1991 earthquake, which devastated areas around Limón on the Caribbean Coast, slowed development for a while and severely damaged the Teatro Nacional. Some of the city's downtrodden appearance is a result of the quake, which left cracks and fissures in walls and streets.

But Chepe, as Ticos call their capital, is slowly revitalizing. Several parks have been manicured, the Catedral Metropolitano has undergone a facelift and the Plaza de la Cultura, long the hub of tourists, vendors and thieves, has been shut down indefinitely, ostensibly for a slow-

moving reconstruction. Government plans to reduce traffic congestion and air pollution are regular fare in the daily news. It seems that San José may finally get the attention it needs.

GENERAL INFORMATION

The **Costa Rica Tourism Institute** (Instituto Costarricense de Turismo or ICT) (222-1090, Caja Building at the intersection of Avenida 2 and Calle 7, is woefully inadequate and unreliable. In 1996 the ICT closed down its main information booth in the Plaza de la Cultura and left travelers wandering about in confusion, without even a sign to direct them to other offices. For now, the visitor information office is on the eleventh floor of the gray Caja Building. Visitors can stop by to collect a free map, brochures and sparse information, Monday to Friday from 8 AM to 4 PM.

The **National Park Office** (283-8004 or 283-8094 FAX 283-7118 or 283-7343 is headquartered in San José, though its offices tend to move about. It operates a hot line (192, for questions and information about Costa Rica's biological reserves, national parks and protected areas. Information can also be obtained by phoning the **Ministerio del Ambiente y Energia Minea (MINAE)** (257-0922 FAX 223-6963.

Travel agencies abound in the San José area, and they are the best source for up-to-date information. Most hotel and streetside agencies distribute maps and make tour, car-hire and hotel reservations. Several of the country's major adventure travel companies (with day trips to San José's outlying areas) are also headquartered inside the city (see TRAVEL AGENCIES in TRAVELERS' TIPS, page 242).

Emergencies

For fire, police, health or other emergencies in San José dial 911. A recommended hospital for English-speakers is **Hospital Clinica Biblica** (257-5252 EMERGENCIES (257-0466, Calle 1 at Avenida 14.

WHAT TO SEE AND DO

Downtown San José attractions are within easy walking distance of each other and most sit at the edge of a plaza or park with benches for resting and regrouping. The best place to start exploring is the **Museo Nacional** (257-1433, Avenida Central between Calles 15 and 17, housed in the imposing, bullet-ridden Bellavista Fortress built in 1870. The bullet holes on the south side of the imposing gray-brown fortress were left during the civil war of 1948. The museum includes a large collection of pre-Columbian and religious art. It's closed on Monday.

The stark, imposing concrete **Parque de la Democracia** slants down a slight hill in front of the fortress. The park's design shows none of the warmth it represented when built in 1989 to commemorate President Oscar Arias's key role in establishing peace in Central America. Folk art and souvenir vendors are relegated to a permanent open-air structure at the foot of

ABOVE: A child delights in chasing pigeons in the square adjacent to the Teatro Nacional.

the plaza; treasures lie waiting amidst Guatemalan textiles and manufactured trinkets.

The **Palacio Nacional**, which houses the national legislature, is across Avenida Central from the museum on Calle 15. Demonstrations blocking the surrounding streets are common, especially around election time. About 85 percent of the population votes in local and national elections, and Ticos are both philosophically and physically involved in their local governments.

One block north, at Calle 15 and Avenida 1, the **Parque Nacional** provides a peaceful green belt with bamboo and palm groves and the **Monumento Nacional.** This frothy white marble sculpture depicts four women who represent the spirits of the Central American nations; potential conqueror William Walker is shown fleeing from the powerful woman representing Costa Rica. A statue of Juan Santamaría, the country's national hero, stands at the park's southwest corner. The **Biblioteca Nacional** opposite the park is the country's largest library. Visitors can browse through the stacks. Also in the neighborhood at the far end of Avenida 3 between Calles 21 and 23 is the **Museo Ferrocarril**, once the terminus for the Jungle Train from Limón to San José. The long brick building, constructed in 1907, now holds a collection of photographs of the old train line, which ceased operation after the April 1991 earthquake. The museum is used for large fairs and concerts and is not open on a regular basis. If you do find it open, take note of the tiled floor and wood carvings on the walls and ceiling.

Around the Plaza de la Cultura

Though metal barricades surround its vast expanse of cement, the **Plaza de la Cultura** remains the heart of the tourist zone.

Bordered by Avenida Central and Avenida 2, and Calles 3 and 5, the plaza is in the center of a five-block-long pedestrian zone. The government closed the square-block plaza in 1996 for remodeling (and to deter crime), a project that seems likely to last interminably. In the past, the Plaza de la Cultura was San José's main gathering spot, where hawkers sold popcorn and souvenirs. The vendors have been relocated and the loungers have transferred their bottoms to the benches in the Plaza Mora Fernández in front of the Teatro Nacional and the Gran Hotel.

Under the Plaza de la Cultura at basement level is the **Museo de Oro Precolombino** (257-0987, Calle 5 at Avenida Central and 2, housing more than 2,000 pre-Columbian gold artifacts. Given the country's paucity of archaeological sites the collection is impressive, with items dating from AD 500 to 1500. The museum is run by the state-owned Central Bank and is protected by gun-toting guards who may request to see your passport before allowing entry. Among the dazzling displays of gold frogs, evil-looking animals and grotesquely distorted humans is the Costa Rican version of armor — a *cacique*, or tribal leader's warrior suit in solid gold. The museum is closed Mondays.

The **Teatro Nacional** (221-1329 at the south side of the plaza, is San José's most striking architectural sight, a tribute to the will and power of nineteenth-century coffee barons. Embarrassed at not having an appropriate venue for traveling artists, the barons put a tax on every bag of coffee they exported to finance a European-style opera house. Ships laden with marble and glass from Italy and France unloaded their precious wares at Limón; from there the valuable materials were brought by train to San José. The official history of the theater states it was built between 1890 and 1897 in an eclectic neoclassic German style; the stone façade underwent changes in 1921. The theater opened on October 10, 1897, with a performance of *Faust* by the Paris Opera and Ballet. Legend has it the 1,040 wrought-iron and carved wood seats weren't ready in time for the show; instead, volunteers hustled up folding chairs from all over town to accommodate the sold-out house.

The best way to view the theater is by purchasing an inexpensive ticket for a show. I saw a performance of the university's guitar orchestra for $5 one night and brought home a compact disc of Latin American guitar classics as a treasured souvenir. The theater has a rotunda ceiling mural of naked cherubs with trumpets and harps painted by

Italian artist Arturo Fontana in 1897. The National Symphony and touring groups appear frequently; tickets range from $3 to $15. Tours when the stage is black are available daily for a nominal fee. Check out the native cedar, mahogany and rosewood doors, floors and ornaments, and the mural of the coffee harvesting scene depicted on the old five-colon note. If you stop for a coffee or dessert at the theater's **Café Ruiseñor** (256-6094, ask for a token to use the grand restrooms.

A standard stop-off for nearly anyone in the area is the **Café Parisienne** in front of the golden yellow **Gran Hotel**, designed by architect Juan Joaquín Jiménez in 1930. The sidewalk tables topped with red umbrellas are the province of travelers and a few regulars who lay claim to their seats for long hours of coffee and conversation. Though I prefer the Ruiseñor, nothing gets you in the touring mood better than a morning coffee or evening beer at the Café Parisienne.

A pedestrian walkway runs east to west along Avenida Central behind the Gran Hotel. Attempts have been made to beautify the strip and a few trees seem to be thriving. This a good way to cut through downtown's madness without dodging cars. There are a few good department stores, takeout eateries and a bank of public phones along the walkway.

Around Parque Central

A hangout for downtown denizens, Parque Central is an elevated square framed by royal palms. It's is a good place to review your maps, sample some sliced papaya or mango from a corner stand and even get a shine for your shoes. The plaza has been landscaped with Guanacaste trees, and bands play at the center *kiosko* bandstand. The hulking gray **Catedral Metropolitano** faces the square. The cathedral has little of the dazzling gilt common in major Latin American churches, and its popularity as a religious center is overshadowed by the Catedral Nacional in Cartago.

The neoclassic **Teatro Melico Salazar** at Calle Central and Avenida 2 hosts live performances, some presented by gringo theater groups who hang out at the Soda la Perla next door. Three blocks west on

Avenida Central at Calle 8, the **Mercado Central** bustles even on Sunday, when most downtown shops are closed. A traditional commercial center since 1880, the market displays the season's delicacies — imported apples for Christmas, ripe mangoes in spring, pineapples and bananas year round. Inside, narrow claustrophobia-inducing aisles lead past fishmongers, butchers, spice and herb stands and trinket salespeople, all competing for your attention. Though it's not as colorfully indigenous as markets in Guatemala or Mexico, the mercado displays

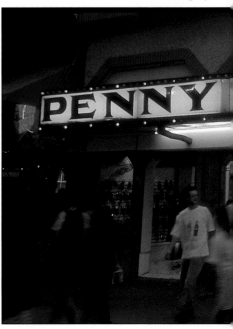

accouterments from every Costa Rican lifestyle. Authentic *vaqueros* (cowboys) study leather saddles and boots; homemakers haggle over the price of chayote, tomatoes and plastic housewares; believers stock up on herbal remedies and religious trinkets; and tourists stick out like plucked ducks. You may be tempted to snap photos while in this hellacious maze. If you do, make sure your valuables are safely tucked out of sight.

The North Side

Downtown San José's prettiest small parks and neighborhoods lie northeast of the Plaza de la Cultura, beginning at the **Parque Morazán** at Calle 7 and Avenida 3.

The continuous activity of the Red Light District ends at the bordello-style Key Largo bar across from the southeast corner of the park. Several bus lines converge on Avenida 3, and streams of commuters flow through the park's pathways during the rush hours. One of my favorite spots for resting and people-watching, the park was relandscaped in 1992 with lawns and benches laid out around the white-domed Temple of Music. The 17-story nondescript Aurola Holiday Inn faces the park's north side; although I would not recommend

America. Bamboo groves, ginger and heliconia blossoms, and intermittent flocks of parakeets make a walk though the park feel like an unexpected commune with nature. On the east edge of the park facing Avenida 5 is the **Edificio Metálica**, a metal building that is said to have come from the Eiffel company in France. The building, now painted light yellow, is an elementary school. The **Casa Amarilla**, a yellow colonial-style mansion housing the State Department, stands guarded on the northeast side of the park.

staying there, you might want to visit the top-floor casino and lounge for a view of the city at night.

If creepy, crawly creatures are of interest (or you want to bone up on possible sightings in the wild), take a detour to the **Serpentarium** (255-4210, Avenida 1 between Calles 9 and 11. The spooky collection of live tropical reptiles and amphibians will inspire a healthy respect for the outback.

A block east of Parque Morazán, the **Parque España** is a more peaceful and densely landscaped refuge with statues of Juan Vásquez de Coronado (a Spanish settler) and Simón Bolívar, the great liberator who attempted to unite the nations of Latin

At the northwest corner of Calle 9 and Avenida 7, the drab high-rise headquarters of the National Insurance Institute (Instituto Nacional de Seguridad or INS) houses one of San José's finest museums, the **Marco Fidel Tristan Museo de Jade** (287-6034, the largest collection of jade objects in the Americas. Located on the eleventh floor with spectacular views of the city, the museum displays an impressive collection of pre-Columbian jade statuettes, pendants, fertility symbols and jewelry. Since Costa Rica has no jade mines, archaeologists speculate that the pieces came from

Signs in English often overwhelm their Spanish competitors along San José streets.

Guatemala or Mexico. The museum is open to the public Monday to Friday from 9 AM to 3 PM.

Facing the west side of Parque España is the **Centro Nacional de la Cultura** (255-2468, at Calle 13 between Avenidas 3 and 5, in a block-square complex of buildings that once housed the National Liquor Factory. *Evelia con Batan*, by world-renowned Costa Rican sculptor Zuñiga stands at the entryway. Art exhibits, live performances and lectures are held in the many yellow buildings which surround an unadorned courtyard. The cultural center is closed on Monday. Ask at the guard desk for a list of upcoming events.

Paseo Colón to Parque la Sábana

At the west side of downtown, Avenida Central becomes **Paseo Colón**, a broad thoroughfare and one of the main routes in and out of town. Hotels, auto dealerships, rental car companies and a few nice restaurants and shops line the paseo, though you must look past a lot of commercial clutter to find the gems. It's about a 20-minute walk from downtown to the best hotels in this neighborhood, sometimes called El Bosco. Tour groups and solo travelers with a bit of cash prefer this neighborhood for their base. It's close to the regional and international airports and the autopista to Escazú, Heredia and points northwest. El Bosco is a good walking neighborhood, with sidestreets leading past small parks, pulperías, arty bars and international restaurants. Work out the travel kinks by taking a brisk walk five blocks south of the paseo to Avenida 10 and the **Cementerio de Obreros**, the deep, wooded municipal cemetery. If you're really into tombstones and floral arrangements check out the nearby Cementerio Calvo and Cementerio Israelita.

Both Avenida 10 and Paseo Colón run west to **Parque la Sábana**, the largest urban park in San José. Once the region's international airport, the park now includes some cement jogging trails along eucalyptus groves, the National Stadium and the National Gymnasium. The **Museo de Arte Costarricense**, housed in the old airfield terminal, contains the works of twentieth-century Costa Rican artists, along with murals and dioramas of the country's history. It is open Tuesday to Sunday from 10 AM to 4 PM.

Neighborhoods

There is much to delight casual wanderers in San José's *barrios,* or neighborhoods, especially those north and east of downtown. **Barrio Escalante**, directly east of the Parque Nacional, which was one of the city's wealthiest neighborhoods at the turn of the century was filled with small farms, gardens and the mansions of coffee barons. Many of the houses, some covered with ornate mahogany carvings, have been lovingly restored by wealthy Ticos. Carefully tended ginger, coffee, coconut and pineapple plants thrive behind wrought iron gates. Wander the sidestreets of Avenidas 5 and 7 for the best sights, including the **Iglesia de Santa Teresita**, the small **Parque de Francia**, and the **Museo Doctor Rafael Angel Calderón Guardia.** Calderón was one of Costa Rica's most liberal-minded presidents, who instituted the national university, the social security system and other measures that seemed too socialist-minded for the elite. His presidency ended in 1948 at the culmination of Costa Rica's civil war. The big yellow mansion is open to the public daily except Monday, and portrays (in a rather self-aggrandizing style) the ex-president's lifestyle and efforts to help the poor.

Several of San José's nicest small hotels are located in **Barrio Amón** and **Barrio Otoya** (roughly bordered by Avenidas 3 to 11 and Calles Central to 17). If you're interested in architecture, get to know these neighborhoods. North of Parque España, steep sidewalks (some covered in handcrafted tiles) lead past restored Victorian mansions. Don't miss the **Castillo el Moro** at the north end of Calle 3. Built in 1925 as a private residence, the Moorish-style white castle is ostentatiously decorated with rows of keyhole windows and plaster crenelations. Strips of handpainted tiles border the castle's dome, which towers beside the main road to Siquirres.

The depressing **Parque Zoological Simón Bolívar** borders Amón and Otoya.

The zoo is only worth visiting on Sunday afternoons, when Josefinos families picnic and party on its lawns. Some of the park buildings have been refurbished, and there are plans to move the animals to a new setting outside the city. For now, the zoo itself is a painful reminder of how animals live in captivity. Still, it attracts hordes of city residents and school kids and is a great place to soak in the local culture. I prefer to slip in for a quick go-round, then wander the hilly *callejones* (alleyways) bordering the park's canyon walls.

students from around the world and has the feel of an ivy league campus. A botanical garden on the campus contains labeled specimens.

Escazú, southwest of Parque la Sábana, feels like a country town within sight of the city lights. Those who can afford to be Josefinos without actually living within the city limits have driven real estate values to the sky in this woodsy enclave. Bus and cab service to downtown San José is inexpensive and accessible (except for those in private residences tucked in a

San Pedro and the University of Costa Rica lie east of downtown en route to the Carretera Interamericana. Home to students, faculty, artists, musicians and suburban dwellers, San Pedro is at first glance a nightmare of through-traffic exiting the city on residential streets. Once out of your car, however, you'll find it a fascinating place. Several small budget bed and breakfasts are located in the area along with the ultramodern San Pedro Mall.

The university of Costa Rica was established in 1940. Its campus covers several blocks of trees and lawns off Calle José María Muñoz. Considered prestigious, conservative and elite, the university attracts

maze of sideroads in the hills). Several good inns and restaurants attract residents and visitors who want the pleasure of country living without having to depend on a car.

Getting Around

Walking is by far the easiest way to see downtown San José, as long as you keep your eyes on your feet when in motion. The sidewalks in many areas are in dreadful condition, with crumbled pavement and potholes nearly as large as those in streets.

A night or two at the Gran Hotel acclimates travelers to the noise and bustle of downtown.

Crossing most streets is another challenge. Pedestrians appear to be considered fair game by drivers, who edge forward at red lights as if their lives depended on a quick getaway. Crossing lights are hung so high that they're difficult to see. Watch the locals instead, and cross with a group.

Despite these drawbacks, you can often reach your destination far more quickly by walking than by riding in a bus or cab. Most of downtown's sights are within a 20-block radius, and walkers can ignore the baffling one way street design that makes driving an utter nightmare.

A few important tips: *avenidas* (avenues) run east and west; *calles* (streets) run north and south. Odd-numbered avenues are north of Avenida Central; even numbered avenues are south. Odd-numbered streets are found east of Calle Central; even numbered streets are located to the west.

Even when walking, directions can be downright baffling. I've had police officers, knowledgeable pedestrians and cab drivers scold me for knowing only the street address of my destination. Landmarks are preferred, usually with some reference to meters. For example, Ticos refer to a city block as being *cien metros,* or 100 meters, long. Nearly all buses to outlying areas depart from the Coca Cola terminal, roughly bordered by Calles 16 and 20 and Avenidas 1 and 3. Mind you, there is no actual terminal building, and the Coca Cola bottling plant for which the area is named was torn down years ago.

Taxis are cheap and abundant and use meters (called *marías*). If the driver says his meter doesn't work, confirm the fare before he starts driving. You can travel from one end of town to another for under $5; the fare is about 20 percent more after 10 PM. Taxis congregate at the Plaza Central and the Plaza de la Cultura.

Buses are equally omnipresent and run the full gamut from dilapidated, smoke-belching contraptions to clean Mercedes Benz machines. The route is written on the windshield. The Cementario-Sábana route runs east-west from Parque la Sábana to downtown.

I've driven many times through downtown San José, despite strong admonitions

to avoid it. Some people love the rush and challenge; I tend to crawl between lanes of cars more dented than my own. It may take a full hour to cross the city in any direction, especially if you stick to the obvious routes. Locals are savvy about alternate routes. Nervous, cautious types are best off renting their cars at the airport or an outlying hotel on the edge of town, although depending on your destination, you still might have to drive through San José.

Sports
Soccer is a national passion so fervently followed that, as one local said, "During a game you could run through the streets of downtown naked and no one would

know." Should you have the nerve to ignore this national passion, you'll find streets, shopping centers and museums virtually empty during Sunday games. Want to watch a game? Stop off at any town square as you travel through the country. Even the smallest village has some sort of soccer field.

Joggers are best off in Parque la Sábana, where trails lead through eucalyptus groves and past a large pond. The park also has a **swimming** pool and **tennis**, **basketball** and **volleyball** courts.

The 18-hole **golf** course at the **Meliá Cariari Hotel (** 239-0022 is open to guests at the Meliá and Sheraton Herradura hotels. Guests at other hotels can call ahead and try to get a tee time; availability is limited.

Shopping

When I first began visiting Costa Rica, it was difficult to find souvenirs other than the ubiquitous wooden bowls made from local hardwoods and miniature painted ox carts from Sarchí. But the art scene has expanded considerably with the growth of tourism, and San José now has several fine shops and galleries. The largest and best of the lot is **Atmósfera (** 222-4322, housed in a block-wide, colonial-style building at Calle 5 between Avenidas 1 and 3. Three levels of galleries feature one-of-a-kind ceramic ware, paintings, masks, sculpture and woodcrafts; all purchases come with a certificate of authenticity and background

The bandstand, *kiosko,* in San José's Parque Central.

information on the artist. The prices are staggering and the quality unsurpassed. **Suriska Gallery** (222-0129 at Calle 5 and Avenida 3, showcases expert woodcrafters Barry Biesanz and Jay Morrison. Morrison also shows his work at **Magia** (233-2630, at Calle 5 between Avenidas 1 and 3. **Annemarie's Boutique** in the Hotel Don Carlos grows larger each year, with several rooms devoted to wooden bowls, plates and boxes, masks (including a few balsa masks from the Boruca Indians), books and a comprehensive sampling of the country's souvenirs. Go there before you begin your travels, and stop back for last-minute purchases. **La Esquina del Café** (257-9868, Calle 3, in Barrio Amón, is a small coffeehouse whose shelves are stocked with interesting objects, including several versions of the traditional coffee maker, called a *chorreadura*, a sock-like contraption inside a wooden frame.

A jumble of shops packed with standard crafts from Costa Rica, Guatemala and Panama fills the arcade at **La Casona,** Avenida Central and Calle Central. Artisans display their wares by the Plaza de la Cultura and the Plaza de la Democracia; good buys include hammocks, woodcarvings and amazingly detailed village scenes painted on the feathers of tropical birds. The **Mercado Central** is always worth some browsing time, but be watchful of your belongings.

The biggest grocery store chain is **MásXMenos,** where you'll find export-quality coffee, local and imported liquor, wine and beer, cheeses from San Antonio de Belén and Monteverde, and most essentials. There are several locations throughout the city and suburbs. **Café Trebol** in the market area on Calle 8 between Avenida Central and Avenida 1 sells excellent coffee beans by the kilogram.

Residents of outlying areas starved for reading matter fill baskets with used books from the shelves at **Book Traders** (255-0508, Avenida 1 between Calles 5 and 7. Shoppers browse through their choices while sipping coffee at the seating area; the back room displays cards, stationery, maps, and books on Costa Rica. **Chispas** (256-8251, on Calle 7 at Avenida 1, specializes in books on science, nature and Costa Rican lore, and also has a fine selection of new novels at reasonable prices.

Most shops are open Monday to Saturday from 9 AM to 5 PM; some close for lunch and all are closed on Sunday except when tourism is particularly high.

WHERE TO STAY

San José has an overabundance of hotels — a situation which encourages competition. Luxurious chain hotels have popped up near the airport, and are best for those wishing to get out of the city as quickly as possible. Refurbished residences, with a dozen or more rooms, are the norm in the downtown neighborhoods. Those closest to the museums and tourist sights are burdened with horrendous street noise; light sleepers are best off in outlying neighborhoods with good bus service to downtown. Most hotels will store your luggage while you travel around the country.

Reserve a room far in advance for the high season — some of the most popular spots are booked solid three months ahead. Don't panic, however. All sorts of circumstances can upset the best laid plans, and rooms sometimes become available in places you would least expect. Rates decrease and availability increases in the green (rainy) season.

Very Expensive

Most of San José's most luxurious hotels are located well outside the city in Heredia (see HEREDIA in AROUND SAN JOSÉ, page 88), close to the international airport. The Marriott, Meliá and Sheraton hotels in this area (about a $15 cab ride from downtown) are full-scale modern resorts with several restaurants, casinos, tour and car-rental desks, fitness and business centers and rooms with air conditioning, satellite television, direct-dial phones and room service. Business travelers hover in this area, along with explorers who want to begin and end their adventures in total comfort.

San José's older resort-style hotels are located just north of Parque Sábana on the autopista to the airport. Their casinos and restaurants cater to business travelers and city dwellers as well as tourists, and are often populated with tour groups getting acquainted. The best choices are the **Corobicí** (232-8122 FAX 231-5834, on the Autopista General Cañas next to Parque Sabana, and the **San José Palacio** (220-2034 TOLL-FREE IN THE U.S. (800) 858-0606 FAX 220-2036, on the east side of Autopista General Cañas.

Expensive

Parque la Sábana provides a green belt on the east edge of the city, and a few of San José's best small hotels are located within walking distance of both the park and downtown. My favorite by far is the 35-room **Hotel Grano de Oro** (255-3322 FAX 221-2782 E-MAIL granoro@sol.racsa .co.cr, Apdo 1157-1007, Centro Colón, San José, Calle 30 between Avenidas 2 and 4; RESERVATIONS IN THE U.S. SJO 36, P.O. Box 025216, Miami, FL 33102-5216. Canadian owners Eldon and Lori Cooke have transformed a turn-of-the-century wooden house into a charmer, with indoor gardens and fountains, a rooftop sundeck with hot tub, and one of the city's best international restaurants. The rooms of various sizes and styles are all decorated with cheery florals and comfy furnishings; room 22 sits beside a fountain and has a private garden. All rooms are nonsmoking; smokers can request rooms with outdoor patios or confine their smoking to the courtyards and sun deck. The hotel's professional and amiable staff, excellent restaurant and accommodating layout are often imitated by envious hoteliers, but not many places achieve the Grano's comfortable efficiency.

Some tour groups use hotels in the neighborhood of Parque la Sábana as their city base. The 39-room **Parque del Lago** (257-8787 FAX 223-1617 E-MAIL parklago@ sol.racsa.co.cr, Apdo 624-1007, Avenida 2 between Calles 40 and 42, San José, is well located across from Parque la Sábana, though pedestrians risk their lives when crossing Calle 42; they should go to the park and use the pedestrian overpass. The decor incorporates carpeting throughout the hotel, mirrored elevators, air conditioning, bathtubs, and good-sized desks next to the windows, which open only at the very top.

Other draws are guarded parking and the hotel's proximity to the autopista, several bus lines, and good *sodas* (coffee shops) and international restaurants.

On the north side of the city proper in Barrio Tournon, the **Hotel Villa Tournon** (233-6622 FAX 222-5211, Apdo 69-12120, Barrio Tournon, is just two blocks from El Pueblo's restaurants and clubs. Sloping wood ceilings, brick walls and gardens give the 80-room hotel the feeling of a country hideaway, yet downtown's museums and sights are within walking distance.

In Barrio Amón, those who plan ahead can claim a room at the elegant **L'Ambience** (223-1598, 222-6702 FAX 230-0481, Apdo 1040-2050, Calle 13 between Avenidas 9 and 11, San José, a restored mansion filled with European and Costa Rican antiques. Six rooms and a suite face a central atrium and courtyard; all have high ceilings, hardwood floors and prints. The gourmet restaurant serves three meals daily; call ahead for reservations. Nearby, the **Britannia Hotel** (223-6667 FAX 223-6411 E-MAIL britania@ sol.racsa.co.cr, Calle 3 at Avenida 11, San José; TOLL-FREE IN THE U.S. (800) 263-2618

Office workers, tourists and street vendors congregate under the umbrellas at the Café Parisienne.

RESERVATIONS IN THE U.S. SJO 3264, P.O. Box 025216, Miami, FL 33102-5216, is in a handsome restored mansion with 24 large rooms and suites.

Overpriced yet convenient, the motel-like **Hampton Inn** (443-0043 TOLL-FREE (800) 426-7866 FAX 442-9532 E-MAIL hampton @sol.racsa.co.cr, Autopista General Cañas, Apdo 962-1000, San José, is a wildly successful, tourist-oriented hotel across the highway from the airport. It's a good choice for quick getaways and is the headquarters for many tour groups.

Several inns and hotels in Escazú offer comfortable, pleasing accommodations in close proximity to the city. Utterly unique and somewhat bizarre is **Tara** (228-6992 FAX 228-9651 E-MAIL iiclayton@magi.com, Apdo 1459-1250, San Antonio de Escazú; RESERVATIONS IN THE U.S. Interlink 345, P.O. Box 02-5635 Miami, FL 33152, sitting atop a steep hill over the town. The white plantation mansion reminiscent of *Gone with the Wind* is almost too much for liberal sensibilities. The lily-white pillars, manicured gardens, fine white linens and almost campy southern-belle style suit those with fantastic imaginations, who luxuriate in the full-scale spa, order rum poolside and dress in costume for formal meals. Far more Costa Rican in style, the **Puesta del Sol** (289-6581 or 289-8775 FAX 289-8766 E-MAIL hhaber@sol.racsa.co.cr; RESERVATIONS IN THE U.S. Department 305, P.O. Box 025216, Miami, FL 33102, is an enchanting bed and breakfast designed from a country estate on a backcountry road near the Nimbé restaurant. The **Costa Verde Inn** (228-4080 or 289-9509 or 289-9591 FAX 289-8591; RESERVATIONS IN THE U.S. Costa Verde Inn, SJO 1313, P.O. Box 025216, Miami, FL 33102-5216, sprawls along a slope overlooking Escazú's neighborhoods. Returning guests settle in for months in the fully-equipped apartments; short-term visitors grab the more modest rooms in several buildings surrounding a garden and tennis court. Some rooms have balconies and gorgeous views; meals are available on request. The inn has a sister property in Manuel Antonio with transportation between the two.

Those relying on foot power and buses are pleased to find the **Amstel Escazú** (228-

1764 FAX 228-0620 TOLL-FREE IN THE U.S. (800) 575-1253, Apdo 4192-1000, San José. The low-lying property sits next to the main road from San José, yet suffers little from traffic noise. Beyond the lobby and family-style dining room the guest rooms surround a small pool. Manicured lawns rise gently towards groves of trees where parakeets and other birds passing through the city find refuge. Located near bus stops and shops on the side highway through San Rafael de Escazú is the **Hotel Sangildar** (289-8843 FAX 228-6454 E-MAIL pentacor@sol.racsa .co.cr, Apdo 1511-1250, Escazú. Modern in terms of creature comforts and services, the hotel has a full-service restaurant, a pool and large air-conditioned rooms, and is popular with small tour groups.

Moderate

A number of interesting small hotels are scattered through downtown's barrios. Even if you're not staying amidst the ferns and fountains at the venerable **Hotel Don Carlos** (221-6707 FAX 255-0828 E-MAIL hotel@doncarlos.co.cr, 779 Calle 9 between Avenidas 7 and 9, RESERVATIONS IN THE U.S. SJO, Department 1686, P.O. Box 025216, Miami, FL 33102-5216, be sure to check out its excellent gift shop and courtyard café complete with gurgling fountain and rock walls covered with reproductions of pre-Columbian masks. The hotel was founded by Carlos Balser, an art collector and major contributor to the jade museum. The 36 rooms are spacious and comfortable, but many face the street and are plagued with traffic noise.

In Barrio Amón, guests gather in the covered courtyard to breakfast on wonderful breads and fresh fruit at **Edelweiss** (221-9702 FAX 222-1241, Avenida 9 between Calles 13 and 15. The Canadian owners here have taken two adjoining houses and divided the space into 16 rooms with floral wallpapers and stencils, exotic wood floors, private bathrooms (some with tubs) and handmade furniture including desks. Nearby, the **Vesuvio** (/FAX 221-7586, 1333 Avenida 11 between Calles 13 and 15, has a good restaurant and basic rooms with pastel walls, ceiling fans, carpeting and small televisions. **La Casa Verde de Amón** (223-

0969 FAX 257-1054, Avenida 9 and Calle 7; RESERVATIONS IN THE U.S. Department 1701, P.O. Box 025216, Miami, FL 33102-5216, is well situated in Barrio Amón, and each of the large, airy, comfortable rooms and suites is distinctly decorated. The green Victorian house is itself quite beautiful, with several covered patios and indoor salons, one with a grand piano.

Behind the to-be-avoided Holiday Inn is the elegant **Hotel Santo Tomás** (255-0448 FAX 222-3950 E-MAIL hotels@sol .racsa.co.cr, Avenida 7 between Calles 3 and 5; RESERVATIONS IN THE U.S. SJO 1314, Box 025216, Miami, FL 33102-5216, a converted century-old mansion filled with the burnished glow of rare hardwood floors and furnishings. The 20 rooms vary in size and have useful and interesting wall maps of Costa Rica.

Moving on to downtown, the choices grow staggering both in variety and drawbacks. Among the larger properties is the 105-room **Gran Hotel Costa Rica** (221-4000 FAX 221-3501, Apdo 527-1000, San José, Calle 3 between Avenidas Central and 2. This Plaza de la Cultura landmark has a promising setting, but the noise factor outweighs the charm. Having spent my requisite night here, I much prefer hanging out at the hotel's Café Parisienne and finding accommodation elsewhere.

Architect Juan Joaquín, who designed the Gran in 1930, also designed the refurbished 104-room **Hotel del Rey** (221-7272 FAX 221-0096, Avenida 1 at Calle 9. The pink, neoclassic building is just next to Parque Morazán, in the heart of hooker heaven. Services include a good travel agency, a sport fishing desk run by Richard Krug (223-4331 FAX 221-0096 (who is the fishing columnist for the *Tico Times*); an American-style deli, and a raucous bar and casino. Choose your room carefully here. Those that face the street can be unbearable; this is the first hotel I've stayed in where the noise level increases as the night wears on and peaks at about 2 AM. The pink **Fleur de Lys** (223-1206 or 257-2621 FAX 257-3637, Calle 13 and Avenida 2, Apdo 10736-1000, San José, near the Museo Nacional is a peaceful small hotel with 20 rooms in a converted mansion, a good restaurant, friendly well traveled clientele and efficient staff.

Inexpensive

Fanciful and gay, the **Hotel KéköLdi** (223-3244 FAX 257-5476 E-MAIL kekoldi@sol .racsa.co.cr, Apdo 12150-1000, San José, Avenida 9 at Calle 3, is decorated with a melange of pastel murals with a Caribbean flair. Each step to the second-floor rooms is painted pink, green, yellow or blue; each wall is a different color. The effect is surprisingly soothing, as if guests are trapped in a heavenly fantasy. The 14 rooms attract a mixed international crowd who mingle in the downstairs lounge and breakfast room.

The German owned and operated **La Amistad Inn** (221-1597 or 221-1614 FAX 221-1409 E-MAIL wolfgang@sol.racsa.co.cr, Apdo 1864-1002, Avenida 11 at Calle 15 San José, in Barrio Otoya attracts a European clientele to its 22 economically-priced rooms, all with ceiling fans and private bath. Breakfast is included in the rate.

Those on a bottom-line budget who plan ahead will be lucky to grab one of the 105 beds in 19 rooms at the **Toruma Hostel** (/FAX 224-4085, Avenida Central between Calles 29 and 31.

For homestays in suburban San José, contact Audrey or Vern of **Bell's Home Hospitality** (225-4752 FAX 224-5884, Apdo 185-1000, San José. Vern Bell is the author of *Bell's Walking Tour of Downtown San José, with Some Glimpses of History, Anecdotes and a Chuckle or Two*, a delight to carry along on your city tour.

WHERE TO EAT

San José is one of few places in the country where you can break away from a steady diet of rice and beans and sample a surprisingly wide range of international cuisine. The most expensive dishes contain lobster or shrimp, and fish is usually pricier than chicken. Familiar chain burger and pizza restaurants dot the streets of

---

OVERLEAF: The Meseta Central offers a peaceful green landscape within minutes of San José.

downtown, while some of the finer spots are tucked away in the outlying neighborhoods. Many restaurants in the city have nonsmoking areas, and many of the expensive places are closed on Sunday.

Expensive

Paella, squid, octopus and game are the specialties at the Spanish **La Masía de Triquel** (296-3524, Avenida 2 at Calle 40. **Il Ponte Vecchio** (283-1810, 75 m (246 ft) east and 10 m (33 ft) north of Salón de Patines in San Pedro, is considered to be the best Italian restaurant in the city. Chef Antonio D'Alaimo, a transplanted New Yorker, makes his own pastas and sauces and offers an extensive list of imported wines. **Le Chandelier** (225-3980, 100 m (328 ft) east and 100 m (328 ft) south of the ICE building in San Pedro, has 10 elegant dining rooms in a restored mansion. The chef imports many of his ingredients for both classic French dishes and nouvelle Costa Rican cuisine.

Though often packed with tourists, **La Cocina de la Leña** (223-5416 or 233-9964, at El Pueblo Center in Barrio Tournon, is a festive place to sample Costa Rican cuisine, and the menu (listed on a brown paper bag) features far more than rice and beans. Try the *olla de carne* (boiled beef and vegetable soup), the tamales, and the *chilaquiles* (tortillas stuffed with spiced beef). Though large and sometimes deafening, the restaurant resembles a warm, rustic farmhouse and is as popular with locals as with tourists. **El Fogón de la Leña** (223-5416 or 233-9964, at El Pueblo Center in Barrio Tournon, next door is a bit more subdued and expensive. Both are in the El Pueblo center in Barrio Tournon, where discotheques and shops captivate the crowds at night.

Moderate

My first choice for a quiet, romantic evening (or morning fueling) is the courtyard restaurant at the **Grano de Oro** (255-3322, Calle 30 between Avenidas 2 and 4. The ensalada primavera with asparagus and hearts of palm is the ideal starter, followed by the filet mignon with gorgonzola and, if there's room, a slice of homemade chocolate cake with vanilla ice cream.

In the same neighborhood is **Machu Picchu** (222-1384, Calle 32, N° 124, between Avenida 1 and 3 near Kentucky Fried Chicken, a lively Peruvian restaurant with a glowing reputation. The *pisco sour*, made of Peruvian firewater, packs quite a punch, and there is a variety of seafood soups, tangy ceviches, and well-seasoned seafood plates. **Tin-Jo** (221-7605, Calle 11 between Avenidas 6 and 8, is consistently named the best Cantonese and Szechuan restaurant and has recently added a few Thai and Indian dishes. Try the pineapple shrimp. **Ariang** (223-2838, in the Edificio Colón on Paseo Colón between Avenida 38 and 40, is popular with both locals and the foreign community. This small, comfortable restaurant near Parque la Sábana serves good Korean food and Japanese dishes for lunch and dinner, including sushi, sashimi, tempura and meats barbecued at your table. It's closed on Sunday.

Redolent of gorgonzola, prosciutto and garlic, **El Balcón de Europa** (221-4841, Calle 9 at Avenida Central, is one of the oldest mainstays on the downtown dining scene. The 15 tables fill quickly with tourists in early evening and locals later, all feasting on antipasto, pasta and risotto. It's closed on Saturday. Italian gourmands tend to prefer the more subdued **La Piazzetta** (222-7896, Paseo Colón at Calle 40; closed Sundays.

Escazú is a small dining mecca attracting trend-followers, with a few choices worth a trip from the city. **Nimbé**, just south of the crossroads at San Antonio de Escazú, is a longtime favorite of vegetarians and health advocates. **Oralé**, at the foot of the hill from Parque Sábana to Escazú, may be the best Mexican restaurant in the country; its bar is popular with well-to-do 20-somethings. **La Leyenda** on the main road next to the bridge offers some good competition for Oralé. Its setting in a hacienda-style building beside a river is truly outstanding, and the chef does a good job of replicating regional Mexican cuisines.

Inexpensive

The most inexpensive, filling meals can be found at *sodas*, small diner-like cafés where a full meal of chicken, beef or fish, rice, beans, cabbage salad, fried plantains and coffee costs under $5. You'll find *sodas* in nearly every neighborhood. Downtown, check out the crowded, enduringly popular **Soda la Perla** (222-7492, Avenida 2 at Calle Central, just across from the Catedral Nacional. Try the paella and huevos rancheros. **Soda y Restaurant Vegetariano Vishnu** (221-3549, Calle 3 between Avenida Central and Avenida 1, serves vegetarian dishes including steamed veggies and rice, cheese sandwiches and meat-substitute burgers; granola, honey and whole wheat breads are sold at the cash register.

Patrons dine on sandwiches and casados at sidewalk tables facing an endless stream of traffic at **Soda Tapia**, on Calle 42 across from Parque la Sábana; it's noisy but it's one of the cheapest places in this neighborhood. **RostiPollos** (221-9555, with six locations around San José, serves fast food Tico style, including rotisserie-cooked chicken, beans, rice and patacones. The best location for travelers is 75 m (204 ft) north of the Plaza de la Cultura on Avenida Central.

My favorite escape from downtown's madness is in the Teatro Nacional's **Café Ruiseñor**. Ideally, I claim a table by the few narrow windows looking out to the Gran Hotel and linger over a strong café con leche and flaky apple pie. The cherubic ceiling mural, marble-paneled walls, heavy green drapes and courtly waiters are a relief from the bustle outside. There's a second Café Ruiseñor in the Museo de Arte Costarricense at Parque la Sábana. Across from the theater is downtown's most popular sidewalk hangout, the **Café Parisienne** in the Gran Hotel. The best people-watching spot in San José serves decent, inexpensive meals and good coffee. Vendors wander through, selling newspapers and souvenirs or offering to shine your shoes.

The three dining areas at **Manolo's** make it a standby for nearly everyone in San José. Sightseers meet up over *churros* (fried strips of dough coated in sugar) at the sidewalk tables, while regulars chow down on inexpensive chicken and rice inside the Formica tabletops. Upstairs, lucky diners claim tables by the window, where they pay a bit more than downstairs for formal ambiance, plates of fajitas, lomito and *arroz de la casa*

(a pile of rice topped with sautéed celery, onions and meat), and a pigeon's-eye view of the pedestrian walkway.

ENTERTAINMENT AND NIGHTLIFE

El Centro Commercial el Pueblo is a tourist trap that's been around long enough to become an institution. It's on the north side of the Río Torres, across from Barrio Amón, Parque Simón Bolívar and the zoo. The walk between downtown and El Pueblo is notoriously dangerous at night and hardly

scenic in the daytime. Evening visits are best. Dine early at El Fogón de la Leña, wander through the shops, then dance at Lucas. During daylight hours check out the nearby **Spirogyra** butterfly farm on Avenida 13 past Calle 3.

Downtown's more traditional nightlife scene centers around **La Esmeralda** on Avenida 2 between Calles 5 and 7, home of the local mariachi union. Action doesn't begin until midnight, when dozens of mariachi bands take requests from patrons stimulated by beer, bountiful *bocas* (appetizers) and amiability. **El Cuartel de la Boca del Monte** (221-0327, on Avenida 1 between

A Muse floats above the windowside tables at the Café Ruiseñor at the Teatro Nacional.

Calles 21 and 23, is far more hip and trendy, attracting a young, well-heeled crowd mixed with travelers and neighborhood residents, especially on Wednesday, Thursday and Friday nights, when bands play to a packed house. Some locals put **Chelles** ℂ 221-1369, on Calle 9 between Avenidas Central and 2, at the top of their cheap-eats-and-good-drinks lists, but women going their unaccompanied may find it off-putting. The staff can be unfriendly to single women, perhaps because the taberna is located in the Red Light District.

HOW TO GET THERE

All cars, buses, planes and trucks make their way to San José at some point. All international flights into the country arrive at Aeropuerto Internacional Juan Santamaría; buses from Panama, Honduras and Nicaragua end up at or near the Coca Cola bus station.

AROUND SAN JOSÉ

The Meseta Central in which San José is situated is a panorama of valleys, rivers, pastures and rolling hills surrounded by bold green volcanoes. The country's four main cities, all founded in colonial times, lie within a few kilometers of each other with San José at the center. Cartago, Costa Rica's first capital and the site of its most important basilica, acts as an outpost of resources for travelers headed east to Turrialba and the Volcán Irazú, and south to the fertile Orosí Valley. Alajuela and Heredia, just north of San José, are home to the country's original coffee plantations, rising in swaths of emerald leaves against rich red soil in the foothills of the Barvas and Poás volcanoes.

Once forested and nearly impassable, the Meseta Central is now Costa Rica's most populous region. Nearly one-third of all Costa Ricans, retired expatriates and impoverished immigrants live in the cities and rural neighborhoods bordered by mountain ranges and national parks. The landscape is disciplined here, meticulously planted with tropical plants imported from throughout the world. Lavender jacaranda, yellow palo verde and pink palo blanco blossoms litter the asphalt highways running past white wooden houses framed with bougainvillea, calla lilies and roof-high poinsettia branches. Homeowners tend their lawns with obsessive care, cutting grass even with machetes and sweeping away leaves with plastic brooms. Waist-high fields of shiny green coffee shrubs pose against forests of macadamia trees and billowing sugar cane.

Fed by the ash and mud left from volcanic eruptions and watered with predictable rainfall and the tributaries of mighty rivers, the lands of the Meseta Central are a farmer's paradise. Cattle range in wheat fields and wander across main roads while daring drivers with haughty stares and indifferent *moos*. Horses clomp along roadside trails; ox cart wheels sing their discordant rhythms on gravel paths. And just over the next rise, bridge or patch of rock-strewn mud lies the rain forests of Braulio Carrillo, the cloud forests of Monteverde, the fiery lava of Arenal.

It's hard to stop driving once you begin following winding sideroads through this verdant countryside; more than once I've found myself happily lost. I've made visits to Costa Rica when I never left these outskirts of San José, escaping the city for day trips of river rafting, mountain climbing, horseback riding and general wandering in the always intriguing Meseta Central.

San José sprawls out into the southern regions of Alajuela province; in fact, Aeropuerto Internacional Juan Santamaría is actually in Alajuela rather than the capital. This province is one of the largest in the country, spreading north to the Nicaraguan border, east to the cowboy ranges of Guanacaste and the shores of Lago Arenal, and west to the Río Sarapiquí, Parque Nacional Braulio Carrillo and Heredia.

The country's national hero, Juan Santamaría, was born here; a statue and a small museum are dedicated to his short life.

The **Butterfly Farm** (/FAX 438-0115, in **La Guácima de Alajuela**, is one of the best in the country. Over 75 native plant species in a tropical garden serve as breeding grounds for hundreds of butterflies; guests on the two-hour tour learn about butterfly exportation, an increasingly popular environmentally-friendly business. Tours to the farm, located near the airport, are available from hotels in San José, Heredia and Alajuela.

Densely populated near the capital, Alajuela quickly becomes remote and unexplored — only one road runs through the province to Nicaragua. Beyond the city are several major attractions: the artisans' center at Sarchí, the gardens of Zarcero, Volcán Poás and the Sarapiquí region. Travelers headed to Monteverde, Arenal and both coasts have a wide range of choices for day and overnight visits in Alajuela.

ALAJUELA

What to See and Do
The city of Alajuela has little to offer the traveler, other than a few hotels near the airport and a maze of bus-clogged streets.

A far superior alternative to visiting the Parque Bolívar Zoo in San José is the **Zoológica de Aves** (433-8989, in **La Garita de Alajuela**, about 15 minutes from Alajuela city. The former coffee plantation is now home to more than 1,000 birds and mammals, many recovered from accidents, poachers nets and other precarious situations. The collection includes all the species of monkeys found in Costa Rica, both green and scarlet macaws and many of the rain forest birds. The cages are labeled so you can bone up a bit on your bird facts before heading into the wilderness.

OPPOSITE: Folk art galleries present the works of the country's best artists. ABOVE: A typical ox cart on the side of the Monteverde–Arenal road.

Where to Stay and Eat

Hotels near the airport but well outside the city are a good choice for those with rental cars. Many inns in the area offer transportation to and from the airport and tours to nearby attractions. The inns in the Alajuela countryside are convenient for those headed on to the Pacific Coast, Poás or the Sarapiquí region.

I stopped in for a short visit but stayed an entire morning at **El Cafetal Inn** (446-5785 FAX 446-5140 (moderate), which is about 20 minutes west of the airport near Atenas, Apdo 105, Atenas. Like many small business owners in Costa Rica, Romy and Lee Rodriguéz invested everything they had in their gorgeous inn and plantation with views of the Río Colorado Valley and the Poás, Barva and Irazú volcanoes. Their two-story inn is an architectural wonder with a waterfall in the downstairs lounge and some curved glass walls in some upstairs rooms. Ten of the rooms here have private baths — the best is the huge tower room with a 180-degree panoramic view of the countryside. The grounds are equally beautiful, with fountains and waterfalls around hammocks and bougainvillea-lined paths leading to the large shamrock-shaped pool. Papaya, citrus and yucca trees ring the pool area, where a large tiled bar and dining area are used for special parties and weekend brunches. Romy whips up extraordinary breakfasts (included in the room rate) and elegant gourmet dinners are available if you make reservations in advance. Tours to the volcanoes, orchid and butterfly farms, waterfalls and over a dozen nearby sights are available.

Las Orquideas (433-9346 FAX 433-9740 (moderate), about 10 minutes north of Alajuela on the way to Poás, is set in the midst of orchid gardens. There are 18 large rooms in the main building, a geodesic dome suite and a flower-framed pool.

How to Get There

Alajuela is 16 km (10 miles) from downtown San José; the city of Alajuela is three kilometers (two miles) from the airport. Buses run from San José throughout the day and night.

MESETA CENTRAL

SARCHÍ

Traveling northwest from Alajuela city, follow the signs for Sarchí, the most popular crafts town in the country. Just 30 km (19 miles) from the town of Alajuela and 47 km (29 miles) from San José, Sarchí is almost overwhelming in its quaintness — even the trash cans and trucks are decorated with fanciful designs that resemble Penn-

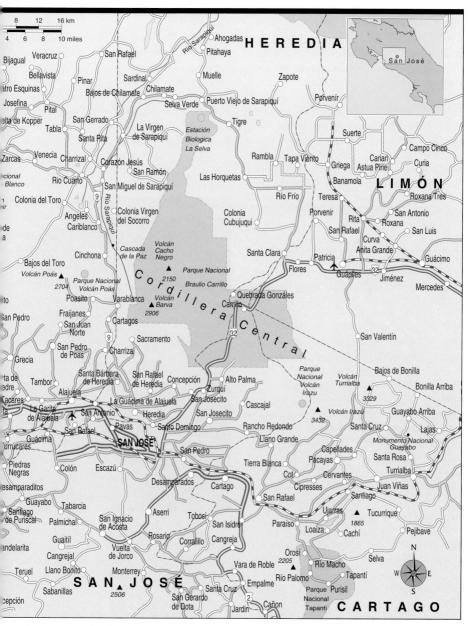

sylvania Dutch plaques combined with Moorish tiles. The designs have appeared on wooden ox carts since at least the early 1900s, and at one time each region in the country had its own typical design.

Ox carts were the main means of transport throughout Costa Rica's countryside until the mid-1900s, and can still be seen nearly everywhere, from the market streets in San José to the sandy beach paths

in the Burica Peninsula. The artisans of Sarchí have transformed the traditional ox cart into every sort of souvenir cliché imaginable. In store after store and roadside stand after roadside stand, tourists comb through miniature ox cart business-card or napkin holders, trays, liquor cabinets and toys. Full-sized ox carts can also be purchased and shipped in case you need a garden ornament. More practical, perhaps, are the handsome wooden rocking chairs with leather seats and backs which fold for easy shipping. The shops also display a mesmerizing array of tropical wood bowls, plates, cups, platters — you name it, they've got it. As I've learned more about Costa Rica's woodcrafters, I'm less attracted to these manufactured goods, though the mahogany, cedar and, purple-heart wood bowls make great inexpensive gifts. I still long for the purple-heart wood jewelry box with glass-like beveled edges that I saw in a Manuel Antonio gallery a decade past. Buses run from San José and Alajuela to Sarchí throughout the day.

ZARCERO

In the competition for the most picturesque colonial town in the country, Zarcero wins hands down. An absolutely charming blue and white church dominates the plaza, where topiary artist Evangelisto Blanco wields his pruning shears on cypress bushes. Precious elephants, rabbits, bulls and matadors, or whatever strikes his fancy, pose against green lawns like hallucinations, begging to be photographed if only to assure the onlooker that they really exist. I've been told Don Evangelisto was offered a job by the Disney company, but he turned them down, saying he didn't want to work anywhere where he couldn't leave his shears overnight next to his current project.

Zarcero is in the center of rich, scenic agricultural lands where fields in every shade of green check the foothills. Roads in this region twist and turn dizzyingly, and turnoffs are few. If you're tired, stop by a roadside stand to sample *cajeta* (candy of caramelized goat milk), *palmito* (the local soft white cheese, not to be confused with hearts of palm) and whatever fruits may be in season.

CIUDAD QUESADA

The commercial capital of the northern agricultural zone, Quesada (also called San Carlos) is the largest city on the road to Volcán Arenal and lake (see LAGO ARENAL

and PARQUE NACIONAL VOLCÁN ARENAL in CENTRAL AND NORTHWESTERN GUANACASTE, pages 111–117; see also A MOUNTAIN WITH AN ATTITUDE in TOP SPOTS, page 18). Fuel up your car, do your marketing and take care of any other business here, and if you're inclined to stay in the area, book a room at the **Hotel el Tucano Resort and Spa (** 233-8936 or 460-3152 FAX 221-9095 or 460-1692 (expensive), eight kilometers (five miles) north of Ciudad Quesada on the road to Aguas Zarcas. Thermal waters feed the pools, steam rooms and whirlpool tubs; mud

baths, tennis, fitness equipment and a natural health clinic are also available. El Tucano has grown considerably since I first visited in the early 1990s; it is now a full-fledged country inn with 90 rooms, often filled with small tour groups using the resort as their base for exploring Arenal. Near El Tucano is La Marina Zoo, where wounded and abandoned jaguars, eagles and toucans are cared for.

VOLCÁN POÁS

Directly north of Alajuela (altough by an indirect route) is the simmering Volcán Poás looming 2,709 m (8,885 ft) over the Meseta Central. The road weaves up the mountains during the 90-minute ride from Alajuela to the crater, passing vistas of regimented rows of coffee plants, swirls of smoke rising from cattle ranches and rivers flowing in deep green valleys. The air feels moist and chilly as you climb, and a gray-white mist streaks the sky. For blue skies and shimmering vistas, see Poás early in the morning before fog shrouds the peaks, though visiting in a shroud of drizzle and mist is enjoyably eerie as well.

Poás is by no means inactive; its first recorded eruption was in 1747, its biggest on January 25, 1910. Poás spewed ash, stones and steam again in the 1950s, and the area was temporarily closed in 1989 when gases and ash belched from the crater. The unmistakable smell of sulfur draws visitors to the edge of the volcano's main crater, a short walk from the ash-covered parking lot at the entrance to Parque Nacional Volcán Poás. On clear days you may spot the milky green lake cupped in the barren crater and see plumes of muddy water spewing in the air. Trails lead from the main crater to Laguna Botos, a lake formed from rain collecting in an inactive crater. Poás has five craters in all, and several trails lead through stunted forest to misty groves filled with bromeliads, epiphytes and a variety of bird species.

Many visitors arrive at Volcán Poás on bus tours from San José, spend an hour or so taking snapshots of the moon-like terrain, then depart for other attractions. I prefer to visit the volcano (and the rest of the area) in a rental car or to ride with a hired guide.

My favorite part of the trip may be the steaming cup of Café Britt coffee served at the park's restaurant after a chilly hike. And I've always thought it would be wonderful to spend the night at the **Poás Volcano Lodge** (/FAX 482-2194 (moderate), 16 km (10 miles) southeast of the crater. The lodge, resembling an English country manor, is situated high in the cool mountain air, over 1,829 m (6,000 ft) above sea level. The lodge offers rooms in the main house and in several outlying cottages, and breakfast is included in the room rate. **Restaurante Vara Blanca** near Poasito is the best place to stop for a meal.

How to Get There

Poás is 37 km (23 miles) north of Alajuela and 53 km (33 miles) north of San José. The most direct route is on Highway 9 toward Varablanca. You may be able to catch sight of Volcán Barva in a protected area of Braulio Carrillo Park to the east. Turn left at the signs for the volcano at Poasito; the road is paved all the way to the park entrance. Public buses don't go all the way to the volcano. If you don't have access to a car either hire a car and driver at your hotel or join an organized tour that arrives at the

crater by 9 AM (the park is open from 7 AM to 4 PM). Allow for at least one full hour at the main crater.

SARAPIQUÍ REGION

Northeast of Poás, the Sarapiquí region is beginning to attract mainstream tourists; for the moment it's a delightful off-the-beaten-track destination for wanderers, bird watchers and rafters.

Just to the north of Poasito the highway descends past the oft-photographed

OPPOSITE: Steam billows from a Volcán Poás crater surrounded by layers of ash from recent eruptions. ABOVE: A turkey buzzard scans the horizon for its next meal.

Cascada de la Paz and continues on to the small town of San Miguel where you can fuel up on gasoline and groceries. At San Miguel one road leads west to San Carlos; the other heads northeast to Puerto Viejo de Sarapiquí in Heredia province. Though there are easier ways to reach this region via the highway from Heredia, I prefer this mystically scenic route through cloud forest on rough back roads that seem to lead into mysterious haunts.

The mighty Río Sarapiquí, which flows south from Nicaragua's Río San Juan, feeds

largest town in the region with some 7,000 residents, sits at the crossroads to further wilderness explorations or the road south to Las Horquetas, the Parque Braulio Carrillo and the Guápiles Highway between San José and Limón.

What to See and Do
The Sarapiquí region borders the remote northern zone of Parque Nacional Braulio Carrillo, one of the largest national parks in the country. The park's entrances are farther south off the Guápiles Highway, but

into smaller rivers crisscrossing the region's forests with waterfalls. And where there is water, there are birds. During a bird census in December, 1996, bird watchers counted 315 species of birds in the region in one 24-hour period. The road runs past **La Catarata San Fernando**, through the rural towns of **La Virgen de Sarapiquí**, **San Miguel de Sarapiquí** and **Chilamate**, all worth a stop for refreshments and a stretch. A few special lodges provide comfortable accommodations for those wanting to explore this area further. Hikers, birders and naturalists find a wealth of trails in the Estación Biológica la Selva, Selva Verde private reserve and the banks of the Río Sarapiquí. Puerto Viejo de Sarapiquí, the

several private reserves add a buffer zone in the northern region. The **Estación Biológica la Selva** (240-6696 FAX 240-6783 E-MAIL reservas@ns.ots.ac.cr, near Puerto Viejo, is essentially an outdoor laboratory for researchers from all over the world. Now operated by the Organization of Tropical Studies (OTS), Apdo 676-2050, San José, La Selva began as an experimental farm owned by Leslie R. Hodridge, who began planting pejibaye, cacao and laurel trees amidst primary and secondary forest in the 1950s. Today La Selva is a living research center for visiting scientists. The reserve covers more than 1,215 hectares (3,000 acres) and has some 56 km (35 miles) of trails. Day visitors must be accompanied by a guide; tours are offered twice daily. The hike begins at the Stone Bridge, a long suspension bridge over the Río Puerto Viejo that leads to a compound of cabins, classrooms and greenhouses where researchers study everything imaginable, from arthropods (over 200,000 species have been identified in La Selva) to poisonous frogs. In the space of two hours we saw a bat falcon eating a pigeon, several violatius trogons, a chestnut mandibled toucan that posed for photographers for at least 10 minutes and a full grown red poisonous dart frog no bigger than a baby's fingernail.

La Selva has rooms for overnight guests, but they must be reserved far in advance and are usually set aside to accommodate visiting scientists. Reservations for day visits must also be made in advance, since only 10 guests are allowed on the trails at any time. To reach La Selva turn south at Puerto Viejo towards Las Horquetas.

Selva Verde (not to be confused with La Selva) is a private reserve and lodge in **Chilamate**. Trails lead through 214 hectares (529 acres) of tropical lowland forest by the Río Sarapiquí. Guided hikes and self-guided trail maps are both available; unless you're an expert it's always best to walk with a guide who can spot oropendulas, toucans, river otters and monkeys. **The Botanical and Butterfly Garden** is a delightful resting spot after a long hike. Wear a bright shirt and the butterflies might mistake you for a flower. The reserve has a wonderful lodge for overnight guests (see WHERE TO STAY below) and the trails and gardens are open to the public for a fee.

River rafting on the Sarapiquí is another big attraction in the area, though the river has lost some of its power since a hydroelectric dam was built, despite much controversy, on the northern end of the river. It's possible to travel all the way to Tortuguero through a chain of rivers; local lodges can set up the trip.

Where to Stay and Eat

Lodges in the Sarapiquí region are beginning to attract small tour groups, and they fill quickly in the high season. Reserve a room in advance by fax, and confirm your reservation when you enter the country. Most lodges serve meals for an additional fee (with little choice for outside dining). There are small sodas in the towns of San Miguel, La Virgen, Chilamate and Puerto Viejo de Sarapiquí.

VERY EXPENSIVE

Rara Avis (/FAX 253-0844, near Las Horquetas, is indeed a rare gem (its name means "rare bird"), as is its owner Amos Bien. Unlike most sensible hoteliers, Bien built his beautiful Waterfall Lodge before slashing a good road through the rain forest to reach it. At first guests endured an infamous three-hour tractor-drawn cart ride through mud and rivers, or hiked for nearly a day to reach the reserve. Such adventures only make Rara Avis more desirable for those who feel Costa Rica has gotten too soft. But even Amos Bien has begun to relent, and gravel and bridges now make the trip just a bit easier. Once inside the reserve guests are enfolded in the atmosphere of a true rain forest where the annual rainfall is over six meters (20 ft) and a dry season doesn't exist. Patient hikers slogging through the mud can spot howler, spider and capuchin monkeys. Near the Waterfall Lodge hummingbirds glitter in the spray given off by a 55-m (180-ft) double cascade. Rooms are available in several settings. **Albergue el Plástico**, closest to the main road, is a former prison barracks turned hostel with several rooms containing 30 beds with shared baths and hot showers. The impressive **Waterfall Lodge** has eight rooms with private baths and hammocks on the balconies which look out on the forest. There is also a two-room cabin set away from the lodge. Meals are served family style in a separate dining room.

EXPENSIVE

Guests sleep in 40 rooms built of tropical hardwoods linked together by palm-covered walkways at **Selva Verde Lodge** (766-6077 FAX 766-6277 E-MAIL selvaver@ sol.racsa.co.cr; TOLL-FREE IN THE U.S. ((800)

Clouds nestle in forested hills in Parque Nacional Braulio Carrillo.

451-7111, just off the main road in Chilimate. Meals are served cafeteria style in the large dining hall with its riverview deck; those not staying here are welcome to walk the trails, visit the butterfly garden and join the meals, with advance reservations. Canoeing, river rafting, horseback rides and nature hikes are available.

MODERATE

Simple and comfortable, **La Quinta de Sarapiquí** (/FAX 761-1052 is located down a dirt road in La Virgen. Take care when you drive over the slippery bridge that crosses the Río Sardinal as you come in to the compound. Part nature reserve, part lodge, La Quinta has 11 rooms in several buildings hidden behind blooming ginger and heliconia bushes. The large rooms — with ceiling fans, good screens and powerful hot showers — have terraces facing flower beds where hummingbirds feed. Meals are served family style in the central lodge beside the river; hammocks hang on the large river deck for lounging to the sound of splashing water. A small swimming pool by the river was nearly completed when I visited, though it's more fun to splash around in the real thing, especially during a rafting trip arranged through the hotel. Guests can also schedule tours to Estación Biológica la Selva and Selva Verde, go horseback riding on riverside trails, travel by boat up the river to Tortuguero, photograph monarch butterflies in a netted garden, or simply lounge through the frequent rain showers in swinging chairs. Owners Beatriz and Leonardo are great promoters of the region and do everything possible to make their guests feel at home.

HEREDIA

Like Alajuela, the province of Heredia borders San José and extends north to Nicaragua. The city of Heredia, about eight kilometers (five miles) north of San José, is the capital of the province and home to the Universidad Nacional de Costa Rica's. Several of the finest hotels near the airport are located in Heredia's small communities south of the city, while the spectacular rain forests of Parque Nacional Braulio Carrillo are spread out between Heredia and the province of Limón. Northern Heredia encompasses the Sarapiquí river and region and Oro Verde, an out of the way nature reserve.

What to See and Do

Heredia is one of the country's few colonial-era cities. Its pretty **Parque Central** faces the **Basílica de Imaculada Concepción**, a rather dumpy edifice that has withstood several earthquakes since its construction in 1797. The population of the city fluctuates with the schedule at the University, which attracts hundreds of international students. The city's youthful ambiance encourages the survival of small inexpensive sodas, coffee houses and vegetarian restaurants, and the market is one of the cleanest and most pleasant in the country.

Coffee plantations cover the countryside in Heredia province. One of the most popular and well organized tours from San José is a visit to the coffee plantations and roasting plants of **Café Britt** (260-2748 FAX 238-1848, three kilometers (two miles) north of Heredia city. Britt is Costa Rica's largest coffee exporter, and their distinctive green and red foil packets of beans or ground coffee are sold in nearly every market and souvenir shop in the country. Their multimedia presentation covers every aspect of coffee growing, harvesting, roasting and shipping; naturally, their coffee and logo-imprinted gift items are sold in the shop. The plantation tour can be arranged through any hotel or travel agency in the area.

Moravia, less than 10 km (six miles) northeast of San José, is a good alternative to Sarchí for folk art shopping. Several small shops frame the pretty **Parque Central**. Though much of the merchandise is the same that you find elsewhere in the country, some shops here carry work by the indigenous Bribrí; others sell local leather crafts.

OPPOSITE: Rain ponchos, binoculars, tripods and cameras all come in handy on hikes through Parque Nacional Braulio Carrillo. OVERLEAF: Cenizero trees spreads their leafy umbrellas.

Where to Stay

Several smaller communities lie between San José and the city of Heredia and are home to some fine country inns and resort hotels within a short distance from the airport. These hotels have become very popular with tourists and business travelers who don't need to stay in the capital. Advance reservations are advised year round.

VERY EXPENSIVE

Finca Rosa Blanca (269-9392 FAX 269-9555, Apdo 41, Santa Bárbara de Heredia, may well be the loveliest small inn in the country. Set amidst the shiny green leaves of coffee plants, the stark white inn with its windowed dome appears from afar as an apparition rising 1,300 m (4,264 ft) above sea level. The eight balconied rooms are constructed from salvaged tropical woods and white plaster; each is decorated individually with wall murals, antiques and contemporary furnishings. Light streams from the dome into the atrium-style lounge, where overstuffed couches encircle the fireplace. Breakfast is included in the rate.

One of the original luxury hotels near the airport is the 220-room **Meliá Cariari** (239-0022 TOLL-FREE (800) 336-3542 FAX 239-2803 E-MAIL cariari@sol.racsa.co.cr, Apdo 777-1000, Heredia, on Autopista General Cañas at San Antonio Belén Intersection, Heredia, refurbished to meet the competition of the Nineties. It's right off the airport highway. Public buses to downtown stop in front of the hotel; coming back from town by bus you're faced with the challenge of vaulting the highway median to get to the other side or riding to the next stop and taking the inbound bus back to the hotel. The Meliá feels remote because it's set on 54 hectares (134 acres). Amenities include a large free-form swimming pool, fitness equipment, an 18-hole golf course, excellent Costa Rican beef served in the **Los Vitrales** restaurant, a nice selection of high-quality folk art in the gift shop, and the inevitable casino.

Dramatic and strangely isolated, the **Marriott Hotel and Resort** sits against the mountains, a pseudo-hacienda visible from the autopista. The handsome estate with golden stucco walls, red-tiled roofs, arches, cupolas and towers is filled with gorgeous folk art and colonial touches — domed brick ceilings, heavy hardwood beams, handpainted tiles and a swimming pool in a lush courtyard. The rooms have all the latest gadgetry, including satellite televisions, mini-bars, in-room safes and hair dryers; three good restaurants offer guests a range of dining options within the resort grounds. The big drawback is the location, which requires a $10 to $15 cab ride from downtown San José.

In the same neighborhood, and with similar prices, the **Sheraton Herradura** (239-0033 TOLL-FREE (800) 245-8420 FAX 239-2292, on Autopista General Cañas at San Antonio Belén Intersection, Heredia, hosts many business meetings and international conferences.

EXPENSIVE

Architecture befitting the mountainous setting (and Costa Rica's enduring reputation as the Switzerland of Central America) defines the **Hotel Chalet Tirol** (267-7371 FAX 267-7050, Apdo 7812-1000, San José, near San Rafael de Heredia. Individual chalets and a gourmet Swiss restaurant are nestled in pine-scented forest. The hotel is near the Barva entrance to Braulio Carrillo park (see below).

MODERATE

The uninspired modern-motel architecture belies the charm at the **Hotel Bougainvillea** (244-1414 FAX 244-1313 E-MAIL bougain villea @centralamerica.com, Apdo 69-2120, San José, in Santo Domingo between San José and Heredia town. The interior design is reminiscent of a ranch manor with stone walls, wood-beam ceilings, original art and fireplaces. The 44 carpeted rooms are comfortable, well-lit and tastefully furnished. The gardens are not to be believed: Every imaginable shade of bougainvillea grows in hedges along paths to the large swimming pool, tennis court, condominiums and forested jogging trails. The dining room is also exceptional. I took the shuttle from San José's Hotel Villa Tournon to the Bougainvillea one morning and had one of the best breakfasts of an entire month in the country. Strong, export-quality coffee,

French toast layered with fresh cream cheese and sautéed fruit, fresh papaya-orange juice — it was superb, as was the view to the lawn and gardens. The hotel is about 15 minutes from San José and the shuttle runs from 6 AM to 11 PM. Next time I'll go out for dinner.

Parque Nacional Braulio Carrillo

Heredia is the launching point for Highway 32, also called the Guápiles Highway, to Limón and the Caribbean Coast. The highway runs right through Parque Nacional Braulio Carrillo, a spectacular moist, green, muddy wonderland of waterfalls and virgin rain forest just 20 km (12 miles) northeast of San José. The park and highway

were jointly conceived from the need for an efficient road between San José and Limón and the desire to protect 45,899 hectares (113,415 acres) of mountainous forest and the Meseta Central's most critical watershed. The park was established in 1978 and the highway, an extraordinary feat of engineering versus nature with the country's only mountain tunnel, opened in 1987.

Despite its proximity to the paved road, Braulio Carrillo is not an easy park to visit — don't expect picnic tables and toilets beside the road. There are, however, several view points where you can pull off the highway and appreciate the extraordinary lush, green landscape. There are short paths

El Fortín stands guard over Heredia town.

formed by adventurous walkers by most of the turnoffs, but don't wander far on your own. Curiosity has led to a number of lost hikers, accidents and even deaths within the park's embrace.

Two official park entrances with ranger stations are located at **Zurquí**, and **Quebrada Gonzáles** (also called Carrillo). Both have short hiking trails. Reports of car break-ins at both entrances and other parking areas along the highway are common. Although it's tempting to undertake a hike while en route to your next destination, you

may return to find your possessions (and even your car) gone. Braulio Carrillo's interior is more easily accessed from the **Volcán Barva** ranger station 29 km (18 miles) north of San José. Barva is the highest point in the park at 2,906 m (9,535 ft) and contains 12 eruption points and several crater lakes. Trails lead from the station to the lakes, which can be visited on day hikes. Overnight camping is allowed near the ranger station; permits must be arranged in advance through the San José office.

Several private reserves and lodges extend the park's natural habitat at the north in the Sarapiquí region (see SARAPIQUÍ, page 85). This area is technically within Heredia province and can be

reached from Highway 32 on the road to Las Horquetas or from Alajuela via the route to the Volcán Poás and Varablanca. Be sure to check in at the ranger station wherever you enter the park, and wear mud boots and a rain poncho.

What to See and Do

Near, if not at, the top of most travelers' lists for day trips from San José is a ride above the forest canopy in the **Teléferico del Bosque Lluvioso**, the Rainforest Aerial Tram (257-5961 FAX IN SAN JOSÉ 257-6053, at the east edge of the park. The brainchild of American naturalist Donald Perry, the tram is an engineering wonder. Perry, a devoted rain forest fanatic, refused to use tractors to erect the poles and attach the cables for the skyway; instead, he enlisted the help of Nicaragua's Sandinistas and their combat helicopters in the construction. A film on Perry's work begins the tram tour. For more information you can purchase his fascinating book, *Life Above the Jungle Floor,* at the gift shop. The tram ride itself is a thing of wonder. Twenty cable cars whoosh almost silently into and above the forest canopy, offering a bird's-eye view of epiphytes, orchids, mosses and ferns. Don't expect to see a lot of animal or bird life unless you arrive when the tram opens at 6 AM; Perry himself warns that the ride is not a zoo, but rather a hanging garden. His fascination, which may become yours, is with the vegetation, the tree ferns that reach higher than the treetops, the vines twisting like acrobat's wire.

The parking lot outside the 450-hectare (1,000-acre) reserve is filled with tour buses whose drivers typically stay with their vehicles, so your car is relatively safe here. The entire tour of the rain forest trails, classrooms, film and tram ride takes about three hours. Be sure to bring a rain poncho and binoculars.

Where to Stay

There are no hotels within the park's boundaries, and few along Highway 32 until you reach Guápiles. The best places to experience a similar climate and topography to the park are located in Sarapiquí (see above) and near the Volcán Barva.

MODERATE

Wounded parrots, toucans and tanagers along with weary travelers find refuge at **Casa Río Blanco** (382-0957 or 710-2652 FAX 710-6161, Apdo 241-7210, Guápiles. This small lodge with cabins and rooms for 12 people is as much an educational center as it is a hostelry. Owners Thea and Ron are experts in sustainable tourism and the concept that lodgings can be nature-friendly. They take in wounded animals and provide a gorgeous setting above the Río Blanco in the rain forest. Several not-to-be-missed attractions are within a half-hour's drive, and you could easily spend three or four nights here resting in hammocks after day trips to the aerial tram, Braulio Carrillo, Rara Avis, the Río Sarapiquí and Limón or San José.

While driving the highway to Limón one time I was pleased to discover **Río Palmas** (760-0330 or 760-0305 FAX 760-0296, in Guácimo. The location, nearly midway between San José and Limón, is ideal for those who want to explore the park and byways. And the setting right beside the highway and above the river is astounding. A swimming pool is fed from a natural waterfall and trails lead along the river banks through luxuriant tropical gardens into the rain forest. A one-story building framing a central courtyard has 15 guest rooms, some with hot water and television. The large restaurant under a thatched roof is the perfect spot for a break from driving.

How to Get There

Highway 32 runs northeast from San José to the park and Limón. Despite it's modern appearance, it is one of the most terrifying roads in the country. North of Heredia the slick asphalt lanes climb quickly to 2,000 m (6,560 ft) and almost certain mist, fog or rainfall. Temperatures drop, visibility decreases and trucks barrel down hills. Mud and rock slides (*derrumbes*) are common, and the highway is frequently closed as workers use bulldozers to clear natural debris or vehicular accidents. Road closures can last from a few hours to days; traffic is directed to lengthy alternate byways through Turrialba or Sarapiquí. Don't even think of driving this road after dark; always start out as early in the day as possible.

There is a ranger station at Zurquí just outside the highway tunnel with a few short trails that take you far enough into the forest for good bird watching. Take extreme care on the trails — robberies have occurred here. Check in at the ranger station before and after your hike. Buses from San José to Guápiles will drop you off and pick you up at the ranger station.

The Volcán Barva ranger station is 29 km (18 miles) north of San José at the end of the road to Sacramento and San José de la Montaña. A precarious but passable dirt and mud road runs four kilometers (two and a half miles) from Sacramento to the Barva station; four-wheel drive is essential year round, but the road may be completely impassable in the rainy season.

CARTAGO

The colonial capital of Costa Rica until 1823, Cartago is now the capital of the province of the same name and the gateway to the south-central region of the country. Travelers rarely spend the night here; instead, they stop to view the town's colonial structures before heading on to Turrialba, Orosí or the Volcán Irazú.

A busy, populous city of 13,500 inhabitants, Cartago has bits of colonial charm left from the days when it was first founded by Juan Vázquez de Coronado in 1563. Its greatest attraction is the **Basilica de Nuestra Señora de los Angeles**, the most important Catholic church in the country.

If possible, visit the church on a Sunday when you'll see Costa Ricans from surrounding towns dressed in their finest spending the day at the church and nearby park. I was fortunate to arrive on a Sunday when there was a big soccer game on television (thus clearing the streets of traffic) and First Communion was being held at several churches in the area. It seemed everyone in town had brought their daughters and sons dressed in frilly white dresses and stern suits to be photographed in front of the church; the children, regardless of their fine attire, were soon chasing pigeons around the dull

---

Coatamundis become acclimated to nature guides along popular trails in Parque Nacional Braulio Carrillo.

gray cement plaza that faces the basilica. The church itself is the most imposing in the country, a massive gray hulk with white domes. An earthquake nearly destroyed the church in 1926; it was quickly rebuilt with Byzantine touches.

Crowds pack the interior on Sundays, lined up against the wood-paneled walls under stained glass windows. Equally popular is the shrine behind the church devoted to La Negrita, the country's patron saint. La Negrita, also called the Virgin of Los Angeles, is said to have appeared to a

gious statues for help with whatever ails them. Picnic tables, a basketball court and ice cream vendors surround the shop.

Five blocks from the church are the ruins of **La Iglesia de la Parroquí**, which was originally built in 1575. The church was destroyed by earthquakes and volcanoes several times and was rebuilt each time until it completely crumbled in the earthquake of 1910. The stone walls draped in scarlet bougainvillea remain, and a garden fills the interior courtyard which is very occasionally open to the public.

small girl on a rock below where the church is built; some say the virgin was a doll made of black stone. Her statue is above the main altar. The shrine behind the church is built around a spring whose waters are said to have curative powers. Believers wait their turn to touch the spring's water, splashing it over their heads and faces, drinking it and filling bottles of every size and shape imaginable with water to take home.

Across the street behind the church is **El Sancturario Exvotos y Articulosos Religiosas**, a shop packed with T-shirts depicting the virgin, holy cards, prayer books and glass counters filled with *milagros*, tiny metal arms, hearts, spines and other body parts used by the faithful to deposit at reli-

How to Get There

The Bernardo Soto Highway (for the most part unlabeled) travels southeast from San José 18 km (11 miles) to Cartago. A large parking lot is across from the basilica; there is a small charge for parking but the lot is guarded and it has clean restrooms. Public buses from San José stop directly opposite the church.

VOLCÁN IRAZÚ

Usually visited on a day trip from San José, the Volcán Irazú looms 3,432 m (11,260 ft) high above Cartago province's agricultural valleys. The road from Cartago quickly climbs past ranches and farms to a nearly barren, veritable moonscape of rock and ash in the Parque Nacional Volcán Irazú. Bring a jacket and umbrella or poncho; the annual rainfall is more than two meters (more than seven feet), and the average temperature is 11°C (52°F). The volcano's name comes from the word *istarú*, which means "Thunder and Earthquake Mountain," an apt description, for Irazú has been active and highly destructive at least since colonial times. The first recorded eruption took place in 1563, the latest in 1963 when United States President John F. Kennedy

was visiting the country. This volcano has been dormant since 1965, though occasional bursts of steam, gas and ash and underground tremors inspire respect. A trail leads from the parking lot to the main crater, one of five. Stubby trees and scrub grasses attempt to thrive in the ash, but little life can exist near the craters. It's said that you can see both coasts from the craters on a clear morning, though a cold mist and fog will likely obscure the view. John Lloyd Stephens, who climbed the volcano in the 1840s, witnessed the clouds lifting from under the volcano's peak:

"*The lofty point on which we stood was perfectly clear, the atmosphere was of transparent purity, and, looking beyond the region of*

San José and the Meseta Central

desolation, below us at a distance of perhaps two thousand feet, the whole country was covered with clouds and the city at the foot of the volcano invisible.

"*By degrees the more distant clouds were lifted, and over the immense bed we saw at the same moment the Atlantic and Pacific Oceans. The points at which they were visible were the Gulf of Nicoya and the harbor of San Juan, which were not directly opposite but nearly at right angles to each other, so that we could see both oceans without turning the body.*"

Accommodations are sparse near the park, but you must stop at the wonderful **Restaurante Linda Vista** (380-8090, a mountain cabin with wooden walls covered with business cards, passport photos and friendly notes from visitors who have traveled here from all over the world. When I last stopped by on a freezing, rainy morning I was the only guest except for two dripping wet motorcycle cops. We three sat in front of a roaring fire drying our clothes and sipping strong coffee as the rain pounded outside. There are two simple, inexpensive cabins behind the restaurant available for overnight guests.

How to Get There

Irazú is 32 km (20 miles) north of Cartago on a good paved road. Most visitors arrive on tours from San José. Make sure your tour arrives at the park early in the day. Those driving on their own can combine a visit to the volcano (about two hours from San José) with stops in Cartago and the Orosí Valley. The only bus to the park travels on weekends, departing from San José's Gran Hotel. Check at the hotel for information and schedules.

OROSÍ TO CACHÍ DAM

One of the most beautiful drives in the entire country begins in Cartago and heads south through Paraíso and the Orosí Valley over the Río Reventazón and the Cachí Dam. The first stop is at the **Jardín Botánico Lankaster** (552-3151, just outside Paraíso, a paradise for orchid enthusiasts. British

OPPOSITE: The Basilica in Cartago is the country's most important church. ABOVE: First communion in Cartago.

naturalist Charles H. Lankaster began the garden in the 1950s; it now belongs to the University of Costa Rica. Plant lovers are enamored with the 10.7-hectare (26-acre) botanical gardens, and they can spend hours wandering the paths, viewing more than 40 species of bamboo surrounding a Japanese temple, a startling cactus and succulent garden that seems out of place in the humid setting, several palm groves and vivid clusters of heliconia. Lankaster was particularly interested in epiphytes (plants that live on other plants), and you can see

simple adobe church built in 1735, peaks over a cluster of small neat houses. The small museum next to the church holds a fascinating collection of religious paintings and icons.

The road (part pavement, part dirt) continues on to the Río Palomo and **Parque Nacional Tapantí**, one of the wettest spots in the country. Scores of rivers and streams run through the park, making it an important watershed. The Costa Rican Electric Institute (ICE) has constructed a hydroelectric dam here on the Río Macho. Birders and

this phenomenon of interdependence in the brilliant pink, red and yellow bromeliads hanging from tree trunks and branches. Greenhouses and the orchid trail contain approximately 800 species of these delicate, showy flowers; the best time to see them in bloom is from February to May. The road to the garden is just west of Paraíso; look for the sign and sky-high electricity transformers on your right. Buses from Cartago to Paraíso will let you off at the entrance.

The road south from Paraíso cuts through a jumble of bougainvillea, ferns and coffee plants to the village of Orosí tucked in a small valley. The red-tiled roof of the **Iglesia de San José de Orosí**, a

hikers revel in the park's dense vegetation and, bundled up in jackets and rain gear, slog along trails through the forest; the **Sendero la Pava** leads from the **Sendero Oropendola** to a powerful waterfall over the Río Grande de Orosí. There are restrooms and picnic shelters near the ranger station, but lodging is not available in the vicinity. Most visitors arrive on day trips from San José.

Back at Río Macho another road curves east and north to the village of Cachí and the lake of the same name, formed by a dam built by ICE through the Río Reventazón. At the side of the lake is the astonishing **Casa el Soñador**, the House of the Dreamer. Covered in woodcarvings, the house is home to the Quesada family, who will give you a tour of the interior and offer woodcrafts for sale. The road continues on through coffee plantations to a lookout point with views Ujarrás, of one of the most picturesque colonial villages in Costa Rica. Follow a narrow, winding road down to the village to see the ruins of the **Iglesia de Nuestra Señora de la Limpia Concepción**, built in 1693. The main road continues back to Paraíso and Cartago; the entire circuit takes about three hours.

TURRIALBA

An agricultural town adjacent to the ríos Reventazón and Pacuaré, Turrialba is becoming an increasingly popular destination for travelers. Sugar cane fields and coffee and macadamia nut plantations surround the crowded town, which has become headquarters for workers constructing yet another hydroelectric dam nearby on the Río Pacuaré. Several rafting companies use Turrialba as their launching point for trips down both rivers, and Costa Rica's largest archaeological site, Guayabo, is nearby.

What to See and Do

The town of Turrialba is worth a quick go-round if you're in need of groceries or other supplies. From town, one road leads southeast to the Turrialba Valley and the best accommodations in the area, while another runs north to **Monumento Nacional Guayabo**, a site well worth visiting if you are interested in Costa Rica's pre-Columbian history. The road to Guayabo runs through small settlements outside Turrialba, and turns from pavement to rock and dirt intermittently. After climbing through forest and clouds you'll spot a turnoff to the ruins on the left; from here to the ruins is a slow four-kilometer (two-and-a-half-mile) drive, which took me more than a half-hour to traverse in a rented sedan.

The archaeological site is in far better condition than the road and covers about 20 hectares (50 acres), though only a portion has been excavated. The **Sendero de los Montículos** through the site is marked with signs describing the archaeological

and natural importance of each section. The park contains the only primary forest left in Cartago province, along with secondary forest. At least 173 species of birds, 14 of mammals and 15 species of snakes have been spotted here — the snakes include the deadly terciopelo or fer-de-lance, much feared and respected throughout Central America. Wear sturdy hiking boots when walking these trails.

Archaeologists believe Guayabo may have been inhabited as early as 1400 BC, and had about 500 residents (their origins

are unknown) at its peak. Most of the structures uncovered thus far were built between AD 300 and 700. Construction seems to have halted and the site to have been abandoned by 1400 AD. Important structures that have been excavated include three tombs where bodies were buried on top of each other with pottery and food and several rock monoliths with paintings and carvings. The **Monolito Jaguar y Largarto** with carvings of the gods of water and earth sits by the path, and workers have unearthed tools and materials believed to

OPPOSITE: The Casa el Soñador, House of the Dreamer, in Orosí Valley. ABOVE: School vacations coincide with the coffee harvest so children can help pick the ripe beans and earn colones.

have been used in creating sculptures and petroglyphs. You can see most of the excavated site from atop **El Mirador Encuentro con Nuestros Origenes**, "The Encounter with Our Origins Lookout Point" before climbing downhill to the main aqueduct and *tanque de captacion* (water tank) that shows the Guayabo people to have used advanced methods of agriculture. Wide cobbled *calzados*, or roads, connect various parts of the site. Guayabo is closed on Mondays, and open from 8 AM to 3:30 PM the rest of the week.

Where to Stay

Several small hotels are available right in Turrialba town, but traffic noise and the blare of a siren every morning at 6 AM are major deterrents to staying here. Far preferable are the lodgings near the Río Reventazón southeast of town.

VERY EXPENSIVE

Spend a lazy afternoon sipping coffee on your terrace as the rain feeds the Reventazón and you may decide to extend your stay at **Casa Turire** (531-1111 or 531-1309 FAX 531-1075, Apdo 303-7150, Turrialba. Designed as a country estate in the midst of sugar cane, coffee and macadamia fields, this 16-room inn is indeed exquisite

and serene. Formal gardens and lawns line the driveway to the peak-roofed, golden-colored Casa. A two-story atrium in the lobby leads to a wood-paneled formal library, a cozy bar that opens to a verandah and the dining room with French doors leading to the patio and pool. The 12 standard rooms are spacious, decorated with antiques and filled with light from glass doors leading to balconies; the large bathrooms have showers and bath tubs (a true luxury) and hair dryers. Each of the four suites has a separate seating area. A trail leads along the banks of the river, where you can spot blue morpho butterflies, hummingbirds, parakeets and oropendulas. Horseback rides through the Hacienda Atirro property of the Rojas family (who own the hotel) lead through cane fields and up steep mountain trails. Rafting, mountain biking, hiking, kayaking and tours to Guayabo are available.

INEXPENSIVE

A rough road leads up the mountainside 11 km (seven miles) from Turrialba to **Pochotel** (556-0111 FAX 556-6222, Apdo 258, Turrialba. This six-cabin, rustic hostelry, sits atop a mountain with fabulous night views of the lights of Turrialba (from below, the hotel's illuminated Coca Cola sign looks like a red beacon in the sky). The restaurant, serving the basic rice, beans, chicken and beef, is a favorite of river rafters who drip their way in at lunch. The rooms have private baths and undependable hot water.

A Giant rain forest locust ABOVE and a Howler monkey RIGHT find their lunches in trees.

Central and North-western Guana-caste

GUANACASTE PROVINCE doesn't start until you cross the Río Lagarto, but political boundaries can't disguise the fact that Costa Rica's cowboy country begins just north of Puntarenas. Cattle ranches sprawl on both sides of the Carretera Interamericana, populated with sturdy zebu stock with big floppy ears and immense humps, imported from India (via Brazil) more than a hundred years ago because their temperament is ideal for the region's hot, dry climate.

Although 75 percent of the province is flat, a chain of towering volcanoes snakes up its eastern flank, a primeval landscape of smoldering cinder cones and cloud forest that harbors more plant and animal species per hectare than any other part of the Americas. The Río Tempisque meanders through central Guanacaste, carving out a massive flood plain that harbors crocodiles and profuse bird life before it empties into the Golfo de Nicoya. Guanacaste encompasses a huge portion of northwest Costa Rica, including Lago Arenal, much of the Nicoya Peninsula's Pacific coastline and several national parks. The fiery Volcán Arenal and the cloud forests of Monteverde lie beside Guanacaste's eastern borders.

BACKGROUND

The sabaneros (cowboys) of Guanacaste have always considered themselves different from their countrymen. And for good reason. Their ancestors were among the earliest European settlers in Central America, settling the region in the late sixteenth century. When the region broke away from Spanish rule in the 1820s, Guanacaste nearly became a small independent nation wedged between Nicaragua and Costa Rica. Locals voted to become part of Costa Rica, but the province remained nominally independent for another 30 years.

There is still a great deal of local pride, reflected in the fact that Guanacastans continue to cherish their cultural heritage — music, dance and cowboy skills demonstrated at scores of local fiestas and rodeos during the dry season (November to April).

Bullfights and equestrian parades are also popular, especially on July 25, a provincial holiday which commemorates Guanacaste's "independence" from Nicaragua. The province's trademark — and Costa Rica's national tree — is the huge, leafy guanacaste (also called the "ear tree" because its dark gray seed pods resemble a pair of ears).

Although ranching still dominates the local economy, Guanacaste also supports a thriving sugar cane industry. Tourism has become increasingly important in recent

years thanks to the area's many national parks, reserves and beaches. The Carretera Interamericana allows quick access from San José, with most of the major sights within a three or four hour drive of the capital.

MONTEVERDE

Monteverde (Green Mountain) is a lush plateau that hovers at a breezy 1,400 m (4,592 ft) above the Guanacaste plains. The mist-shrouded Cordillera de Tilarán and its fabulous cloud forest tower behind, an ever-present reminder that Monteverde lies at the edge of Costa Rica's greatest wilderness. **Santa Elena** is the area's only village, but Monteverde's built-up area stretches

PRECEEDING PAGES: In the Monteverde Cloud Forest LEFT, it rains 300 inches per year. Visitors to the Butterfly Garden RIGHT, in this damp region, get close to hundreds of species of these ephemeral creatures. OPPOSITE: Salvadorian writer Marcelino García Flamenco's grave is perched over Bahía Salinas; and the Cordillera de Guanacaste looms over grazing lands in the northwest.

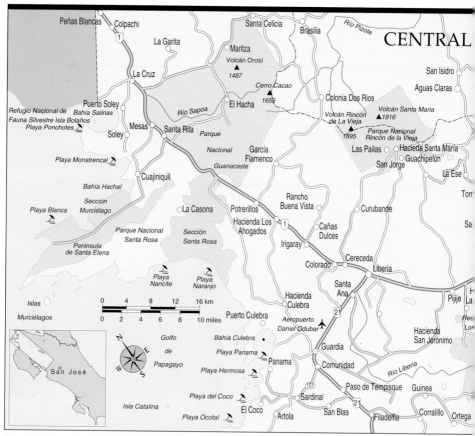

for six kilometers (nearly four miles) along the plateau, alternating between pasture-land, pine groves and rustic hotels that seem more like something out of the Canadian Rockies or Grand Tetons than something you would expect to find in Latin America.

BACKGROUND

The human history of Monteverde is almost as fascinating as its natural heritage. Once upon a time (1951) a dozen Quaker families fled the United States in search of a country without an army or military service. They found exactly what they were looking for in Costa Rica, which had abolished its army several years earlier. The Quakers purchased a large tract of virgin land in the Tilarán mountains and went to work building a new community. Dairy farming seemed natural here because of the alpine climate and the verdant local

pastures, and this evolved into a cheese-making business that still thrives today. Although the Quakers are now a minority in Monteverde, their presence is still strong. Their cheese factory is the area's largest single employer, they own many of the hotels and shops on the mountain, and the Friend's Meeting House doubles as an active community center.

In the early 1950s, the Quakers decided to preserve a large section of woodland as a watershed for their power plant and various rural enterprises. But they were also conscious that the local rain forest would eventually disappear if land clearance wasn't stopped. The Quakers opened the area to scientific study and eventually set aside part of the watershed as a small conservation zone. In 1975, the **Reserva Biológica Monteverde** came into being.

Now managed by a private trust called the **Centro Científico Tropical** (Tropical Science Center of Costa Rica), the preserve

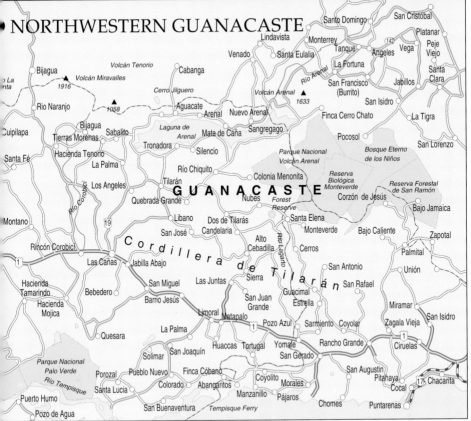

NORTHWESTERN GUANACASTE

encompasses 10,500 hectares (26,000 acres) of unspoiled rain forest on the upper reaches of the Río Peñas Blancas. Over the years the park has been expanded and augmented with grants from a number of international organizations including the World Wildlife Fund, the Nature Conservancy, the Rare Animal Relief Effort and the governments of Canada, Denmark and the United States.

WHAT TO SEE AND DO

Monteverde's **Reserva Bosque Nuboso** (Cloud Forest Reserve) is extraordinary — a lush mountain habitat formed by a combination of high humidity and low cloud cover from trade winds that blow across the cordillera. The area receives between three and five meters of rain each year, water which provokes incredibly lush plant growth: ferns and moss, orchids and magnolia and huge zapote trees with their

buttress roots. Animal life is also abundant: more than 1,200 species of reptiles and amphibians, 400 types of bird and 100 different mammals are found here. Jaguars and puma are known to exist in the park, but sightings are rare because they live deep in the forest. Nearly everyone sees monkeys, either howlers or capuchins. Most people come for the bird watching, especially a chance to spot the resplendent quetzal, sacred bird of the Maya, which is found in greater number at Monteverde than any other place in Costa Rica.

All told, there are about 120 km (74 miles) of hiking trails, but the most popular walks are in the western corner, an area called **The Triangle** that fans out from the entrance gate and visitor center.

Sendero Bosque Nuboso (Cloud Forest Trail) is a self-guided nature walk with numbers that correspond to a booklet that can be purchased at the entrance. This trail offers probably the best quetzal spotting in the park, as well as a chance to stride the Continental Divide. Be forewarned: these lovely birds are easier heard than seen. The **Sendero Pantanoso** (Swamp Trail) crosses over a marshy region on wooden boardwalks. **Sendero Río** (River Trail) hugs the banks of Quebrada Cuecha, with an observation deck that looks over a double waterfall.

Most people walk the park unescorted, but you can join a guided tour if you like. Bird-watching tours and night tours are also available. The preserve is open daily 7 AM to 4 PM.

The **Santa Elena Forest Reserve**, another private rain forest park, is six kilometers (nearly four miles) north of town, off the Tilarán Road. In many respects Santa Elena is a carbon copy of the large Monteverde preserve. But there is one unique attraction: a rain forest canopy tour that takes you high into the trees in a harness attached to pulleys running between elevated wooden platforms — a bird's-eye view of the cloud forest that you won't soon forget. Entrance fees support reserve operations and local high school education.

Although it is still largely off-limits to the general public, another important wilderness area is the **Bosque Eterno de los Niños**, the Children's Eternal Forest, which wraps around three sides of the Reserva Bosque Nuboso. This reserve traces its origins to nine-year-old Roland Tiensuu, a Swedish schoolboy who penned a letter to the Monteverde Conservation League in 1987 asking what children could do to save the rain forest. Roland and his classmates later raised enough money to purchase six hectares (15 acres) of Costa Rican forest. Soon kids from 21 countries were raising funds to buy more forest. Today the Bosque Eterno de los Niños covers more than 13,000 hectares (32,000 acres), with plans for expanding further along the cordillera.

Bajo del Tigre, or Jaguar Canyon, a small section of the Bosque de los Niños near downtown Monteverde, is open to the public. It has a children's nature center, a small arboretum and self-guided trails. The Bosque de los Niños and its efforts to protect additional lands are managed by

the **Monteverde Conservation League** (645-5003 FAX 645-5104 E-MAIL acmmcl@ sol.racsa.co.cr.

Other tourist attractions in the Monteverde area include the **Butterfly Garden** (entrance fee includes guided tour); the **Serpentario** snake farm; and the **Finca Ecológico**, a private game reserve where you can see local species such as coatamundi, sloth and white-faced capuchin monkeys.

DOWNTOWN MONTEVERDE

Downtown Monteverde is a bustling little village area that surrounds a grassy square about halfway between Santa Elena and the Monteverde Reserva Bosque Nuboso entrance. Lots of distractions here: **Casem Gallery** displays souvenirs and handicrafts made by local artisans. **Café Monteverde** is a pint-sized coffee factory where you can watch the roasting process and buy beans for home consumption. **Stella's Café** doubles as a bakery and art gallery for original works by sisters Stella and Meg Wallace. There's a small grocery store, too. Up the road is **La Lechería**, the cheese factory, which sells 16 varieties. If you happen to visit in January, catch the **Monteverde Music Festival**, a month-long jamboree that features artists from around the globe.

WHERE TO STAY

Monteverde offers a wider range of accommodations than any other nature area in Costa Rica except Manuel Antonio. Lodges fill quickly in the dry season; make reservations far in advance through fax or e-mail.

Expensive
The top of the line is the **Monteverde Lodge** (645-5057 FAX 645-5126 E-MAIL costaric @expeditions.co.cr, Apdo 6941-1000, San José. What do you say about a place that has a huge Jacuzzi inside a glass-walled atrium at one side of the lobby? You can soak in the pool, sip a margarita and watch the sunset over the Golfo de Nicoya — something you can't do anywhere else on the mountain. The gourmet restaurant is

equally renowned. And the rooms are of rare quality: wood and glass decor, modern, American-style bathrooms, comfortable furnishings. The staff, however, can seem a cold and indifferent at times.

It might well be difficult to find a more romantic abode than the **El Sapo Dorado** ℂ 645-5010/5184 FAX 645-5180/5181 E-MAIL elsapo@sol.racsa.co.cr, Apdo 9-5655, Monteverde. The creation of local rancher Geovanny Arguedas and his Quaker partner Hannah Lowther, the "Golden Toad" sprawls across a wooded hillside with

miles) up the road, and the hotel will organize backcountry trips to Peñas Blancas and San Gerardo.

For an all together different experience, try out the **Ecolodge San Luis** ℂ/FAX 380-3255 or 645-5277 E-MAIL smithdp@ctrvax .vanderbilt.edu, Apdo 36, Santa Elena de Monteverde. Situated 40 minutes southeast of Santa Elena, the Ecolodge is part of a 66-hectare (162-acre) coffee plantation and fruit farm that bills itself as a model of sustainable tropical ecotourism. All of the usual Monteverde activities are available

lavish views in all directions. The chalets include 20 rooms with private baths, fireplaces and terraces or balconies. El Sapo Dorado also offers five kilometers (more than three miles) of trails through the neighboring woodland.

Moderate

Hotel Fonda Vela ℂ/FAX 661-2551, Apdo 10165, San José, occupies a 14 hectare (35 acre) farm on the edges of the cloud forest. Hardwoods and native stone abound in this delightfully rustic inn. Views from the guest rooms and restaurant look across emerald-green pastures and ranch land to the Golfo de Nicoya. The reserve is two kilometers (less than one and a quarter

to guests, and the lodge offers a unique opportunity to meet local farmers, participate in research programs and get your hands dirty on various farm chores such as picking coffee and delivering it by horseback to the processing plant. Accommodations are in spacious cabinas with private baths, or at the bunkhouse.

Originally built by Quakers and Costa Ricans to serve biologists visiting the cloud forest, rustic charm and friendliness prevail at the **Hotel de Montaña Monteverde** ℂ 645-5046 or 224-3050 FAX 645-5320 or 222-6184 E-MAIL monteverde@ticonet .co.cr, Apdo 2070-1002, Paseo de los

Roses bushes frame tame green lawns behind the Monteverde Lodge.

Estudiantes, San José. There are 26 rooms (including a suite with Jacuzzi overlooking the forest), all with private bath and hot water.

The closest hotel to the Monteverde Reserva Bosque Nuboso is the **Villa Verde** (645-5025 FAX 645-5115, about one kilometer (a little over half a mile) from the park entrance. Run by Costa Rican nature-lover Irene Villalobos and her two affable sons, the Villa Verde is a rustic lodge built of wood, stone and glass. The rooms are tidy, the bathrooms are large and have hot water. The food is excellent, from hearty breakfasts to superb Tico cuisine at night. In the evenings guests gather around the stone fireplace.

Inexpensive

Hotel el Bosque (645-5221 FAX 645-5129, features 21 cabinas that sprawl across the forested hillside in helter-skelter fashion. Each has a private bath and hot water. The wood-paneled restaurant is one of the best in Monteverde.

Santa Elena has half a dozen pensions within a block of the bus station. One of the better of these is **Pensión el Tucán** (645-5017 FAX 645-5462, a modest but pleasant, small hotel that's run by Rosa Jiménez and her family. The wood-paneled rooms come with private or shared bath with hot water. El Toucan can organize horseback riding trips.

Pensión Manakín (645-5080 FAX 645-5517, named after a local bird, is farther up the road towards Monteverde reserve. Nothing fancy here, but the price is right and the owners will treat you like a part of the family.

WHERE TO EAT

Many of the hotels at Monteverde offer excellent meals. Locals say **El Sapo Dorado** has the best food and probably the most romantic atmosphere — a hilltop location overlooking the forest. The menu specializes in vegetarian fare (for example, grilled tofu), but there's plenty on offer for carnivores, including steamed shrimp and clams, white sea bass and beef tongue with asparagus. There's also a good wine selection.

Another gourmet choice is the **Monteverde Lodge**. The glass-enclosed dining area seems to hover over the mountainside and is a magical place at sunset. The menu ranges from filet mignon and grilled chicken with palm hearts to dorado and pasta alfredo. The wine cellar includes labels from France, Spain, Chile and California.

For local food, both the **Villa Verde** and **El Bosque** offer wholesome Tico cuisine in large quantities.

The influx of tourists in recent years has lead to the establishment of a number of Italian restaurants. **Da Lucia** (on the same road as the bull ring and butterfly farm) has fairly good Italian cuisine, but you may have to wait for a table because this place is very popular. **La Pizzeria de Johnny** offers basic Italian fare (pizza, pasta, garlic bread) with bright decor and a friendly staff.

Stella's Café is without a doubt the best place in Monteverde to forget about your diet. Offerings range from fresh coffee, hot chocolate and fruit milk shakes (avocado, papaya, banana, blackberry) to mango pie, chocolate brownies and fresh-baked bread. Stella's also serves breakfast and light lunches. **Chunches Café** in Santa Elena offers espresso along with its selection of used books and foreign newspapers, and the café doubles as a laundromat.

If you're in the mood for nightlife, try **Taberna Valverdes** in Santa Elena, with music and cold beer that attracts a young crowd of locals and tourists. If the tunes are too loud for you, sit beneath the pine trees in the garden.

HOW TO GET THERE

The turnoff point for Monteverde is a tiny place called Lagarto, on the Carretera Interamericana, about two hours from San José. The junction is marked by a large sign and two roadside cafés with cold drinks and toilets. The 35-km (22-miles) route up the mountain is almost as legendary as the place itself — one of the worst roads in a country which is known for horrible highways. A four-wheel-drive vehicle is not necessary, but it would help in negotiating the countless potholes, ruts and protruding stones.

Monteverde can also be reached via a 40-km (25-mile) backroad from Tilarán. Despite rumors to the contrary, this route is no worse than the road from Lagarto to Monteverde and it's much more scenic, through rolling ranch country where you're sure to come across cowboys and ox carts.

An alternative when leaving Monteverde is combined horse and water travel. **Leonel Quesada (** 645-5087 or 645-5354 provides horseback trips through the San Gerardo Valley to Lago Arenal, where a boat takes you across to the north shore.

and dairy farms reminiscent of central California and southern Spain. A highway snakes around the west and north shores, but east of Nuevo Arenal most of the road is unpaved.

Activities in the lake area include fishing, boating, windsurfing, horseback riding, mountain biking, hiking and camping on small islands. Arenal is said to be well-stocked with game fish including *guapote* (rainbow bass), *machaca* (shad) and the tasty African tilapia. This lake is also wonderful for swimming, with water

From there, take a taxi to La Fortuna or any of the Arenal hotels.

Express buses run twice daily between San José and Monteverde (four hours). Buy your return ticket as early as possible because buses back to San José are often full.

temperatures hovering at 20°C (68°F) year round. Windsurfing enthusiasts flock to Arenal from around the globe to catch the lake's strong, consistent winds — 15 to 35 knots during the winter season from November to April. The "bump and jump" is excellent.

LAGO ARENAL

In 1973, the Costa Rican government built a large earthen dam on the Río Arenal, creating **Lago Arenal**, a 30-km (19-mile)-long reservoir that is now the prime recreational lake in all of Central America. Arenal is surrounded by rolling hills — a picturesque landscape of cattle ranches

WHAT TO SEE AND DO

Two towns serve the lake region. **Nuevo Arenal** is on the north shore, created in 1973 to resettle villagers displaced by the rising waters. **Tilarán**, five kilometers (three miles) south of the lake, crowns an

The porch is an essential ingredient of a Lago Arenal vacation.

emerald-green ridge. It's more of a cowboy town than a resort village, with rodeo and livestock shows in April and June. Tilarán is an important crossroads: Cañas is 23 km (14 miles) to the west via a good paved road that links up with the Carretera Interamericana; Monteverde is two hours or 42 km (26 miles) to the southeast on a rough and tumble backroad that starts at Quebrada Grande.

In addition to the lake, there are several worthwhile sights in the immediate area. **Jardín Botánica Arenal**, five kilometers

(three miles) east of Nuevo Arenal, offers a lavish assortment of tropical plants and flowers, created by American Mike LeMay. **Lago Coter** is five kilometers (three miles) northwest of Nuevo Arenal. A lodge that overlooks this tiny crater lake (see below) offers horseback riding, hiking and mountain biking on 740 hectares (300 acres) of private forest. You can also kayak and fish the lake.

The recently created **Parque Nacional Tenorio**, which embraces a 1,916-m (6,284-ft) volcano of the same name, is due east of Lago Arenal. The turnoff to the park is at Río Piedras. There are no visitor facilities at the present time.

Water sports occupy the much of the visitor's time here. **Tilawa Viento Surf** (695-5050 TOLL-FREE (800) 851-8929 FAX 695-5766 E-MAIL tilawa@sol.racsa.co.cr, rents Hobie Cats and windsurfers. Equipment includes Nash custom and Mistral production equipment. Windsurfing classes from beginner to advanced are available. A Norwegian named Stein runs the show.

Tico Wind (/FAX 695-5387 E-MAIL 106346 .510@compuserve.com, rents windsurfing equipment including Ezzy Wave and Transformer sails, BIC and Gorge Animal custom boards. Classes from beginner to advanced, including several clinics each year with five-time world champion Rhonda Smith, are available.

JJ's Fishing Tours (695-5825 offers half- and full-day fishing excursions including all equipment, lunch and drinks. **Tree Dwellers** (225-4049 has Lago Arenal boat tours, fishing trips, water skiing and island camping.

Horseback rides into the forest around Lago Coter can be arranged through **Stables Arenal** (694-4092 FAX 695-5387.

WHERE TO STAY

Expensive

The first accommodation on the road from Tilarán is the very unusual **Hotel Tilawa** (695-5050 TOLL-FREE (800) 851-8929 FAX 695-5766 E-MAIL tilawa@sol.racsa.co.cr, Apdo 92-5710, Tilarán. The Tilawa bills itself as the Costa Rican version of the ancient palace of Knossos in Crete, a fantasy land of ochre columns, colorful handpainted frescoes, handmade textiles and custom-made furniture. The guest rooms are modern and spacious, with air conditioning and private baths. Amenities include swimming pool, tennis courts, a windsurfing center, car rental, horseback riding and fishing trips.

The **Hotel los Héroes** (/FAX 441-4193, Apdo 5542-1000, San José, is a Swiss-owned establishment that wouldn't look out of place in Zermatt or Interlaken. It's situated near the lake's eastern extreme, where pastureland gives way to rain forest. The 12 rooms are spartan but spanking clean, with private baths. The restaurant serves Swiss and Austrian specialties.

Moderate

Perched on a hill above the lake's western shore is **Mystica Lodge** (/FAX 695-5387 WEB http://members.aol.com/mysticacr/index.html, Apdo 29, Tilarán. Barbara and Francesco, a delightful Italian couple, run the spacious, six-room lodge with a family style touch, including hearty meals; their pizza is said to be the best in the Arenal region.

Chalet Nicholas (/FAX 694-4041, Apdo 72-5710, Tilarán, is another family establishment, although it's difficult to tell who really runs this place — John and Cathy Nichols or their three great danes! About five minutes from Nuevo Arenal, this topnotch bed and breakfast has three unique rooms that overlook either lake or forest. Breakfast is prepared with organic fruits grown on the property (try the macadamia pancakes). Cathy tends an orchid garden, John tinkers in a woodworking shop, and either is happy to show you the ins and outs of their hobbies.

The **Eco Lodge Lake Coter** (257-5075 FAX 257-7065, Apdo 8-5570-1000, San José, is almost a world unto itself. Poised on the edge of tiny Lake Coter, the lodge offers 24 rooms (most with shared bath) and 16 cabins (all with private bath) in a wilderness setting. The main building here has a restaurant, lounge with fireplace, game room with pool table, bar and library. Activities include hiking, horseback riding, boating and fishing.

Inexpensive

Equestrian and aquatic are the main themes at **Xiloe Lodge** (259-9806 FAX 259-9882, Apdo 35, Tilarán. Like many of the hotels at the lake's western extreme, Xiloe caters to windsurfers. But it's also big on horses, arranging scenic rides into the nearby hills. The lodge has a cowboy-themed restaurant, the **Equus BBQ**, down on the lake shore. Accommodations are in bungalows with refrigerators, or cabins with small kitchens. All units have private baths and hot water.

WHERE TO EAT

Where you dine depends largely on which end of the lake you're staying. At the western end try **Mystica Lodge** for pizza, the **Equus BBQ** for chicken and steaks or **Soda la Macha** in Río Piedras village for other Norte Americano food in a spectacular open-air dining room (with fireplace) which overlooks the lake. A good place for

lunch is **La Rana de Arenal**, which has an outdoor terrace, fabulous garden and superb lake views. **Rosetta** restaurant at the Hotel Tilawa has probably the best menu on this side of the lake.

Near the eastern end, try **Sabor Italiano** for pizza, **Restaurante Picapiedra** at La Alondra Lodge for other Italian fare or **Los Héroes** restaurant for Alpine specialties such as fondue, smoked pork cutlets and wiener schnitzel. Nuevo Arenal's most popular eateries are **Pizzeria Tramonti** and **El Toro Bravo**. **Toad Hall**, next to the Marina Club,

offers homemade cakes, cookies and brownies, which you can munch on the open-air terrace overlooking the lake.

HOW TO GET THERE

Lago Arenal can be approached from two directions: the via Cañas and Tilarán or via Fortuna. Either way the lake is a three- to four-hour drive from San José along fairly good roads (by Costa Rican standards). The road between Cañas and Tilarán runs through heavy duty cattle ranching country, deforested tracts that have evolved into

OPPOSITE and ABOVE: Lago Arenal is a playground for boaters, anglers and windsurfers.

rolling hills that straddle the Continental Divide. There is daily bus service from San José to Nuevo Arenal and Tilarán.

PARQUE NACIONAL VOLCÁN ARENAL

Many visitors feel that Volcán Arenal is the most spectacular sight in all of Costa Rica, and for good reason. This behemoth erupts at least once every hour, spewing molten lava and noxious gases, hurling house-sized stones and clouds of ash into the deep blue sky, and rumbling with the ferocity of an angry giant. Arenal is mesmerizing at any time of day, but it's especially magical at night, when a river of red-hot magma flows down its northern slopes.

BACKGROUND

Formed roughly 4,000 years ago, Arenal, 1,633-m (5,356-ft)-high, was sacred to the pre-Columbian Indians who inhabited this area. It was dormant in modern times and covered in thick rain forest — until July 1968, when the mountain trembled and suddenly blew its top. The eruption destroyed the villages of Pueblo Nuevo and Tabacón, killing 77 people. Magma flowed freely for nearly five years, creating massive lava fields around the mountain's base. Another large eruption occurred in the late 1970s, creating a second cinder cone at the summit. The last major explosion was in 1993. But every day presents a pyrotechnic show of one sort or another. Arenal rarely disappoints its many fans.

WHAT TO SEE AND DO

The best view of the nightly lava flow is on the northern flank, from Tabacón Springs anywhere along the Fortuna-Nuevo Arenal road. However, there are no trails into the lava fields on this side. Trails and guided tours start on the south side, primarily from the Arenal Observatory Lodge. Even if you're sleeping somewhere else, spend at least a day exploring the lodge and its environs. There's a volcanology museum with a seismograph and a glass-enclosed

restaurant-bar, where you can enjoy a meal or sip a cold beer as Volcán Arenal works its magic.

Four trails lead away from the lodge. The short Cascade Trail (90 minutes) leads to a small waterfall in the jungle. The Cerro Chado Trail (four to five hours) cuts trough a macadamia plantation and up a dormant volcano shrouded in thick rain forest. Inside the crater is an aquamarine lake which can be explored by canoe. The Old Lava Field Trail (two hours) cuts through a jungle-shrouded valley and up Arenal's south flank to the rocky remnants of the 1968 eruption. You can also walk to the New Lava Field (three hours) inside the national park — dark-gray stones that rushed down the western slope in 1993. Just below (buried beneath millions of tons of rock) is Pueblo Nuevo.

Parque Nacional Volcán Arenal, created in 1994, covers the volcano area and rain forest on the southeast shore of Lago Arenal. The only ranger station is five kilometers (just over three miles) south of the Fortuna-Nuevo Arenal road. Self-guided trails lead to the New Lava Field, which is open 8 AM to 10 PM. Bring a flashlight when you hike at night.

Under no circumstance should you attempt to scale Arenal. Tourists have been killed and injured by volcanic activity in recent years because they ignored warnings to stay off the mountain. Hired guides (available at the Observatory Lodge and the ranger station) can take you to about 1,000 m (3,280 ft), but that's as close as you can get to the summit without risking life and limb.

Rest your weary feet at Tabacón Hot Springs on the mountain's northwest flank. Probably nowhere else in the world can you lie on your back in a hot water pool, margarita in hand, and watch bright-red lava flow from a volcano. That is what makes Tabacón so special. Most people come here for at least half a day, roaming between the hot pools, water slides, mud and massage treatments and the swim-up bar. Tabacón's steamy waters (temperatures range from 27 to 39°C or 81 to 102°F) are reputed to cure any number of maladies,

The Volcán Arenal is often shrouded in haze.

including arthritis and dermatological problems. Amenities include changing rooms, towels, lockers, shower blocks and a restaurant. It's open 10 AM to 10 PM.

WHERE TO STAY

EXPENSIVE

The best abode in the entire region is the **Arenal Observatory Lodge** (695-5033 or 257-9489 FAX 257-4220 E-MAIL arenalob @sol.racsa.co.cr, Apdo 321-1007, Paseo Colon, San José. Owned and operated by

the Aspinall brothers, who also run the adjacent macadamia plantation, the lodge was built in 1987 as a volcano observatory for the University of Costa Rica and the Smithsonian Institute. Now open to the general public, the lodge represents rustic elegance at its finest. Try to book rooms 29 or 30, which feature picture windows that frame the steaming volcano and the rain forest below. You can literally lie in bed and watch the fireworks. Horseback riding trips and guide services are available, including marvelous night walks and a hike to the New Lava Field each morning.

A mixed bag of anglers, naturalists, bird watchers and volcano enthusiasts flock to

Arenal Lodge (228-3189 TOLL-FREE (800) 948-3770 FAX 289-6798 E-MAIL arenalodge @centralamerica.com. The lodge is perched on a ridge near the eastern end of Arenal, with panoramic views of both the lake and volcano. The 42 rooms have private baths. Amenities include a library and bar, stone fireplace, game room with pool table, and an inner patio with solarium.

MODERATE

Montaña de Fuego Inn (382-0759 or 479-9106 FAX 479-9579 offers a dozen A-frame

cabins on a grassy knoll eight kilometers (five miles) west of Fortuna. Each unit has private bath, hot water and a balcony with superb views of the volcano.

WHERE TO EAT

Arenal Observatory Lodge has an excellent breakfast buffet and a good selection of beef, chicken and seafood meals for lunch and dinner. The **Hot Springs Restaurant** inside the Tabacón spa, serves both North American and local dishes with a view of the volcano from almost every table. Another dining room with a view is the **Novillas Steak House**, a modest al fresco eatery on the road between Tabacón and Fortuna.

HOW TO GET THERE

Volcán Arenal can be reached from San José via either Tilarán or Fortuna, but the latter route (which also runs through Zarcero and San Carlos) is shorter — about three hours in total. Buses run daily from San José to Fortuna and Nuevo Arenal; from Fortuna you can take a taxi to the national park or hotels around Arenal's base. If you're on the Nuevo Arenal bus, ask the driver to let you off at the turnoff

fiestas, including Palm Sunday when a street market and carnival erupts around the arena.

PARQUE NACIONAL PALO VERDE

Palo Verde is the closest thing that Costa Rica has to North America's Everglades or Australia's Kakadu — a massive area of swamp and forest that hugs the north banks of the ríos Tempisque and Bebedero. The park embraces 12 different life zones including mangrove swamp, marshes, savanna

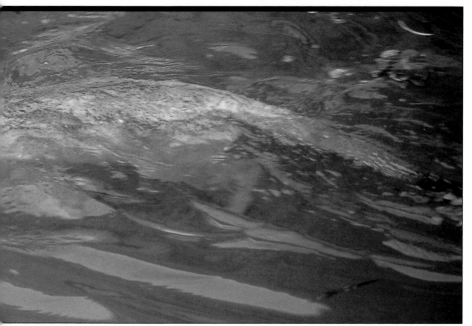

to the Observatory Lodge, about 15 km (nine miles) west of Fortuna.

LAS CAÑAS AND PARQUE NACIONAL PALO VERDE

The sleepy cowboy town of **Las Cañas** (population: 21,000), at the junction of the Carretera Interamericana and the Tilarán-Arenal, road is named after the wild cane that grows in this part of Guanacaste. The streets, some of the worst in Costa Rica, are a gauntlet of potholes and bumps.

The local bullfight ring (Plaza de Toros Chorotega) is located on the main road opposite the town cemetery. Bloodless bullfights are staged here during local

grasslands, lagoons and various forms of tropical forest. The park takes its name from the *palo verde* (green stick) tree, but the area harbors more than 150 different tree species.

Most people come to Palo Verde for the birds, the largest gathering of waterfowl in all of Central America, including storks, herons, egrets, spoonbills, ibises and ducks. Also famous are the rare scarlet macaws that nest in this park, reduced to about a thousand mating pairs throughout the country because of rampant poaching

OPPOSITE: The view from the porch at the Montaña de Fuego Hotel. ABOVE: Pumas are rare, but still inhabit many forests in Costa Rica. OVERLEAF: An arcade of saplings leads into the countryside below the mighty Volcán Arenal.

in the past. Other denizens include the howler monkey, iguana and saltwater crocodile, a known man-eater which is just about impossible to see in the other Pacific Coast parks.

Palo Verde is under water for most of the rainy season, and even during dry season (December to April) the park is virtually impossible to tour without a boat. Several companies offer guided boat tours of Palo Verde, including Liberia-based **Asmiturli** (666-1606 and **CATA Tours** (669-1026 or 296-2133. You can usually hire your own boat

and local guide in the village of Bebedero, 14 km (nine miles) west of Las Cañas.

WHERE TO STAY

There is no lodging available inside the park, and permission to camp must be gained from national park authorities. The nearest hotels are in Las Cañas and Lago Arenal.

HOW TO GET THERE

Headquarters and the Estación Biológica Palo Verde are in the reserve's central sector, 38 km (24 miles) down a rough flagstone road that starts at Bagaces on the Carretera Interamericana. **Bebedero**, 14 km

(nine miles) southwest of Las Cañas, is the jumping of point for motor launch trips to Palo Verde.

RINCÓN COROBICÍ

Though there is no town of significance here, the bus stop and locals call the area Rincón Corobicí, meaning the "corner" of Corobicí. This riverside hamlet has developed into the tourist hub of south-central Guanacaste. Three distinct attractions bring visitors to the region: river rafting on the Río Corobicí, Las Pumas Wildlife Center and La Pacífica hacienda.

HOW TO GET THERE

The bus stop and sideroads to the area's three attractions are located six kilometers (three and a quarter miles) north of Las Cañas on the Carretera Interamericana.

RÍO COROBICÍ

Rapids in this stretch of the Río Corobicí are rated at class-one and -two, which means that rafting is more of a gentle float than a raging white-water adventure. But it's one of the more pleasant things you can do in Guanacaste and a terrific way to see wildlife. The trip is also a great opportunity to view the Guanacaste backcountry and various forms of rural life.

Floating down the Corobicí, directly down river from the bridge, you'll see a few shanties; this is an aspect of country life that isn't always visible from the Carretera Interamericana. The shanties eventually give way to hacienda country with grazing horses and cattle. Soon the pastures evolve into riverside jungle. It's easy to spot howler monkeys and iguanas in shoreline trees. Bird life is phenomenal: snowy egrets and blue herons flit back and forth across the water, ospreys ride the thermal updrafts, huge tiger herons hide among the reeds and various types of night herons stalk the undergrowth. Vegetation is also fantastic, with giant mahogany, kapok and guanacaste trees shading much of the river. The trip lasts about two hours. **Ríos Tropicales** (233-6455 FAX 255-4354, is the best of the raft companies, with professional guides, good equipment and a tasty riverside lunch at the end of the journey.

LAS PUMAS WILDLIFE CENTER

It is difficult to see big cats in the wild because they've been hunted to extinction in most parts of Costa Rica. The Las Pumas Wildlife Center offers an opportunity to view indigenous felines and support a good cause at the same time. The brainchild of Lilly Bodmer de Hagnauer, a transplanted Swiss environmentalist, this animal orphanage shelters a number of rare or endangered species including jaguars, puma, jaguarundi, ocelots and marguays. It also sustains a fair number of birds and at least one white-tailed deer.

The big cats are not taken from the wild — they come to Las Pumas as orphaned babies whose parents were killed by poachers, or as exotic pets that got too big (and dangerous) for suburban houses. Lilly and her small staff nurse them back to health or into adulthood. Originally her goal was to release the animals back into the wild, and to track them by radio transponders to observe their range and behavior — a Costa Rican version of *Born Free*. However, she has ceased this practice as the animals were being quickly dispatched by hunters. A group of marguays, for instance, was wiped out within a couple weeks of their release.

Lilly (a spirited septuagenarian) has lived at Las Pumas for 37 years. While she gets many of the orphaned animals from the National Wildlife Service, the center doesn't get a penny from the Costa Rican government. It's supported entirely by donations from visitors. Contributions go towards the purchase of food, vitamins and medicine for the cats, as well as better homes (a recent $1,000 donation from the BBC built a jaguar enclosure; $500 from German television gave the pumas a new roof).

The big cats snooze in the daytime, but begin to wake up in the late afternoon, which is probably the best time to visit. Las Pumas Wildlife Center is situated behind La Pacífica and the Safari Corobicí offices, about a hundred meters down a dirt road lined with cactus plants and trees.

LA PACÍFICA

This combination cattle ranch, preserve and resort hotel strives to prove that agriculture, tourism and conservation can pursue mutual goals which don't destroy the land. The hotel lies on the south bank of Río Corobicí between Las Pumas Wildlife Center and the rafting center. The 2,000-hectare (4,940-acre) hacienda is on the north bank, where it sprawls into the foothills of the cordillera. The property was founded in the

early 1900s by former president Don Bernardo Soto, and named after his wife, Dona Pacífica Fernández, whose other claim to fame was designing the Costa Rican flag.

You can explore La Pacífica on horseback, on foot or on a mountain bike, and you can watch cows being milked at the dairy plant or cattle being herded across the Guanacaste savanna. Howler monkeys, iguanas and more than 200 bird species dwell in the hacienda's Roca Blanca, Tenorito and Frog forests. La Casona, the historic ranch house, has a small museum

OPPOSITE: The Río Corobicí flows peacefully through southern Guanacaste. ABOVE: Jaguars are protected in reserves such as Las Pumas, but are rarely sighted along nature trails.

dedicated to frontier life. There are also a good many pre-Columbian archaeology sites on the property.

Where to Stay

Hotel Hacienda la Pacífica (669-0050/ 0266 FAX 669-0555, Apdo 8, 5700 Cañas, offers comfortable accommodation at good prices in cabinas with private baths. Their restaurant offers local and international cuisine in a garden setting.

RESERVA BIOLÓGICA LOMAS BARBUDAL

These "bearded hills" are an island of tropical dry forest in heart of cattle country, with thickly wooded rolling terrain that serves as a refuge for monkeys, coatis and coyotes, as well as a stopover for migratory birds such as egrets and herons. Scarlet macaws visit from nearby Palo Verde and the park is endowed with more than 230 bee species. There are also many rare trees including mahogany, rosewood, gonzalo-alvis and Central American redwood. Perhaps the best time to visit is March, when the cortéz trees are in full yellow bloom.

Park headquarters on the banks of the Río Cabuyo offers information and picnic tables. There are walking trails along the river and several swimming holes. Founded in 1986, Reserva Biológica Lomas Barbudal covers about 2,270 hectares (5,607 acres).

Where to Stay

There is no lodging in the park other than primitive camping near the ranger station. The nearest hotels are in Liberia.

How to Get There

Don't blink or you will surely miss the turn-off from the Carretera Interamericana: a tiny hamlet called **Pijije** about 10 km (six miles) north of Bagaces and 16 km (10 miles) south of Liberia (look for the KM 221 marker). It's then 30 minutes down a rough flagstone road to the park headquarters.

LIBERIA

The capital of Guanacaste province hugs the banks of the Río Liberia which flows down into Parque Nacional Palo Verde

and the Río Tempisque. Dubbed the Ciudad Blanca (White City) because of chalky soil and whitewashed houses, this languid outpost of 23,000 people was founded 1769 — seven years before the United States became a nation.

Liberia doesn't look that old, although some of the buildings around the central plaza still bear a colonial flavor. Huge leafy matalpo trees shade many of the streets, but can't disguise the fact that Liberia is hot and dusty for much of the year. Most tourists don't give the town more than a passing

glance; they're too busy heading for the coast and the nearby national parks. But, Liberia is the only place in Guanacaste that makes an attractive hub for visiting the best of both beach and nature attractions.

WHAT TO SEE AND DO

La Agonia (The Agony) is a charming nineteenth century church at the eastern end of Avenida Central. **Casa de Cultura** near the town center has a small museum with exhibits about *sabaneros* or local cowboys and a tourist information service called **Asmitourli** (666-1606, which offers brochures, maps, hotel reservations and guided tours to various Guanacaste attractions.

Liberians let their hair down on July 25, a fiesta day that celebrates the province's separation from Nicaragua in 1824 as well as the **Feast Day of St. James**. Events include bullfights, rodeos, cattle shows, marimba bands, food stalls, folk dancing and horse parades. There's a youth parade called the **Posada del Niño** on Christmas Eve each year and a local cultural week (Semana Cultura) each September.

WHERE TO STAY

Moderate

Anyone with a hankering for motel life should try **Hotel el Sitio** (257-0744/0746 FAX 290-5909 or 257-0745, Apdo 134-5000, Liberia. Located just south of the big intersection on the road to the Aeropuerto Daniel Obudar, El Sitio is popular with Costa Ricans on their way to the beach. The 52 rooms feature private baths, hot water, air conditioning, satellite television and safe-deposit box. Amenities include two swimming pools, gym, sand volleyball court, restaurant and bar, laundromat and a babysitting service.

    Las Espuelas (666-0144 FAX 225-3987, Apdo 1056-1007, San José, sits in a large grove of trees off the Carretera Interamericana and has comfortable rooms with private baths, hot water, air conditioning and satellite television. The garden features a pool and hammocks strung between the giant shade trees.

Inexpensive

Hotel Boyeros (666-0722 FAX 666-2529, Apdo 85-5000, Liberia, is on the Carretera Interamericana, a block south of the big crossroads. The spacious rooms have private baths, hot water, air conditioning and balconies. Expansive matalpo trees shade the open-air restaurant and the nearby playground.

WHERE TO EAT

El Bramadero, at the Pan-Am Highway junction, is popular with Costa Rican travelers, offering hearty portions of comida tipico and ice cold beer. **Restaurant Pokopi**, opposite Hotel el Sitio, serves everything from

burgers to seafood. Pokopi's tiny discotheque is the only place in Liberia that swings at night. The **Hotel Boyeros** restaurant features simple but filling international and local Tico dishes.

HOW TO GET THERE

Liberia is roughly 220 km (136 miles) from San José via the Carretera Interamericana. The journey takes three to four hours, depending on traffic conditions. There are numerous daily bus services from San

José, as well as other Guanacaste destinations including Las Cañas, La Cruz, Nicoya, Santa Cruz, and the major beach resorts. Most buses headed for Nicaragua will also pick up passengers in Liberia.

    There is a small airport 12 km (seven and a half miles) west of Liberia where international charter and regional flights arrive. The airport is called Aeropuerto Daniel Obudar, though locals usually refer to it as the Liberia airport. TravelAir has four flights every week from San José to

OPPOSITE: A drive along the Carretera Interamericana is filled with unexpected sights and ever-changing scenery. ABOVE: Churches in rural Costa Rica have little ornamentation and serve as the village gathering place.

Liberia, with return flights on the same days. There are car rental desks at the airport, but they are only open when major flights arrive.

PARQUE NACIONAL RINCÓN DE LA VIEJA

One of Costa Rica's best-kept secrets, Parque Nacional Rincón de la Vieja is a sprawling area of 14,000 hectares (34,580 acres) in northern Guanacaste that harbors a wide range of natural attractions: an ac-

which last erupted in 1984 and 1991. Unlike Arenal, which is far too dangerous to climb, you can climb up Rincón and peer down into its steaming caldera. Rincón is a composite volcano that features nine different eruptive spots or craters. The round trip from the ranger station is roughly 15 km (nine miles), but the journey usually takes all day because of the steep ascent. If the weather is clear, you will be able to see Lake Nicaragua and the Nicoya Peninsula. The summit trail also passes Von Seebach, an adjacent crater which has a beautiful aqua-

tive volcano, mud pools and hot springs, dry coastal forest and cloud forest and myriad forms of wildlife. The park is a walker's paradise, with more than 100 km (62 miles) of well-marked trails.

Park headquarters is at **Santa María**, due north of Liberia. But most people enter through **Las Pailas**, where there's a ranger station (with maps) and the park's only campground. Trails spread out in three directions from Las Pailas.

The **Central Trail** leads up to Rincón de la Vieja Volcano, 1,898-m (6,225-ft) high,

marine lake. Be sure to take water and a windbreaker or jacket in case the weather turns nasty at the summit.

The **Eastern Trail** (Sendero Las Pailas) skirts the campground (a great place to spot iguanas) and crosses the Río Colorado on a small suspension bridge before heading into a large thermal zone called Las Pailas (The Cauldrons). You can veer right or left after the bridge; the trail is a seven-kilometer (four-and-a-third-mile) loop through the various volcanic attractions including boiling, bubbling mud pots, steaming fumaroles and hissing gas vents. At the far end of the loop is the start of another trail that leads six kilometers (just under four miles) to **Los Azufrales**

ABOVE: A boa constrictor strangles its prey, a hapless iguana, at Rícon de la Vieja. OPPOSITE: Mud pools and boiling thermal waters bubble at Las Pailas, The Cauldrons, Rincón de la Vieja.

(The Sulfurs) hot springs, which bubble at a blistering 42°C (108°F). One kilometer (just over half a mile) beyond the springs is Santa María ranger station.

The **Western Trail** (Sendero de Cataratas) breaks off from the volcano route about half a kilometer (a third of a mile) from the ranger station. It crosses the Río Blanco on a suspension bridge and plunges deep into the dry tropical forest. There are huge trees all around, and this is a great place to spot wildlife including howler and white-faced monkeys, coatimundi, armadillo, agouti and myriad avian creatures (the park has more than 300 bird species). This trail eventually splits: The north fork runs two kilometers (one and a quarter miles) to the four **Cataratas Escondidas** (Hidden Falls). The south fork leads another two and a half kilometers (one and a half miles) to **Catarata la Cangreja**, a 40-m (131-ft)-high waterfall that plunges into a brilliant turquoise-colored pool. This is a perfect swimming hole, so bring your suit.

A curious side note: The name Rincón de la Vieja means "corner of the old lady", but nobody seems quite sure how the mountain got that tag. There is a legend that suggests that the matriarch of the Spanish family that first settled this area in the late eighteenth century lived by herself at the base of the volcano. Another story is reminiscent of Romeo and Juliet: a young Spanish woman, spurned by her lover's family, lived out the rest of her years on the mountain, turning her back on the conservative colonial society that destroyed her romance. Either way, Rincón de la Vieja remains a haunting and beautiful place.

WHERE TO STAY

Moderate

The most convenient base is **Rincón de la Vieja Volcano Mountain Lodge** (695-5553 or 284-3023 FAX 256-5410 E-MAIL rincon@sol. racsa.co.cr, Apdo 114-5000, Liberia. The lodge is three and a half kilometers (just over two miles) from Las Pailas ranger station and offers various means to explore the park including guides, horses and mountain bikes. It also stages a forest canopy tour on private land outside the park. Accommodation is in rustic cabins or rooms with private bath (but no hot water or air conditioning). It has a small swimming pool and an outdoor bar, frequented by a chatterbox parrot and two friendly dogs. The meals are basic but filling. The beer is always cold.

Inexpensive

A further five kilometers (just over three miles) down the mountain is the **Hacienda Lodge Guachipelún (** 284-2040 or 442-2818 FAX 442-1910, Apdo 636-4050, Alajuela. The ranch house, built in the 1870s, was transformed into a cozy but rather basic bed and breakfast. This place feels much more like a working ranch than the Volcano Mountain Lodge. The seven rooms have private baths with cold water but do not have air conditioning.

Camping

Las Pailas campground is top-notch by Costa Rican standards, with a new toilet block, fresh running water and picnic tables.

HOW TO GET THERE

The Las Pailas ranger station is about 25 km (15.5 miles) from Liberia. Take the Carretera Interamericana five kilometers (just over three miles) north to **Guadalupe**, turning right onto a very rough unpaved road which leads 12 km (seven and a half miles) to a sleepy village called **Curubande** and then another eight kilometers (five miles) to the park entrance. There is no public bus service and it's doubtful that a Liberia taxi would be willing to tackle this road. However, Volcano Lodge will fetch you from Liberia or the Guanacaste beaches if you're staying with them.

HACIENDA BUENA VISTA

Buena Vista Lodge (/FAX 695-5147, Apdo 373, Liberia, bills itself as a "mountain lodge and adventure center" but it is also a working hacienda — 648 hectares (1,600 acres) of cattle pastures and forest that are criss-crossed by horse and hiking trails. Some people just call it paradise, and that's not far from the truth. The lodge nestles at 800 m (2,624 ft) in the volcanic foothills of Rincón de la Vieja volcano with panoramic views of the Guanacaste plains, Santa Elena Peninsula and the Pacific Ocean in the distance. On clear days you can see the southwest coast of Nicaragua from up here. It's the kind of place you come to for a day and stay for a week.

The property is adjacent to Parque Nacional Rincón de la Vieja, and much of the wildlife found in the park spills over onto the Buena Vista land: monkeys, white-tailed deer, anteaters and myriad bird species (including a pair of talkative green amazons that live in a tree outside the lodge entrance).

WHAT TO SEE AND DO

One of the prime reasons for coming to **Buena Vista** is the ranch's famous mud baths and hot spring which are said to cure just anything ails your skin. The horseback trip to the thermal area takes about one hour, traversing rolling hills punctuated by spreading guanacaste trees and gentle streams. On arrival at the spa (and changing rooms) you spread mud over every inch of your body, let it dry in the sun to the consistency of chalk and then submerge yourself in a stone hot tub. You can also dip in a nearby cold water stream fed by mountain springs.

Buena Vista also organizes horseback and hiking tours into Parque Nacional Rincón de la Vieja, including trips to the volcano summit and the hidden waterfalls. Back at the ranch, the local *vaqueros* demonstrate cowboy skills in a corral near the lodge and swap tales in a rustic bar. Four-wheel drive, bird-watching and entomology tours (for butterfly lovers) can also be arranged.

The lodge offers inexpensive accommodation in 37 cozy rooms, most of them with private bath (but no air conditioning because Buena Vista's mountain clime is

OPPOSITE: Boiling thermal waters bubble at Las Pailas in Parque Nacional Rincón de la Vieja.

quite cool compared to the Guanacaste plains). Roughly 60 percent of the food served at the lodge restaurant is produced on the hacienda, including beef, chicken, eggs, cheese, milk and organically grown vegetables. The water is heated with solar panels; power is generated by a small hydroelectric system on the hacienda. Hearty hacienda lunches and dinners are all you can eat.

HOW TO GET THERE

Buena Vista Lodge will arrange pickup in Liberia. Those driving their own vehicle should head north from Liberia on the Carretera Interamericana and turn right onto the flagstone road that leads through **Cañas Dulces**, continuing 12.5 km (seven and three-quarter miles), and across the Río Tizate on a primitive wooden plank bridge. The palm trees along this road are used by locals to make a potent moonshine called *viña de coyol*.

PARQUE NACIONAL SANTA ROSA

Costa Rica's oldest national park, Santa Rosa was founded in 1971 to safeguard vast tracts of tropical dry forest and the nation's two most important battlefields. The Sección Murciélago was added in 1979, with land expropriated from former Nicaraguan dictator Anastasio Somoza. President Oscar Arias declared the land between Murciélago and Santa Rosa to be a part of the park in the late 1980s, so that Santa Rosa could cover the entire Santa Elena Peninsula (about 50,000 hectares or 123,500 acres in total).

This is an eclectic park that includes historical sights, massive tracts of wilderness, offshore coral reefs and miles of unspoiled beaches on the Santa Elena and Papagayo gulfs. Landscape and vegetation vary widely. Within the space of an hour you can travel from tropical dry forest to savanna-like pastureland to thorn scrub with cacti and agave to mangrove swamp. There is also a wide array of life forms: tapirs, sloths, anteaters, opossums, coatimundi, iguana, white-tailed deer, howler and spider monkeys, jaguars, ocelots and more than 300 bird species and 5,000 types of butterflies and moths. Santa Rosa's beaches provide nesting sites for three sea turtle species, including the largest arribadas of olive ridley turtles in tropical America.

HOW TO GET THERE

The park's entrance gate is just off the Carretera Interamericana. Maps and booklets are for sale. Two kilometers (one and a quarter miles) beyond the entrance station is a turnoff to the right leading to the *tan-quetas* — rusty armored vehicles captured from Nicaraguan troops in 1955 during Somoza's ill-fated invasion of Guanacaste.

The park headquarters is at **La Casona**, seven kilometers (four and a third miles) west of the Carretera Interamericana. This is also headquarters for the Guanacaste Conservation Area, a loose confederation of the northwestern national parks, nearly one million hectares (2,470,000 acres) of coast, mountain and forest. La Casona also has a campground and scientific research center — one of the world's most important stations for tropical dry forest study.

WHAT TO SEE AND DO

La Casona Hacienda has been beautifully restored, and is now a museum commemorating the battle in which 9,000 Central American volunteers beat back William Walker and his Yankee marauders. In front of the house is a huge guanacaste tree that shades 200-year-old stone corrals where much of the fighting took place. On the hill behind is **Los Héroes**, a monument to the brave Costa Ricans who turned back Walker's mercenary threat in 1856 and Somoza's invasion in 1955. The sunsets are fabulous from here. Nearby is an excellent nature walk called the **Sendero Indio Desnudo** (Naked Indian Trail) which loops a kilometer (two thirds of a mile) through dry tropical forest. The trail takes its name from the resident red-bark trees which are said to resemble disrobed Indians.

Longer trails include the **Sendero los Patos** (Ducks Trail), **Sendero Valle Naranjo** (Naranjo Valley Trail) and **Sendero Palo Seco** (Dry Trees Trail) which offer the park's best possibilities for wildlife spotting. The ideal times for animal watching and photography are early morning and late afternoon.

Santa Rosa also offers fabulous coastline. During dry season you can drive the 13 km (eight miles) from La Casona to the **Golfo de Papagayo**, but even then you'll need a four-wheel drive to make the journey. The road forks before hitting the beach. The southern (left) route leads to **Playa Naranjo**, one of the best surf spots in Central America, according to those who

base for the Contras, then a grassy airstrip on the left that was used by Oliver North and company to supply the Nicaraguan rebels. Despite this sordid history, Murciélago's scenery is gorgeous — unspoiled beaches and coral reefs backed by thick forest. **Playa Blanca** 17 km (10.5 miles) from the Murciélago ranger station with its soft white sand is one of the most beautiful strands in Costa Rica. Five kilometers (three miles) from the Murciélago ranger station, Bahìa Hachal offers a stony gray beach and turquoise water.

ride the waves. Also in this area are Laguna el Limbo with its resident waterfowl. Off the coast is **Peña Bruja** (Witch's Rock) which is popular with both surfers and aquatic birds. The northern (right) fork leads to the secluded **Playa Nancite** on the north side of the **Estero Real** (Royal Estuary), where as many as 100,000 olive ridley turtles nest during rainy season (September and October).

Sección Murciélago occupies the northern flank of the Santa Elena Peninsula and is reached via a rough flagstone road from Cuajiniquil on Golfo de Santa Elena. Before you reach the park entrance you'll pass a national guard camp on the right which was once Somoza's hacienda and a CIA training

Those in quest of still more beach tranquillity should make for the western parts of Santa Rosa such as **Cabo Santa Elena**, **Playas Coloradas** and **Bahía Potrero Grande** (another great surfing spot), which are accessible only by boat. You'll have to hump in everything, including food and water. Questions about visiting Santa Rosa should be directed to the head of the park's ecotourism program: **Marcela Mora Peralta (/FAX (506) 695-5598 or 695-5577.

ABOVE: La Casona Hacienda, in Santa Rosa, houses a museum commemorating the battle between Central Americans and the American William Walker's mercenaries.

WHERE TO STAY

Santa Rosa's only indoor lodging is the **Centro de Investigación Daniel Janzen** (/FAX 695-5598, Apdo 169-5000, Liberia. This research station provides inexpensive accommodation in the form of eight-person bunk rooms at La Casona, but visiting scientists and researchers get first crack at the beds. Be prepared for shared baths with cold water. Cooking facilities are available.

Camping is permitted at six different areas inside the park. There are improved campgrounds with toilets and running water at La Casona and Murciélago ranger station. Primitive camping is allowed at **Puesto Argelia** on **Playa Naranjo** and **Estero Real** near **Playa Nancite**, as well as **Playa Blanca** and **Bahía Hachal** in the **Sección Murciélago**. Arrange camping in advance through the **National Park Office** (257-0922 FAX 223-6963, in San José.

HOW TO GET THERE

The Santa Rosa turnoff on the Carretera Interamericana is 35 km (22 miles) north of Liberia. La Casona is seven kilometers (four and a third miles) west along a good paved road. Buses will set you down near the park entrance, where it's easy to hitch a ride to La Casona. Taxi service is available from Liberia or La Cruz.

The turnoff to the Sección Murciélago is eight kilometers (five miles) further north — a paved road that curves down to Cuajiniquil on the Golfo de Santa Elena, where a rough flagstone road leads to the ranger station and Playa Blanca.

PARQUE NACIONAL GUANACASTE

The twin volcanic cones of Orosí, 1,487 m (4,877 ft), and Cerro Cacao, 1,659 m (5,441 ft), dominate Parque Nacional Guanacaste. Established in 1989, the reserve protects 85,000 hectares (209,950 acres) of tropical dry forest and cloud forest on the opposite side of the Carretera Interamericana from Santa Rosa. Together, the two parks form a single giant wildlife corridor stretching from the arid Pacific Coast beaches to the steamy Caribbean lowlands.

A patchwork of former hacienda property, the park harbors an amazing array of flora and fauna — more than 300,000 plant and animal species — with more discovered every year by researchers who inhabit three field stations inside the park. Among the larger animals dwelling here are jaguar, puma, peccary, coyote, white-tailed deer, ocelot, marguay, sloth, anteater and coatimundi.

This is not a visitor-friendly park. The roads are horrible and the field stations are for the convenience of visiting scientists rather than tourists. Still, there are ways to explore Guanacaste. **Cacao Biological Station** in the southern part of the park is the best jumping off point for treks up Volcán Cerro Cacao. Even if you don't make the climb, a trip to **Cacao** offers a chance to explore the cloud forest around the field station. **Maritza Biological Station** is near the base of Volcán Orosí in the northern part of the park. You can clamber up the volcanic slopes or explore the **Llano de los Indios** (Plain of the Indians) with its ancient petroglyphs at **El Hacha** and other sites. **Pitiya Biological Station** is on the eastern side, with researchers who study the Caribbean watershed.

Before entering the Parque Nacional Guanacaste, it's best to check on road conditions and accommodation availability at the administrative office of **Guanacaste**

ABOVE: Cattle graze in Guanacaste where the Volcán Orosí OPPOSITE looms.

Conservation Area (695-5598, at **La Casona** in Santa Rosa park.

WHERE TO STAY

Guanacaste doesn't have any overnight visitor facilities *per se*, but you can bunk down or camp at any of the research stations with prior permission from national park authorities. Contact Marcela Mora Peralta, head of ecotourism for the **Guanacaste Conservation Area** (/FAX 695-5598 or 695-5577, Apdo 169-5000, Liberia.

HOW TO GET THERE

The turnoff to Cacao is 23 km (14 miles) north of Liberia on the Carretera Interamericana, at a small hamlet called **Potrerillos** on the banks of the Río Tempisquito. Follow the rough dirt road through Quebrada Grande, park your vehicle on the south bank of the Río Gongora and walk the remaining distance to the field station.

The Maritza turnoff is 50 km (31 miles) north of Liberia on the Carretera Interamericana, at the same junction as the road to Cuajiniquil and Sección Murciélago. Head east along a primitive dirt road through virgin forest and savanna lands.

Santa Cecilia, 28 km (17 miles) east of La Cruz by paved road, is the jumping off point for Pitiya Biological Station.

LA CRUZ

Sleepy, sultry La Cruz is the last major town before the Nicaraguan frontier. It perches on a volcanic escarpment 250 m (820 ft) above Bahía Salinas, an imposing landscape reminiscent of East Africa's rift valley. Other than the whitewashed grave of Salvadorian writer and patriot Marcelino García Flamenco, the town doesn't have much to offer visitors.

WHAT TO SEE AND DO

Several nice beaches are nearby including **Playa Pochotes** on Bahía Salinas, **Playa Monstrencal** at Brasilito on Bahía Junquillal, and secluded **Playa Jobo** at the tip of the unspoiled Descartes Peninsula. Boats for exploring **Salinas Bay** can be rented at the fishing village of Puerto Soley, six and a half kilometers (four miles) west of La Cruz. Further afield is the lovely beach at **Bahía Junquillal** or **Cuajiniquil Recreation Area**, 27 km (17 miles) to the southwest via Cuajiniquil.

Refugio Nacional de Fauna Silvestre Isla Bolaños floats in the middle of Bahía Salinas, accessible only by boat. This 25-hectare (62-acre) reserve provides a home for various bird species, including the frigate bird, brown pelican, oystercatcher and black vulture. It's forbidden to disembark on Isla Bolaños without permission from park authorities in San José or Santa Rosa, but you can watch the avian action from boats anchored offshore.

The border post is 19 km (12 miles) north of La Cruz on the Carretera Interamericana, at **Peñas Blancas** on the banks of the Río Sapoa (which flows into Lake Nicaragua).

WHERE TO STAY

Moderate

An unexpected touch of class (and bastion of modern art) in the northwest is **Amalia's Inn** (/FAX 679-9181. There's nothing quite like it anywhere in Costa Rica — a cozy little bed and breakfast perched on the edge of the escarpment, with sweeping views across Bahía Salinas and the Santa Elena Peninsula. The rooms are furnished with double beds, black leather sofas and Picasso-esque original artwork by Amalia herself. All rooms have private baths with hot water. There's a small pool on the terrace. Amalia will treat you like one of her own family.

Another quite interesting place to bunk down is **Los Inocentes Lodge** (679-9190 or

WHERE TO EAT

Ehecatl Restaurant in La Cruz is remarkable both for its food and location. The name means "God of the Wind" in the Chorotega Indian language, an apt description for this unique eatery. Poised on the brink of the escarpment with panoramic views of Bahía Salinas, this carefree, casual place serves delicious lobster, shrimp, fish, octopus, mussels, ceviche and other seafood delights. Try for a table

265-5484 FAX 265-4385, Apdo 1370-3000, Heredia. Just outside Parque Nacional Guanacaste's northern boundary, this ecolodge offers overnight accommodation as well as horseback and walking trips to the nearby forest and Volcán Orosí. Named after the family that pioneered this area, the hacienda was built in 1890 — a handsome wooden house that was remodeled into a modern lodge in 1982. Even if you don't spend the night, come here for a ride and lunch. Los Inocentes is reached by turning off the Carretera Interamericana about three kilometers (two miles) south of La Cruz (look for signs to Santa Cecilia) and driving 16 km (10 miles) along a good paved road.

on the second floor. Ehecatl has another location at **Potrerillos**, on the Carretera Interamericana between Liberia and Santa Rosa.

HOW TO GET THERE

La Cruz is 55 km (34 miles) north of Liberia on the Carretera Interamericana. There are daily buses from Liberia and San José.

OPPOSITE: Out on the range a cowboy shades his eyes with the traditional wide-brimmed cotton hat. ABOVE: A round-up at Cañas Dulces.

Guana-caste: Pacific Coast and Nicoya Peninsula

CATTLE COUNTRY tumbles down to the sea along the Guanacaste Coast, which features more resorts than any other part of Costa Rica. Hot, dry weather for much of the year, and a shorter rainy season than the rest of the country, make this region ideal for sunbathing and water sports. It's especially popular with expatriate surfers and sport fishermen, who find conditions among the best on the planet.

Guanacaste province has a good highway network (fewer potholes than other parts of the country) and most of the

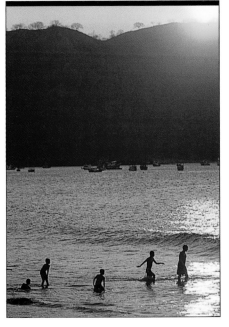

beaches are within a four- or five-hour drive from San José. As a consequence, Ticos flock to this coast on school breaks and national holidays. During Christmas and Easter it's nearly impossible to find an empty hotel room in Hermosa, Coco, Flamingo, Brasilito and Tamarindo. At other times of year, many of the strands are empty, especially around the Golfo de Papagayo and on beaches south of Tamarindo.

The arid climate makes the Guanacaste beaches an extreme contrast to Caribbean and Central Pacific strands. The dry coastal forest is more open and much browner than the rain forest found elsewhere in Costa Rica, especially during the dry season when the region takes on desert-like traits.

Rolling hills, sugar cane plantations and cattle ranches dominate the landscape between the coast and the Río Tempisque. Although the residents are friendly, market towns such as Santa Cruz and Nicoya sustain a rough edge gleaned from several hundred years of cowboy life. It's still not unusual to see mounted riders amble up to an open-air bar or restaurant.

Farther south, the Nicoya Peninsula is virtually cut off from the rest of the northwest coast. The roads are dreadful, impassable for much of the year and a bone-jarring adventure even at the best of times. Isolated expatriate communities and budding beach resorts exist at Sámara and Nosara on the peninsula's west coast, as well as Tambor and Montezuma in the south. Nicoya's rugged beauty and welcome seclusion offset the area's inaccessibility.

HOW TO GET THERE

The beaches of Guanacaste and Nicoya, located geographically side-by-side, can be difficult to reach. Those in the north are best accessed by air from San José or by road from Liberia. The southern beaches are best reached by ferry from Puntarenas.

GOLD COAST BEACH RESORTS

PLAYA DEL COCO

Playa del Coco is the northern hub of Costa Rica's self-proclaimed Gold Coast. It's about four and a half hours from San José, on paved road, which makes Coco the most accessible beach in the region. Because of this, there's nothing remotely serene or silent here, especially during national holidays and school breaks when thousands of Ticos flock to Coco from San José and environs.

El Coco, the only village on the bay, is not especially attractive by Costa Rican standards. Fishing used to be the primary

PRECEEDING PAGES: The Río Tempisque empties into the Golfo de Nicoya. Playa Hermosa RIGHT, "Beautiful Beach," lives up to its name. OPPOSITE: Several species of parrots and parakeets thrive in the northern forests. ABOVE: The sun shines more frequently along northern Pacific beaches than it does in the damp south.

occupation (there's still a fishing pier and a few boats bobbing in the offshore swell) but tourism is now firmly entrenched as the number one money spinner. The town plaza, where buses and taxis gather, is dominated by shabby tourist stands and the local police station.

Where to Stay

MODERATE

A unique places to stay in the Playa del Coco area is **Rancho Armadillo** (670-0108 FAX 670-0441 E-MAIL sirena@sol.racsa.co.cr,

Apdo 15-5019, Playa del Coco. Built by Texan Jim Proctor in 1978, after he discovered Costa Rica on an around-the-world sail, Armadillo is an inland estate rather than a beach hotel. Surrounded by lush jungle, the hacienda-style lodge features five cabins with rustic wooden floors and ceilings, as well as spacious bathrooms, hot water and either air conditioning or fan. The pool area offers a sweeping view of the Golfo de Papagayo. Armadillo also has a restaurant and bar with satellite wide-screen television.

A bit closer to the beach is **Villa del Sol** (/FAX 670-0085 E-MAIL villasol@sol.racsa .co.cr. Owned and operated by expatriate Canadians, this modest bed and breakfast features five rooms with private baths (hot water), fans and balconies, a pleasant garden and a small pool with hot tub.

A favorite with sport fishermen is the funky **Flor de Itabo** (670-0011/0292

Sportfishing for sailfish and marlin is a rewarding activity along the Pacific Coast.

FAX 670-0003, Apdo 32, Playa del Coco, with a range of poolside rooms and two-story bungalows to choose from, all with private bath and air conditioning. The hotel features its own small casino and a tasty Italian restaurant. The only drawback is its remoteness (a kilometer or just over half a mile) from the beach.

INEXPENSIVE

A favorite backpacker haven is the cozy **Luna Tica** (670-0127 FAX 670-0459. Owner Emilia Barahona doesn't speak too much English, but she keeps things neat and tidy. And it's only steps from the beach.

Where to Eat

There are many choices but nothing truly outstanding. **San Francisco Treats** has light snacks and the adjacent **California Café** offers typical gringo eats such as pizza, lasagna, chili and roast beef sandwiches. **Le Bistro Oasis** tenders French food with a Tico slant, including fish, chicken and steak dishes. **Papagayo** on the main road has probably the best seafood in town. **Da Beppe** at the **Hotel Flor de Itabo** is the hot Italian spot. **Astillero Disco Club** is the only place to dance the night away.

What to See and Do

Coco is one of the best headquarters for SCUBA diving in the north Pacific. Shore diving and trips to offshore dive spots are easily arranged. Serious divers get excited about trips to Isla Catalina, a half-hour from shore, and Islas Murciélagos, about 90 minutes by boat from Coco. Experienced divers find an abundance of sharks at Murciélagos and rays at Catalina. **Mario Vargas Expeditions** (670-0351, offers PADI instruction and SCUBA trips, as well as fishing charters and scenic boat trips. "Mario Vargas is generally considered to be the most experienced divemaster in Costa Rica," says *Skin Diver* magazine. **Rich Coast Diving** (/FAX 670-0176 E-MAIL SCUBA @divecostarica.com, also offers top-notch SCUBA instruction and trips. Other services include sport fishing, surfing, water skiing, kayaking, sailing and snorkeling. **Spanish Dancer** (670-0332/0415 is an

GUANACASTE:
PACIFIC COAST AND
PENINSULA NICOYA

Pacific Ocean

11-m (36-ft) catamaran with daily trips, which include swimming, snorkeling and lunch.

How to Get There

Playa del Coco is 255 km (158 miles) from San José and 35 km (22 miles) from Liberia. The turnoff is opposite the El Tamarindo gas station in the town of **Comunidad** on the Liberia–Santa Cruz highway. Coco is 15 km (nine miles) west of this junction, on a meandering country road that leads past shrimp farms, sugar cane fields and cattle ranches. Just before the coast, the road forks. The north (right) fork heads for Playa Hermosa. The south (left) fork leads to Coco.

There are daily express buses from San José and regular buses from Liberia. Taxis running from Liberia town and airport, or other nearby beaches, serve Coco.

PLAYA OCOTAL

Only three kilometers (two miles) west of Coco, Playa Ocotal has become something of an international buzzword for great diving and sport fishing. And for good reason: the offshore waters here are rich in marine life and local hotels tend to cater to SCUBA and fishing aficionados. But that's not to say that landlubbers won't enjoy the place.

Bahía Ocotal is rather small by Guanacaste standards, but it's a lovely stretch of gray and black sand framed by rugged cliffs. Punta Gorda, the headland west of Ocotal, is surrounded by reefs and excellent dive spots such as Las Corridas. **El Ocotal Diving Safaris** (670-0321 offers PADI instruction and SCUBA trips to the islas Catalina and Murciélagos.

Where to Stay

EXPENSIVE

Poised on a bluff above the bay is the superb **Hotel el Ocotal** (670-0321 or 222-4259 FAX 670-0083 or 223-8483 E-MAIL ocotal@ centralamerica.com WEBSITE www .centralamerica.com/cr/hotel/ocotal.htm, Apdo 1, Playa del Coco. The place is flush with SCUBA and sport fishing enthusiasts. This is also a great place for anyone who wants to relax at the pool or beach. The rooms are spacious and well-equipped including satellite television, refrigerator, air conditioning and queen-sized beds. Both bungalows and suites are available. The newer rooms have Jacuzzis and sun decks. El Ocotal has SCUBA diving and sport fishing facilities.

MODERATE

Hotel Villa Casa Blanca (/FAX 670-0448 is one of Costa Rica's best bed-and-breakfast establishments. Nestled on a tropical cove

with sweeping views of the Golfe de Papagayo, this pleasant Spanish-style ranch is run by Canadians Jim and Jane Seip. Lush tropical gardens surround the swimming pool, which also has a swim-up bar. The rooms here feature private bath, hot water and either air conditioning or fans. On the hillside behind are a honeymoon suite and condominiums.

Where to Eat

El Ocotal Restaurant offers excellent seafood and other international dishes with stunning views of the coast. The **Father Rooster Bar**, in a turn-of-the-century ranch house on the beach, serves tacos, nachos and other typical fair on a breezy verandah.

How to Get There

Playa Ocotal is three kilometers (two miles) west of Playa del Coco. Bus service from San José and Liberia terminates in El Coco, where you can easily pick up a taxi or walk to Ocotal.

PLAYA HERMOSA

Hermosa is a beautiful U-shaped bay protected by a pair of coral-fringed headlands covered in typical Guanacaste scrub. The atmosphere is much more cultivated than

including two swimming pools, tennis courts, a playground, a volleyball court, a discotheque and five restaurants. The 54 rooms in the main block all have fabulous beach views and there are 24 spacious villas with their own pools.

MODERATE

The best on the beach is a romantic little place called the **Hotel el Velero** (670-0310 FAX 670-0330. Thirteen clean and spacious rooms each have private bath, hot water and either fan or air conditioning. Velero

nearby Playa del Coco and the region's relaxed ambiance makes Hermosa an excellent place to seek quiet and solitude. A couple of kilometers offshore are the Islas Pelonas which offer good snorkeling and SCUBA diving.

Where to Stay

EXPENSIVE

Dominating the hillside above the bay is the **Sol Playa Hermosa** (670-0405, 290-0560 TOLL-FREE (800) 572-9934 FAX 670-0349 or 290-0566 E-MAIL hermosol@sol.racsa.co.cr, Apdo 12169-1000, San José. Under the banner of Spain's famous Sol Meliá Group, this international resort hotel provides everything you need for a family vacation,

has a very good restaurant and a sailboat for coastal excursions. Special package rates (including full breakfast) are available for stays of three days or more. The proprietor is a former Royal Canadian Mountie who entertains guests with tales of crime-fighting exploits in the frozen north.

The **Playa Hermosa Inn** (670-0163 FAX 670-0451 is a friendly bed and breakfast recently taken over by new owners and managed by the cordial Susan Fletcher. The place is basically an old

OPPOSITE: Weekends bring youngsters from throughout the country to Playa Hermosa. ABOVE: Dry hills curve beside beaches and bays on the Nicoya Peninsula.

house with large, airy rooms converted into guest accommodations. Each of the nine rooms includes air conditioning or fan, as well as private bath. There's a pool that overlooks the beach and you can count on a hearty breakfast.

INEXPENSIVE

One of the best bargains in all of Costa Rica is the new **Villa del Sueño** (/FAX 670-0027. A Tico-style villa set around a garden and swimming pool, it has clean spacious rooms with tiled floors, high hardwood ceilings and private baths.

Just five minutes walk from the beach is **Villa Huetares** (284-9410 or 460-6592 FAX 670-0439. Not much character, but the place is tidy and the management friendly. The cabinas, which feature private baths and kitchens, sleep six people.

Where to Eat

Nearly everyone who comes to Playa Hermosa eventually finds their way to the ever-popular **Popeye and Daddy-O's**, a blue and yellow house one block up from the beach which serves hot pizza, ice-cold beer and more. Popeye's (670-0245 also delivers. **El Velero** has great seafood and pasta in an outdoor seaside setting. For inexpensive Tico-style food try dinner at the **Restaurant Bahía Culebra**. Sol Playa Hermosa offers five restaurants ranging from the international cuisine of the upscale **El Roble** to a poolside snack bar called **Las Gaviotas**.

General Information

Aqua Sport (670-0156 has a good number of marine activities including snorkeling, windsurfing, surfing, kayaking and sailing. **Bill Beard's Diving Safaris** (/FAX 670-0012 E-MAIL diving@sol.racsa.co.cr, offers matchless instruction and expeditions to some of the best dive spots in the area, including the Catalinas, Punta Gorda, Los Meros and Escorpiones.

How to Get There

Follow essentially the same directions for Playa del Coco (above). Hermosa is about six kilometers (four miles) north of Coco along the coast road. Express buses from

San José and regular buses from Liberia stop daily in Hermosa. Taxis run from Liberia, Aeropuerto Daniel Obudar and other nearby beaches.

BAHÍA CULEBRA AND PLAYA PANAMA

There is nothing even faintly serpentine about Bahía Culebra (Snake Bay), a massive U-shaped bay on the Golfo de Papagayo that marks the northern frontier of the Guanacaste beach resort belt. The wild and rugged **Llano de la Palma** (Plain of the

Palms) and Parque Nacional Santa Rosa are just north of the bay; Hermosa and Coco beaches are due south. So Culebra is ideally situated to take advantage of increased tourism in the region — which is both its fortune and misfortune, depending on which side of the ecological fence you sit.

Almost the entire shore of Bahía Culebra has been slated for development as part of a massive scheme called the Papagayo Project, the largest real estate venture in Costa Rican history, and probably the most controversial. Spread over 2,000 hectares (4,940 acres) and primarily financed by Mexican big business, the project will result in more than 15,000 hotel rooms and condominiums spread across at least 22 properties. The master plan also calls for a large marina, several country clubs and a major road (now only partially built) that would connect the resorts directly with Liberia's airport.

Proponents of the Papagayo Project say it will boost Costa Rica into the tourism big leagues, along with the likes of Mexico and Jamaica. They scoff at notions that most of the rooms will never be filled, espousing a "build it and they will come" attitude borrowed from an American

Where to Stay

VERY EXPENSIVE

At the end of the road that winds up from Playa Hermosa is an all-inclusive resort called the **Malinche Real** (670-0033 or 233-8566 FAX 221-0739, which sprawls across the hillsides above Bahía Culebra. It has everything you would expect of a big resort: swimming pool with swim-up bar, gymnasium, massage and sauna and access to a secluded beach.

The **Costa Smeralda** (670-0044/0032 FAX 670-0379 is part of the controversial

baseball movie. Those who oppose the project say there isn't enough "sun and sea" tourism in Costa Rica to justify such a massive undertaking and that construction will cause permanent damage to the fragile shoreline, mangrove swamps and nearby pre-Columbian archaeological sites.

Several hotels are already up and running (see below), but fortunately they are mostly around Playa Panama. For the time being, most of Bahía Culebra remains pristine and secluded. It's still a wonder why the Spanish never turned this inlet into a major seaport because it's one of the finest natural harbors on Central America's Pacific Coast.

Papagayo Project. This huge resort hotel offers hilltop cabinas overlooking Bahía Culebra, as well as a free-form swimming pool, spacious gardens and a small casino.

EXPENSIVE

Best value for money in the Playa Panama area is **Sulu Sulu Beach Resort** (670-0000 FAX 670-0492. Set beneath cool beachside trees, this friendly hotel has cabinas with private bath, hot water and air conditioning. Sulu Sulu offers numerous activities including horseback riding, jet skiing, mountain biking, beach volleyball, and it has a children's playground.

Parque Nacional Santa Rosa extends along the Santa Elena Peninsula, north of Bahía Culebra.

The **El Wafou** (670-0151 or 231-3463 has 60 spacious rooms, many with views of the sea. Amenities include a swimming pool, tennis courts and sport fishing trips.

Where to Eat

There is not yet a variety of choice, but this should change as the Papagayo Project ripens. For the moment, the only restaurants are in hotels. The Malinche Real has formal dining at **Da Vinci** and informal eats at **La Fonda** and **La Cascada**. Al Wafou and Costa Smeralda have two restaurants each.

General Information

Resort Divers (/FAX 670-0421 at Costa Smeralda offers SCUBA diving instruction and organizes trips to the islas Catalina and Bat; they also organize sailing and sport fishing trips.

How to Get There

Playa Panama is three kilometers (two miles) north of Playa Hermosa along a road that eventually deteriorates into rough flagstone. Malinche Real is at the northern end of this road. A daily express bus from San José and regular buses from Liberia serve the area. Taxis run from Liberia and Aeropuerto Daniel Obudar or other nearby beaches.

The isolated beaches on the northern and western sides of Bahía Culebra are not accessible from Playa Panama except by boat. However, there is a new paved road that runs from Guardia (on the Liberia–Santa Cruz highway) to this area. Look for the "Monte del Barca" sign and follow the road about 14 km (nine miles) through sugar cane fields and cattle pastures. Along the way is a turnoff to Playa Cabuyal and the Horizontes Experimental Forest Station. Eventually the road peters out into three dirt tracks. The left-hand-

most fork leads to empty beaches such as Nacascolo, Pochata, Prieta, Vierador, Blanco, Palmares and Zapatillal. A four-wheel-drive vehicle is recommended for reaching the more secluded strands.

PLAYA BRASILITO

Brasilito is basic when compared with the super-luxury of neighboring Flamingo and Conchal (see below). The sand here is dull gray rather than pearly white; the accommodation is no-frills rather than flawless. But the people who run the cabinas and beachfront bars along Playa Brasilito are, for the most part, friendly and down to earth.

Where to Stay
INEXPENSIVE
Hotel Brasilito (654-4237 FAX 654-4247 E-MAIL compes@sol.racsa.co.cr, is a long-time favorite with sun-lovers searching for good value and friendly ambiance. Right off the main square in Brasilito and within meters of the tree-shaded beach, the hotel offers tidy rooms with private bath (cold water only). The young German owners have also created a fairly good restaurant.

Where to Eat
Hotel Brasilito is the best bet for eats on this particular beach. Other choices include **La Capannina** for pizza, **La Casona** for Tico cuisine, **Marisquería** for seafood and **Camarón Dorado** for romantic dining near the beach.

How to Get There
Playa Brasilito is 285 km (177 miles) from San José and 65 km (40 miles) from Liberia. The turnoff is at the town of Belén on the Liberia–Santa Cruz highway. Brasilito is 28 km (17 miles) west of this junction via Santa Ana and Huacas. There are daily express bus from San José, regular buses from Liberia and taxis from Liberia, Aeropuerto Daniel Obudar and other nearby beaches.

PLAYA FLAMINGO

Flamingo likes to think of itself as the Miami Beach of Coast Rica, a ritzy resort that draws jet-setters from around the globe. Many Europeans and North Americans — as well as wealthy Costa Ricans — have chosen Flamingo as their retirement spot, living in plush villas on the rocky peninsula. But the truth is that Flamingo has a long way to travel before reaching true international stature.

Still, Playa Flamingo — until recently called Playa Blanca or White Beach because of its fine white sand — has much to offer. Among the local amenities are swank, sophisticated hotels; the only full-service marina between Acapulco and Panama; and an annual sport fishing derby (May to June) which draws marlin hunters from far and wide.

This is definitely the place to make camp if you're hooked on game fishing or accustomed to upmarket service and sanitary standards. But it's certainly a place to avoid if you're searching for nature and tranquillity.

Where to Stay
VERY EXPENSIVE
The **Aurola Playa Flamingo** (233-7233 TOLL-FREE (800) 2-AUROLA FAX 222-0090, Apdo 7802-1000, San José, meets all the standards of an international beach resort. The 88 rooms here, all of them spacious and tastefully furnished, include 25 bay-view kings and eight large surfside suites. Hotel amenities include a SCUBA diving center, a boutique, a casino, a large pool with swim-up bar and childcare service. Aurola also boasts three restaurants and a piano bar.

EXPENSIVE
Perched on a bluff above the yacht harbor is the eclectic **Flamingo Beach Hotel** (290-1858 or 654-4141 FAX 231-1858 or 654-4035 E-MAIL hotflam@sol.racsa.co.cr, Apdo 321-1002, San José. Whether you want to relax in the sun or have an active vacation, the Flamingo has something for everyone, including the tennis player, swimmer, sport fishermen and SCUBA diver. All rooms have private baths and satellite television.

MODERATE
Perhaps the oddest building overlooking Playa Flamingo and one of the few structures that looks Spanish-colonial rather than American-modern is **Flamingo Tower Bed and Breakfast** (654-4231 FAX 654-4275. With its charming decor, bluff-top location and panoramic views of the Pacific, this hotel is ideal for romantic getaways. There are only five rooms, each with air conditioning, private bath, hot water and a small refrigerator. The honeymoon suite occupies the namesake tower, originally built by Harvard University for astronomical

OPPOSITE LEFT: Sandy trails lead through forests to hidden beaches and bays. RIGHT: The Meliá Playa Conchal is a luxury resort on one of the most beautiful beaches in Costa Rica. OVERLEAF: Playa del Coco is a favorite for Tico teens on spring break.

observations. Manager Gene Chamberlain will make you feel at home.

Where to Eat

The **Sunrise Restaurant** at the Flamingo Marina Hotel offers tasty seafood and great views of Playa Potrero on the other side of the bay. Across the street, the **Sunset Lounge** tenders perhaps the most elegant dining on the peninsula. There are several good seafood places at the bottom of the hill including **Marie's and Rosa's Café Rico** (upstairs opposite the supermarket).

fishing and SCUBA diving trips. **Flamingo Bay Pacific Charter** (233-7233 TOLL-FREE (800) 992-3068 FAX 222-0090, at the Aurola Playa Flamingo Beach Resort, is able to handle just about any kind of sport fishing request. **Flamingo Divers** in the shopping plaza (opposite the bus stop) offers classes and trips.

How to Get There

Playa Flamingo is three kilometers (two miles) north of **Brasilito** on the coast road. A daily express bus runs from San José and

Best eats on the beach are at the charming **Catalinas** at the Aurola Playa Flamingo.

Catering to its clientele, Playa Flamingo offers a wider range of nightlife than any other beach in this area. **Amberes**, open-air discotheque, balances on a bluff above the marina. Down the road, **Mariner Inn**, a favorite with visiting yachtsmen, swings to the rhythms of rock and blues on weekends and holidays.

General Information

Costa Rica Diving (/FAX 654-4148 offers tailor-made excursions and PADI instruction. **Papagayo** (/FAX 654-4063, at the Mariner Inn, specializes in sailing charters on a yacht of the same name as well as sport

regular buses from Liberia. Taxis make the journey from Liberia, Aeropuerto Daniel Obudar and nearby beaches.

PLAYA POTRERO

Potrero lounges on a wide turquoise bay on the lower edge of the Golfo de Papagayo — where surf meets turf Costa Rica style — *i.e.,* where Guanacaste cattle country pours down to the seashore. The sand here is pearly white and Potrero is much less touristy than some of its cousins to the south. Better still, a number of largely undeveloped beaches are within striking distance, including Playa la Penca, Playa Danta and Playa Azúcar (Sugar Beach), a remarkable coral beach that many people consider the most beautiful in all of Costa Rica.

Numerous tiny islands lie off Potrero's shores including Santa Catalina, Brumel, Plata and Chocoyas, all of which offer good SCUBA diving and snorkeling with the aid of a charter boat. Closer to shore, there are small reefs around Punta Salinas and Punta Guachipelines at either end of the bay.

Where to Stay
VERY EXPENSIVE

Hotel Sugar Beach (654-4230 FAX 654-4242 Apdo 90, Santa Cruz, is something special, one of Costa Rica's better small hotels and one of its most beautiful beaches all in the same package. You can't beat the location: a secluded bay north of Flamingo. It's not easy to top the rooms too; all of them are spacious, well-decorated (native hardwood ceilings) and recently renovated. The free-form pool, shaded by huge jungle trees, overlooks the beach.

EXPENSIVE

Marked by casual elegance, the American-run **Bahía Potrero Beach Resort** (654-4183 FAX 654-4093, Apdo 45-5051, Santa Cruz, is set in a grove of giant shade trees, the hotel has a fabulous garden (with children's playground) and the best restaurant in these parts. Most rooms face the beach, which is just steps away. Private baths, hot water and air conditioning complete the package.

MODERATE

Casa Sunset House (/FAX (506) 654-4265 is one of Potrero's best bets. Owners Martha and John Herbst (and their frisky dalmatian) make you feel right at home in their guest house, which overlooks beautiful Playa Penca beach. Seven cabinas feature large bathrooms, ceiling fans and covered porches. Guests are welcome to bring their own food and drinks; Casa Sunset will supply the dishes, silverware, ice coolers and cooking facilities at no extra charge.

INEXPENSIVE

Cabinas Christina (654-4006 FAX 654-4128, with its nice garden and small pool, is tucked between cattle pastures about five minute's walk from the beach. **Cabinas Isolina** (654-4333 FAX 654-4313 nestles in a grove of huge shade trees next to the beach.

Where to Eat
Richard's American Restaurant, at the Potrero Beach Hotel, offers the best eats on the strand, serving everything from salads to seafood. Nearby is **Harden's Garden** with homemade pizza, bread, pastries and other baked goods. **Perla's BBQ** is a favorite Tico hangout with a wide range of beach treats, including burgers, hot dogs, steaks, chicken, ribs, chili and ice cold beer. One of the newer spots to chow down is **Bahía Esmeralda Pizzeria**, in Potrero village.

How to Get There
Playa Potrero is three kilometers (two miles) north of Flamingo and six kilometers (four miles) from Brasilito on the coast route (flagstone beyond Flamingo). Playa Azúcar is another five kilometers (three miles) north along the bay. Daily express bus service from San José and regular buses from Liberia terminate in Potrero village. You must walk, catch a taxi or hitch a ride to Playa Azúcar.

PLAYA CONCHAL

Conchal can give Playa Azúcar a run for its money as the most beautiful beach in Guanacaste. This curl of fine white sand and turquoise water lies between Brasilito and a jungle-shrouded headland called Punta Sábana. The name derives from the fact that Conchal is comprised of billions of tiny shells and shell fragments. You can feel them crunch beneath your toes as you walk along the surf.

The valley behind Playa Conchal was a working cattle ranch until very recently, but most of the former hacienda now falls within the bounds of the giant Meliá resort which includes an 18-hole golf course. You can walk to Brasilito along a dirt road that hugs the coast, or you can trek in the other direction to an isolated fishing village

---

Commercial fishing boats cruise the Pacific in search of dorado, tuna and marlin.

called Playa Real (Royal Beach) on the western flank of Punta Sábana.

Conchal's bay is protected from the open ocean, so it doesn't offer much wave action, but it's placid waters are perfect for swimming (be careful of rip tides) and sea kayaking. Offshore you can see the jagged outline of Isla Catalina, a popular diving spot. Snorkelers should head for reef-fringed Punta Sábana.

There's a tiny village called Puerto Viejo perched on the south side of Bahía Conchal where the budget hotels and restaurants are situated.

Where to Stay

VERY EXPENSIVE

A touch of the Spanish Riviera comes to Costa Rica in the form of the **Meliá Playa Conchal** (654-4123, 293-4915 TOLL-FREE (800) 336-3542 FAX 654-4167 or 293-4916 E-MAIL mconchal@solracsa.co.cr, Apdo 232-5150, Santa Cruz. The 310-room Meliá bills itself as the "largest and most opulent resort" in Costa Rica, a title that's difficult to dispute. The hotel has about everything you need for a beach vacation: an 18-hole golf course designed by Robert Trent Jones, a huge free-form swimming pool, Vegas-style casino and adjacent disco, live stage shows each night, four different restaurants (the seafood is superb), a full range of water sports, and one of the most beautiful beaches in Costa Rica.

MODERATE

The **Hotel Condor** (654-4050/4178 FAX 654-4044 E-MAIL ticosport@sol.racsa.co.cr, is a modest alternative to the splashy Meliá. But the rooms have everything you need: king-sized or twin beds, private bath with hot water and air conditioning or fan. The Condor's water sports center can organize SCUBA diving, snorkeling, windsurfing, fishing and other aquatic expeditions.

Where to Eat

The **Hotel Condor** has good food at great value. **Cabinas la Paz** specializes in home-made pizza. Under the umbrella of the **Meliá Conchal** are four restaurants including very good Italian and sumptuous seafood.

How to Get There

Follow essentially the same directions as for Playa Brasilito (above). Take the Liberia–Nicoya highway south to Belén, turn west on the coast resort access road and follow it 24 km (15 miles) to Huacas. From Huacas, a rough flagstone road leads west to Mata-palo four kilometers (two and a half miles) and then further north to Puerto Viejo eight kilometers (five miles).

A daily express bus runs from San José to Brasilito or Matapalo, where you can catch a cab or walk to Playa Conchal. Taxis connect Conchal with Liberia, Aeropuerto Daniel Obudar and other nearby beaches.

PARQUE NACIONAL LAS BAULAS AND PLAYA GRANDE

Spectacular coastal scenery aside, Parque Nacional las Baulas exists for one reason: preservation of giant leatherback turtles that lay their eggs in the warm sands of Playa Grande each evening.

Mother turtles visit Las Baulas through-out the year, but the best time to see them is between October and April, the prime nesting season on the Pacific Coast. Better still, make an effort to visit during high tide on a full-moon evening when as many as 100 leatherbacks are jostling for space along the beach. Other species, including greens and olive ridleys, also use Playa Grande as a nesting site.

Egg poaching was rampant in the past, but in recent years local villagers have been employed as government rangers to guide visitors to nesting sites along the beach. In fact, it's now strictly forbidden to stroll the strand unless you are accompanied by a ranger. Turtle-watching groups are limited in size so as not to disturb these matronly reptiles. Other points to remember: no flashlights, no flash cameras, and be sure to wear sandals or shoes because it's difficult to see what you might be treading on in the dark.

The park also protects rich mangroves of the Estero Tamarindo. Bird life is abundant, but anyone who explores the swamp by boat (rented in nearby Tamarindo town)

Isla de Tortuga is one of the last great escapes in the Golfo de Nicoya.

has a chance of seeing crocodiles, monkeys and deer, too. Beyond the mangroves is the gargantuan **Rancho las Colinas Golf and Country Club** (654-4089 FAX 293-4644, which includes vacation condominiums and an 18-hole championship golf course. The park entrance is adjacent to the Hotel las Tortugas.

By daylight, Playa Grande is a sparkling white curve of sand. The offshore waters (also part of the national park) constitute one of the best surfing spots on the Central America's Pacific Coast.

Where to Stay
MODERATE
Anyone with an avid interest in turtle watching should stay at **Hotel las Tortugas** (/FAX 653-0458 E-MAIL nela@cool .co.cr, Apdo 025215-1869, San José. Proprietors Louis Wilson and Marianela Paston led a successful 15-year struggle to have Playa Grande designated as a national park and their hotel is situated just outside the park boundary. They don't have any rooms facing the beach because the lights might disturb the nesting turtles. But each room does come with private hot water bath and either air conditioning or ceiling fans. The hotel restaurant looks out over the beach. Las Tortugas also rents out apartments and

houses in the Playa Grande area by the week or month.

Also at Playa Grande is **Hotel Cantarana** (653-0486 FAX 653-0491. Situated at the south end of the peninsula between the estuary and the beach, this German-owned and Mediterranean flavored inn offers spacious rooms with private bath, hot water and air conditioning. There's a small pool and an open-air restaurant. Room rates include breakfast.

INEXPENSIVE
The **Restaurante Playa Grande**, opposite the national park information kiosk, offers affordable cabinas and camping under a big shade tree out front. There's also a swimming pool.

Where to Eat
Las Tortugas offers good beachside dining including seafood and salads. **Rancho Diablo** is surfer dude central, with hot American-style food and ice cold beer. **El Bucanero** and **Restaurante Playa Grande** specialize in inexpensive but ample Tico food.

How to Get There
Playa Grande is eight kilometers (five miles) west of Huacas and 69 km (43 miles) from Liberia. Beyond Huacas the route is unpaved all the way through sleepy Matapalo village where you make a sharp left after the town square–soccer field.

No public transport goes all the way to Playa Grande; however, there are buses from San José and Liberia which serve Matapalo, where you can catch a cab or walk to Playa Grande.

PLAYA TAMARINDO

Surf city of the Guanacaste Coast, Playa Tamarindo is a broad strand between Punta San Francisco and the Estuario Tamarindo, the bay protected by a rocky outcrop called Isla Capitán. You're more likely to hear a California twang or Aussie drawl than native Spanish. Blond hair and blue eyes abound along the main drag, especially during the high season between November and April, when every day brings blue skies, abundant sunshine and some of the gnarliest waves this side of Malibu.

But don't think "hang ten" is the only byword at Tamarindo. The resort area offers plenty of other activities including sport fishing, windsurfing, SCUBA diving, golf (at Rancho las Colinas) and jungle boat tours through the nearby Estuario Tamarindo. There's also a good deal of nightlife ranging from merengue-flavored beach bars to surfer nightclubs.

More secluded beaches nearby include Playa Langosta and Playa Avellana. Langosta, three kilometers (two miles) from Tamarindo on the south side of the Estuario de San Francisco, is best reached by boat. The beach is dominated by surfers in the daytime, by nesting turtles at night. Avellana can also be reached by boat, but the quickest way is by road, 15 km (nine miles) via two sleepy inland towns called Villarreal and Hernández. Avellana is another good surf spot.

Where to Stay
VERY EXPENSIVE
There is one local hotel that sits head and shoulders above all the others in terms of service and luxury: **El Jardín del Eden** (653-0137 FAX 653-0111 E-MAIL hotel@jardin-eden.com WEBSITE www.jardin-eden.com/hotel. This small luxury hotel, run by an Italian couple, commands a hilltop overlooking Bahía Tamarindo. Each of the 20 rooms here come with air conditioning, private bath, hot water, mini-bar and safe-deposit box, as well as a balcony or terrace with sea view. Another reason to stay here is the superb French restaurant which serves some of the best food on the Guanacaste Coast. Eden does indeed have tropical gardens, as well as two pools and a 120-m (400-ft)-long private walkway to the beach.

Tamarindo Diria (290-4340 FAX 290-4367 E-MAIL tnodiria@sol.racsa.co.cr, is one of the few local abodes that's right on the water. The 79 rooms feature private baths, air conditioning and fans, cable television, mini-bar and safe-deposit box. The beach is just a step away, as are the Diria's two swimming pools (one for adults, one for

kids). The hotel's open-air restaurant is also one of the best in town.

Hotel Capitán Suizo (653-0275/0075 FAX 653-0292 E-MAIL capitansuizo@ticonet.co.cr, is a longtime favorite with Tamarindo habitués. Buck for buck, this might well be the single best hotel in all of Costa Rica. It certainly has one of the more picturesque settings. Just steps from the beach, the Suizo features eight thatched-roof bungalows and 22 rooms in a two-story block (ground floor rooms have air conditioning, upper floor rooms catch the sea breeze and have fans).

The free-form pool is surrounded by lush tropical gardens. Suizo has its own stables — 14 horses waiting to take you splashing through the surf — as well as a SCUBA center and other water sports facilities.

MODERATE
The European managers of **Hotel el Milagro** (441-5102 FAX 441-8494, have created one of the best mid-range establishments in Tamarindo. Situated opposite the beach, El Milagro is an ideal base for surfing safaris and other coastal pursuits. The 34 rooms feature hot water, safe-deposit boxes and

OPPOSITE: Horses come in handy for traveling along the peninsula's dusty roads. ABOVE: Sea kayaks, high and dry on Playa Conchal.

terraces that catch the sea breeze. Other amenities include a restaurant and bar, swimming pool and shady garden. The management speaks Spanish, English, Dutch, German and French.

INEXPENSIVE

Local hotelier Maria de los Angeles Molina has fashioned what could be Costa Rica's best budget value in the **Cabinas Marielos** (441-4843 FAX 653-0141. Set around a quiet garden with towering coconut palms, the cabinas offer a pleasant family atmosphere

and great rooms when you consider the low rates. Cabinas sleep as many as four people and all have private cold water bath.

Where to Eat

Tamarindo has more eateries than any other beach in Guanacaste. It would probably take a month to feast your way through every single establishment. **Capitán Suizo** has an excellent poolside restaurant with American and continental cuisine. **Jardín de Eden** offers the best French cuisine in town. There are at least half a dozen pizza joints and pasta houses, including **Stella's** and **Las Brusas** (side by side on Calle Guanacaste) and **La Terraza** with its breezy upper-deck dining room. **Tropicana** serves

Mexican cuisine, including fish and salads. **Iguana Surf** does California-style breakfast and lunch. **The Vaquero** offers seafood and Tico dishes with loads of romantic beach-front ambiance while **Coconuts** has a cool terrace that's popular with the surf crowd. **Johan's Bakery** always has something fresh out of the oven.

General Information

Learn to shoot the curl from **Iguana Surf**'s local experts; they also rent surfboards, sea kayaks, mountain bikes and snorkeling equipment. **Tamarindo Sportsfishing** (/FAX 653-0090, offers two vessels (seven and 11 m or 22 and 38 ft) under Captain Randy Wilson, who has been fishing these waters since 1974. Contact **Papagayo Excursions** (680-0859 FAX 225-3648 for diving, windsurfing, water skiing, jungle boat safaris and horseback riding.

How to Get There

Tamarindo is 12 km (7.5 miles) south from Huacas (via Villarreal) and 73 km (45 miles) from Liberia. The drive down from Liberia takes about one hour and the entire route is paved until the last four kilometers (two and a half miles).

Daily express buses run from San José (five and a half hours) and local buses from Liberia and Santa Cruz. Daily flights are available from San José to the Tamarindo airstrip on both TravelAir and SANSA.

PLAYA NOSARA

Nosara is the sort of place where you can either drop in for a couple of days or drop out for the rest of your life. A multitude of foreigners have come to Nosara for a vacation and never left. Many of them own retirement homes in the area. Expatriates control most of the hotels and restaurants in Nosara.

Although everyone refers to the area as Playa Nosara, the actual beach of that name is just one part of a broad coastal valley fed by two rivers, the ríos Nosara and Montaña. The estuary where the streams flow into the sea is a world-famous surf spot. Playa Nosara lies to the north of the estuary; Playa Pelada and Playa Guiones are to the south. All three beaches are popular with sunseekers and surfers. Nosara village is about five kilometers (three miles) inland at the end of a serpentine road that winds down from Nicoya (34 km or 21 miles).

The entire Nosara coast — from Punta India in the north to Punta Guiones in the south — is incorporated into the **Refugio Nacional de Fauna Silvestre Ostional**. The park features lush tidepools, coastal jungle, offshore reefs and patches of sand that serve as nesting sites for the olive ridley

turtle. The ridleys are famous for their *arribada*, or mass arrival, when as many as 100,000 turtles lay their eggs on several consecutive nights. Peak season is August and September, but you can usually find a few turtles on the beach each night between July and the Christmas holidays.

Where to Stay

VERY EXPENSIVE

Big Sur comes to Costa Rica in the form of the **Nosara Yoga Retreat** (233-8057 FAX 255-3351 E-MAIL aroldan@sol.racsa.co.cr WEBSITE www.nosara.com/yogaretreat. A superb spot for a beach holiday in its own right, the retreat offers all kinds of mind–body activities, including full body massage,

breathing and meditation instruction, daily Hatha yoga classes, nutritional counseling, supervised fasting and detoxification. Retreat directors Amba Camp and Don Stapleton have more than 40 years of yoga experience between them.

MODERATE

Set on a leafy ridge with a view looking out over the bay, **Almost Paradise** (/FAX 685-5004 is run with tender loving care by Gerlinde, a former German television producer. The six rooms here are spick and span, each with private bath and balcony. The hotel restaurant has some of Nosara's more savory cuisine.

There's more Germanic ambiance at the **Rancho Suizo Lodge** (222-2900 or 223-4371 FAX 222-5173 E-MAIL aratur@sol.racsa.co.cr WEBSITE www.nosara.com/ranchosuizo, managed by Swiss expatriates Rene Spinnler and Rush Luscher. This pleasant little hotel located near Playa Pelada has bungalows each with their own hot water baths. Amenities here include two bars, as well as and mountain bike and water sports equipment.

Where to Eat

With so many expatriate residents, Nosara offers more dining choice than most Costa Rican beaches. **Bambu Bar & Restaurant** has the "best char-grilled burgers" in Costa Rica as well as Sunday brunch with eggs benedict and Bloody Marys. **La Dolce Vita** features pasta and pizza, while both **Rancho Suizo** and **Almost Perfect** have cafés with a variety of tasty cuisine. Other good bets include **Monkey Business** and **La Lechuza**.

How to Get There

Nosara village is 33 km (20.5 miles) southwest of Nicoya; the beach is five kilometers (3 miles) further west. You can also drive the coast road from Playa Sámara 29 km (18 miles) or take a long scenic journey from Santa Cruz, 63 km (39 miles), that

ABOVE: Most beach towns have one or two small, palm-bedecked hotels OPPOSITE perfect for romantic getaways. Boats of many sizes dodge into sheltered bays ABOVE for an anchor and a swim. OVERLEAF: Day trippers walk the solitary beaches on Isla de Tortuga.

takes you through Caimito, Junquillal, Lagarto and Marbella.

A daily express bus runs from San José and there's a local bus from Nicoya. TravelAir offers daily flights from San José; SANSA flies three times a week.

PLAYA SÁMARA

Sámara is a relatively secluded beach about 26 km (16 miles) south of Nosara on the coast road. The warm gray sands of Bahía Sámara are surrounded by vacation

Central America. The 40 cabinas cling to the hillside above Playa Carrillo, each unit equipped with air conditioning, private bath with hot water, satellite television and safe. Guanamar has its own small fishing fleet — a 7.5-m (25-ft) Boston whaler and an 11-m (36-ft) Hatteras, for expeditions to snag marlin, yellowfin, sailfish, wahoo and other tropical whoppers.

EXPENSIVE

Situated on a forested hill overlooking the coast, **Hotel Mirador de Sámara (** 656-0044

houses and small resorts. Despite its isolation, Playa Sámara offers a good choice of upscale accommodation.

Several good beaches are to be found on either side of Bahía Sámara. Playa Garza to the north offers white sand and sweeping views of the Pacific. Playa Carrillo to the south is framed by palm trees and coral reef. Playa Camaronal is a world-famous surfing spot.

Where to Stay
VERY EXPENSIVE

Guanamar Beach and Sportfishing Resort
(656-0054 or 293-4544 FAX 656-0001 or 239-2405, Apdo 7-1880, San José, has long been considered one of the top resorts in all of

FAX 656-0046 indeed offers splendid views from most of the rooms and an unusual three-story observation tower. Owner Max Mahlich runs a tight ship that includes six large guest rooms with fully equipped kitchens and private baths. The beach is a five-minute walk away.

The **Villas Playa Sámara (** 256-8228 or 656-0104 FAX 221-7222 is another good choice, with 57 air-conditioned villas (one, two or three bedrooms) decorated with rattan furniture and mosaic tiles. The Villa features a restaurant and bar, swimming pool and Jacuzzi and a small casino. Sports include fishing, windsurfing, jet skiing, horseback riding, mountain biking and water skiing.

MODERATE

Best value for money in Sámara is most likely the **Isla Chora Inn** (656-0174/0175 FAX 656-0173. Deluxe rooms include air conditioning, satellite television and safe-deposit boxes and private baths with hot water. There's a swimming pool and the restaurant serves Italian food.

INEXPENSIVE

Hotel Playa Sámara (686-6922 or 656-0190 is occasionally noisy side, but it offers modest rooms with fans and private cold water baths.

Where to Eat

Isla Chora Inn's restaurant serves pizza and pasta dishes, as well as homemade Italian ice cream. **Villas Playa Sámara** has a good international restaurant. Try **Colocho's** for seafood or **Flor de Giruelo** for Costa Rican-style Chinese dining.

How to Get There

Playa Sámara is 38 km (23.5 miles) south of Nicoya along a road that's only partially paved at present. It can also be reached from Playa Nosara along a very rough coastal road.

A daily express bus runs from San José and a local bus from the town of Nicoya which continues on to Playa Carrillo. Both of Costa Rica's domestic airlines offer daily service from San José to Sámara's tiny airport.

EXCURSIONS INLAND

SANTA CRUZ

The crossroads town of Santa Cruz, with a population of 17,000, is a bustling metropolis by local standards, but it's a far cry from the big city. Founded in 1760, Santa Cruz is one of Guanacaste's oldest towns and the official Folklore City of Costa Rica. Traditional folk dancing, country music and (bloodless) bullfighting linger on here, and can be experienced at their flamboyant best during annual town fiestas such as the festival of **Cristo Negro de Esquipulas**, held on January 15, and the celebration of **Guanacaste's annexation**, held on July 25.

During the remainder of the year, there isn't much reason for travelers to pause in Santa Cruz except to fill up their gas tank or change buses. But if you find yourself with spare time, have a look around the leafy town square with its mango trees and the ruined bell tower of an old church that was destroyed in an earthquake a half-century ago.

Twelve kilometers (seven and a half miles) east of Santa Cruz is sleepy **Guaitíl**, where the ancient tradition of Chorotega Indian pottery has been revived in recent

years. The handmade ceramics come in various earthen shades and prices are very reasonable. Members of the village art co-operative are happy to demonstrate the process for visitors, from fashioning with local clay to firing in kilns behind their workshops.

Where to Stay

INEXPENSIVE

La Estancia Cabinas (680-0476 or 255-2981 FAX 680-0348 offers simple but clean rooms with private bath, cold water and fan. The **Hotel Diria** (680-0402/0080 FAX 680-0442, Apdo 58, Santa Cruz, has similar rooms and facilities but with the added advantage of a garden and swimming pool.

Where to Eat

Unless you're into rice and beans, Santa Cruz doesn't present much choice. **Bamboo** restaurant inside the Hotel Diria has a few

OPPOSITE: A rancher on the Nicoya Peninsula.
ABOVE: An evening dip in cool river waters.

international dishes on the menu. **La Taberna** serves average Chinese food. The best local cuisine is at the **Coope Tortillas**, with Tico dishes and fresh tortillas cooked in wood-fired ovens.

How to Get There

Santa Cruz is 55 km (34 miles) south of Liberia and 20 km (12.5 miles) north of Nicoya on Highway 21 and can be used as a base for excursions to Playa Tamarindo, 34 km (21 miles) away, and other beaches on the central Guanacaste Coast.

There are daily express buses from San José, as well as local buses from Liberia, Tamarindo and Nicoya town. Taxis run to and from Nicoya.

NICOYA

One of Costa Rica's oldest towns, Nicoya (population: 11,000) was founded in the mid-sixteenth century as a market town and religious center for the surrounding haciendas, which then relied heavily on Chorotega Indian slave labor. The fulcrum of local culture in Spanish colonial days was the Iglesia San Blas, a gorgeous white-washed church which today simmers like a mirage in the Guanacaste heat. San Blas is

still the town's most impressive structure and includes an archaeological museum with modest pre-Columbian treasures.

The town's biggest celebration each year comes on December 12, feast day of the Virgin of Guadalupe. Like most Guanacaste festivals, this one includes local music and dance, bullfights and livestock shows and ample portions of food.

Nicoya is located on the banks of the Río Grande, half an hour's drive south of Santa Cruz and a good three hours north of Playa Naranjo and the ferry terminal on the Golfo de Nicoya. The town is a convenient jumping off point for excursions to Parque Nacional Barra Honda as well as for the beaches of the northern Nicoya Peninsula, including Playa Nosara, 39 km (24 miles) away, and Playa Sámara, 38 km (23.5 miles) distant.

Where to Stay

INEXPENSIVE

Nicoya doesn't offer much choice when it comes to accommodation. Probably the most comfortable place in town (and certainly the most efficient) is the **Complejo Turistico Curime** (683-5288 FAX 685-5530. Cabinas and rooms include air conditioning, hot water, television and a refrigerator.

Hotel Rancho Humo (255-2463 FAX 255-3573, 27 km (17 miles) north of Nicoya, is a secluded lodge on the banks of the Río Tempisque. The prices here are rather high for what you get, but the ranch has a swimming pool and all rooms have air conditioning. The front desk can arrange boat trips into nearby Parque Nacional Palo Verde.

Where to Eat

Café Daniela has the best pizza in town as well as tasty Tico cuisine. **Restaurant Jade**

offers Chinese with a local flair. **Papatan's Soda & Restaurant** serves up savory Costa Rican dishes.

How to Get There

Nicoya is 20 km (12.5 miles) south of Santa Cruz, 28 km (17 miles) west of Tempisque ferry and 72 km (44.5 miles) northwest of Playa Naranjo.

The Tempisque ferry from the mainland ostensibly departs every 45 minutes during daylight hours; the trip takes 20 minutes. However, the ferry is very unreliable, and you can end up waiting for hours for it to depart. Check with your car rental agency or hotel along your travels; if it sounds like the ferry may leave you high and dry, take

the Interamericana to Liberia and then head south through Santa Cruz. Daily express buses run from San José, as well as local buses from Liberia, Santa Cruz, Nosara and Sámara. Taxis travel to and from Santa Cruz.

PARQUE NACIONAL BARRA HONDA

Barra Honda stands apart from other Costa Rican parks because the main attraction here is below the ground: the country's largest limestone cavern system. More

than three dozen caves and labyrinths have been discovered here over the past 20 years, with the deepest (Santa Ana Cave) gaping more than 200 m (660 ft) below the surface.

The caverns are marvelous, filled with stalactites and stalagmites of a thousand different shapes and sizes. Among the more remarkable caves are Terciopelo, La Trampa, Pozo Hedionda and Nicoa (where prehistoric man once lived). Millions of bats also call these caverns home, as do

OPPOSITE: Rocky islets rise above the water in the Golfo de Papagayo. ABOVE LEFT: Palms flourish in the island nature reserve at Tortuga. RIGHT: Guanacaste's colonial churches mark some of the earliest settlements in the country.

salamanders and fish who have adapted to living in total darkness.

Visitors must have reservations and a ranger guide to enter the caves, which can be arranged through the National Parks Office (257-0922 FAX 223-6963, in San José. Another alternative is to join an organized spelunking expedition offered by a private tour company such as **Ríos Tropicales** (233-6455 FAX 255-4354.

Above ground, Barra Honda offers more special attractions. The dry tropical forest here is home to numerous indigenous species including puma (who have been known to attack humans), monkeys, deer, peccaries, anteaters and myriad bird species. Las Cascades is an above-ground limestone formation that resembles a frozen waterfall. Cerros Barra Honda is a short 442 m (1450 ft) rocky peak. Be aware that trails are not well marked. Lost hikers have died in this park.

Where to Stay

Other than camping, no accommodation is available in the park. The nearest hotel is the Rancho Humo, north of Nicoya town (see above).

How to Get There

The entrance to Parque Nacional Barra Honda is 14 km (9 miles) east of Nicoya via the villages of Piave and Santa Ana. If you are coming directly from San José, the entrance is about 20 km (12.5 miles) west of the Tempisque ferry via a roundabout route that takes you through Quebrada Honda, Tres Esquinas, Nacaome, Pueblo Viejo, and Santa Ana.

Buses depart daily at noon from Nicoya stopping at Santa Ana; it is then a two-kilometer (one-and-a-quarter-mile) walk to the park entrance.

GOLFO DE NICOYA BEACH RESORTS AND WILDLIFE RESERVES

PLAYA NARANJO

Naranjo is the western terminus of the vehicle–passenger ferries that ply the Golfo de Nicoya from Puntarenas, which makes it the jumping off point for excursions to the beach resorts (Tabor and Montezuma) and wildlife parks (Curu, Tortuga and Cabo Blanco) of the southern Nicoya Peninsula. The town of Naranjo is not particularly interesting in itself, but it is a good place to fill up your gas tank and stock up on food supplies before heading west to the wilder parts of Nicoya. Naranjo can also be used as a gateway to central Nicoya, but the road north to Quebrada Honda and Nicoya town is one of the worst highways in northwest Costa Rica.

Where to Stay
INEXPENSIVE

Hotel Oasis del Pacifico (661-1555 is the only place to stay in Naranjo. Rooms have private bath with hot water but no air conditioning. Rates include breakfast. The Oasis has a restaurant and two pools.

Where to Eat

The **Oasis del Pacifico's** restaurant offers a selection of meat and fish dishes "and lots of local food" according to the manager. There are a variety of sodas near the ferry terminal.

How to Get There

If you're coming south from Guanacaste, Playa Naranjo is 69 km (43 miles) south of Quebrada Honda and 72 km (45 miles) from Nicoya town. Heading west from Naranjo along the coast road are Paquera 22 km (14 miles), Playa Tambor 41 km (25.5 miles) and Montezuma 59 km (36.5 miles) via Cobano.

There are at least five daily passenger–vehicle ferries from Puntarenas. Passage takes about 90 minutes. Buses to from Paquera, Tambor and Montezuma arrive near the Naranjo ferry pier.

PAQUERA

The little seaside town of Paquera has become an alternative ferry harbor for southern Nicoya in recent years. There are three services each day from Puntarenas. Bus service is available to Naranjo, 22 km (13.5 miles), Tambor, 19 km (12 miles) and Montezuma, 37 km (23 miles).

REFUGIO DE FAUNA SILVESTRE CURU

This small reserve of 84 hectares (207 acres) near Paquera is privately owned but open to the public. Seven distinct ecosystems thrive, including pristine black sand beaches, mangrove swamp and several types of coastal forest. Birds are abundant, and among the mammals on the reserve are ocelots, white-tailed deer, sloths, anteaters, capuchin and howler monkeys. The owners are trying to reintroduce spider monkeys.

Bahía Curu with its lovely black-sand beach has good snorkeling, but you'll need to bring your own equipment. Permission from the owners is required and must be obtained before visiting the reserve (661-2392 or 223-1739. They live in an old house near the beach and will gladly give you a private tour of the reserve.

ISLA DE TORTUGA

Tortuga is an exquisitely handsome island off the southern Nicoya Coast, about two kilometers (one and a quarter miles) from Curu and within easy reach of Puntarenas. Its wonderful white sand beach is framed by towering coconut palms and warm turquoise waters that are perfect for swimming.

For the last 20 years, Tortuga has been operated as a private nature reserve by the Cubero family of San José. The Cuberos have replanted and reintroduced plant species that had disappeared from the island. They've developed a self-guided nature trail looping around the island that includes a climb to the island's highest point at 172 m (570 ft) and a "canopy tour" ride in leather harnesses attached to a cable.

Tortuga harbors many species of rare and endangered plants including orchids, bromeliads and tropical hardwoods such as the indio desnudo tree and the madrono with its striking white flowers. The island also hosts several animal species including the agouti, as well as providing nesting sights for frigate birds and pelicans.

The beach can be enjoyed free of charge; there's a $5 fee for the nature trail. Tortuga is 90 minutes from the port of Puntarenas by boat. Excursions can be arranged through Luís Fernando Sánchez, at **Bay Island Cruises** (296-5551 FAX 296-5095, San José.

PLAYA TAMBOR

A well-kept secret until a few years ago, Tambor is now being discovered by the jet-set crowd, thanks to myriad articles in international travel magazines and the construction of several five-star resorts.

Tambor village is a cluster of wooden shacks and fishing boats on Bahía Ballena (Whale Bay). The black sand beach here is handsome and clean. Around the bay are several picture perfect strands, such as Tango Mar, which many consider of the most beautiful beaches in Central America.

Where to Stay
VERY EXPENSIVE
Perched on rugged cliffs overlooking a splendid white sand beach, **Tango Mar** (661-2798 or 223-1864 FAX 255-2697 is one of Costa Rica's prime seaside retreats. It's difficult to pick the most delightful thing about this marvelous hotel: the thatched

A guide displays the skull of a man-eating crocodile at Hotel Rancho Humo near Barra Honda.

cabinas, the expansive 51-hectare (125-acre) tropical gardens, the various sports activities (from a 10-hole golf course to beach volleyball) or the gourmet cuisine at Tango Mar's restaurant. If you want to pamper yourself, this is the place.

At **Tambor Tropical** (683-0011/0012 FAX 683-0013, they may have only 10 rooms, but they're among the best in Costa Rica, each with kitchen, private hot water bath and coastal panoramas. This splendid little resort also has a swimming pool and access to multiple recreation activities. *Conde Nast Traveler* magazine calls the Tropical "truly stunning."

EXPENSIVE

Nicoya's first Mexican-style mega resort is **Barcelo Playa Tambor** (661-2039 or 220-2034 TOLL-FREE (800) 858-0606 FAX 661-2069, Apdo 458-1150, San José. With 402 units, it has more rooms than all the other hotels on this coast combined. Rates include all meals and drinks; water sports activities are extra. Rooms feature private hot water baths and air conditioning.

INEXPENSIVE

Los Lagartos (/FAX 683-0236 is located right on the beach. Carlos and Rita Entwes run this simple but pleasant little lodge that's a hit with young American and European travelers. Rooms are with shared or private cold water baths.

Where to Eat

Bahía Ballena Yacht Club offers a range of Mexican, Cajun and Creole cuisine courtesy of the transplanted Louisiana chef. **Tango Mar** offers the best menu on the peninsula, including sumptuous seafood dishes and generous salads.

General Information

Bahía Ballena Yacht Club is a small marina that caters to visiting yachts. It offers SCUBA diving, fishing and sightseeing boat trips, as well as renting out snorkeling and windsurfing equipment and sailboats.

How to Get There

Tambor lies between Paquera, 19 km (12 miles) away, and Montezuma, 18 km

(11 miles) distant. Buses from Paquera ferry pier depart three times daily. Taxis also run to Paquera. Tambor's tiny airfield has three daily services from San José. The larger hotels can arrange boat service from Puntarenas.

MONTEZUMA

If Tambor's chic resorts don't match your expectations of a Costa Rican beach holiday (or your budget), amble down the coast to Montezuma, a sleepy seaside retreat that

has both stunning beaches and reasonable accommodation.

Much like Playa Nosara in northern Nicoya, Montezuma is something of a throwback to the 1960s. Plenty of surfers and long-haired kids. Cold beer and cheap eats. Fair-haired maidens on the beach by day, guitar music in the local bodegas at night. It would be difficult to find a more mellow place in all of Costa Rica.

Montezuma has its share of expatriate residents, many of them retired Europeans and North Americans who consider southern Nicoya their little slice of paradise. Some of them manage the lodges and cabinas along the beach, while others keep a tight watch on development, heading off attempts to turn their tranquil community into a southern version of Papagayo or Flamingo.

Montezuma is blessed with abundant beaches, most of them backed by tropical forest and fronted by coral reefs. Crowds are never a problem, but reaching the beaches can be a challenge. Playa Grande and other beaches situated west of town are easily reached by road. But Quizales, Cocalito, Cocal and other beaches to the east can be reached only on foot, by horseback or by boat.

Where to Eat
Los Mangos is probably the best choice for variety and quality. Try **El Saño Banano** for vegetarian fare and **Chico's** for Tico fare.

How to Get There
Montezuma is 18 km (11 miles) from Tambor and 37 km (23 miles) from Paquera along the coast road. Beyond Cobano, the route is unpaved and may require a four-wheel-drive vehicle. Buses from Paquera ferry pier depart three times daily. Taxis are few and far between in this area.

Where to Stay
MODERATE
The best on the beach is **Hotel los Mangos** (642-0076 FAX 642-0050, which has a choice of bungalows with private hot water baths, rooms with private cold water baths, or rooms with shared baths. Los Mangos isn't air conditioned, but there's almost always a cool sea breeze. Amenities include a restaurant, pool and lots of ocean.

INEXPENSIVE
Hotel Montezuma (642-0058, **Hotel Amor de Mar** (642-0262 and **Cabinas el Saño Banano** (661-1122 extension 272 offer pleasant and cheap accommodation near the beach.

RESERVA NATURAL ABSOLUTA CABO BLANCO

The "absolute" in Reserva Natural Absoluta Cabo Blanca refers to the fact that it's protected against all intrusion and possible future defilement. Cabo Blanco (White Cliffs) was the corner stone of Costa Rica's national park system, founded in 1963 on a dazzling parcel of pristine land at the tip of the Nicoya Peninsula.

The reserve was the brainchild of Olaf and Karen Wessberg, Swedish farmers who

Small craft powered by pedals are an ecologically-sensitive alternative to jet skis. OVERLEAF: An Easter procession winds its way through a Nicoya Peninsula village.

settled in Cabo Blanco in the mid 1950s. When logging and cattle ranching threatened to destroy the cape's wilderness, the Wessbergs launched an international campaign to save the area and create a national park system that would benefit the entire country. Their dream was realized, but not without a dark side: Olaf Wessberg was murdered in 1975 while carrying out an environmental survey of the reserve.

Three decades after its birth, Cabo Blanco remains a special place. It is not difficult to see why the Wessbergs and

the station to the cape and both beaches. **Sendero Central** winds inland, through thick forest, reaching a terminus at Playa Balsita. **Sendero el Barco** leads along the wild bluffs west of Play Balsita.

Where to Stay

There is no overnight accommodation inside the reserve and camping is not permitted. The closest place to stay is Cabuya village, a few kilometers beyond the park entrance, which has a handful of simple cabinas and guest houses.

many others wanted this place preserved for all time. The lush coastal forest protects numerous bird and mammal species, including the puma, peccary, ocelot, white-tailed deer, kinkajou and three different types of monkey. The park's two beaches, Playa Balsita and Playa Cabo Blanco, harbor tide pools and small coral reefs. Cabo Blanco itself is Costa Rica's version of land's end, a windswept promontory that projects into the Pacific. Offshore is Isla Cabo Blanco, nesting sight of myriad sea birds including brown boobies. You'll need a boat to reach it.

Cabo Blanco's ranger station, at the park entrance, has trail maps and other information. **Sendero Sueco** leads from

How to Get There

Cabo Blanco reserve is 11 km (seven miles) west of Montezuma along a rough dirt road, which is often impassable during the rainy season. There is no public transportation to the reserve. Taxis are sometimes available in Montezuma. You can ride horses to the park entrance, but cannot take them into the reserve.

ABOVE LEFT: Playa Hermosa bungalows decorate the hillsides. Catching the last rays at Playa del Coco ABOVE RIGHT and sailing near Playa Hermosa OPPOSITE.

The Central Pacific Coast

COSTA RICA'S MOST POPULAR BEACHES curve into tropical jungles west of the Cordillera Talamanca along the central Pacific Coast. Close to San José and more urbane than the beach towns of the Nicoya Peninsula or the Caribbean Coast, the Pacific communities of Jacó, Quepos, Manuel Antonio and Dominical thrive on tourism.

Though Manuel Antonio in particular is firmly ensconced in the tourist circuit, the central Pacific still feels remote and wild. Spider and capuchin monkeys swing through the trees in parks and settlements all along the humid, lush coastline and in mountain foothills. The Costanera Sur, a semi-paved road that aims to be a coastal highway, runs south from the port city of Puntarenas, where cruise ships, freighters and ferries anchor in the Golfo de Nicoya. The road quickly deteriorates as it reaches the Reserva Biológica Carara, a popular day-trip destination from San José and Puntarenas. The road along continues to Jacó, known for its powerful surf, its party-town attitude and its proximity to the park's primary tropical forest.

Potholes, ruts and knee-deep mud in the rainy season greet travelers headed farther south to Quepos and Manuel Antonio. The road gets so bad in places that signs warn drivers they are traveling at their own risk — an ironic twist when en route to one of the most densely populated beach towns in the country. Quepos, the nearest major town to Parque Nacional Manuel Antonio, has grown over the past two decades from a settlement of less than a dozen families into a hodgepodge of businesses and homes for nearly 15,000 residents. The Quepos–Manuel Antonio area has the country's largest selection of one-of-a-kind hotels and restaurants outside San José, all set amidst forest beside the most beautiful beaches in the country.

The rampant development tapers off as you pass outside Quepos, following along the Costanera Sur as it carves its way south through the coastline, past African palm plantations and identical workers' settlements made up of pink, yellow, green and blue houses built around soccer fields. Hotels, nature lodges and private villas appear again as you arrive at Dominical, a popular surfing spot that's becoming much more upscale than Jacó. Electricity and telephones are scarce in this region, just 42 km (26 miles) south of Quepos. Yet plenty of speculators are betting on its emergence as both a tourist destination and expatriate settlement, and land prices along the wave-beaten shoreline here have skyrocketed. From here south the road passes the remote Parque Nacional las Ballenas and a few hidden surf spots then cuts inland to Palmar Sur and the Carretera Interamericana to Panama.

Fishing, swimming and surf spots are the Central Pacific's great strengths; there are few cultural attributes here. Travelers short on time or money find relatively easy access to great beaches, abundant nature and sufficient options to meet their needs for shelter, food and excitement. To escape the crowds, schedule your visit at the beginning or end of rainy season; room rates will also be lower then.

BACKGROUND

One could say the Central Pacific towns were created for tourism, though there were Indian settlements here long before the European conquest. More recently, the

PRECEEDING PAGES: Isla de Caño LEFT is one of the best places for divers to spot sea fan coral. A dinosaur lizard in Parque Nacional Manuel Antonio RIGHT emerges from its hiding places. OPPOSITE: A rare solitary moment on Manuel Antonio's popular main beach. ABOVE: Quepos has about 15,000 residents, many of whom work in the overabundance of hotels, restaurants and tour companies around Manuel Antonio.

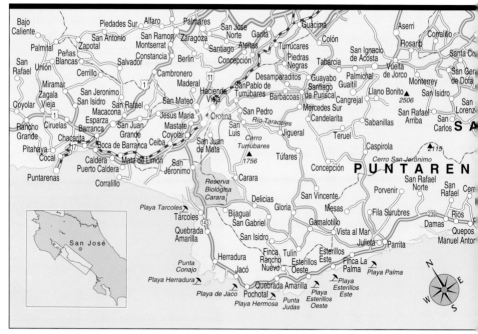

area was the second front of the United Fruit Company, deforested and cleared for banana plantations in the 1930s. The company, already firmly entrenched on the Caribbean Coast, was responsible for the first transport link from the coast to the capital. Once a train line and a road were cleared in the 1960s and 1970s, word of these picturesque beaches spread through the country. By the 1980s, Manuel Antonio was one of the most popular destinations in the country; by the 1990s its national park was swarming with visitors.

PUNTARENAS

The largest city in this region, Puntarenas was a bustling, charming city a century ago when coffee barons shipped their crops to Europe from the port and wealthy Ticos vacationed at nearby beaches. Today, Puntarenas is faded, shabby and sultry, with a few vestiges of charm beneath its hoary exterior. Fishing boats, small cruise ships and the occasional yacht bob in the gentle waters along the downtown waterfront, where seagulls and pelicans are as predominant as people. Larger cruise and container ships dock at Puerto Caldera, which the government constructed about

19 km (12 miles) south of the original port in Puntarenas.

The loss of status as the main Pacific port and the rise of far more scenic coastal resorts tolled the death knell for Puntarenas, but the city is now battling to regain its status. Sewage plants, paved streets and a projected convention center have sparked revitalization. The Paseo de los Turistas pedestrian path along 10 blocks of beachfront north of the city is now lined with sodas, souvenir shops and ice cream stands, though it's still far from scenic.

Few travelers choose Puntarenas as destination, though it is the closest beach to San José. Good highways run the 130 km (81 miles) from the capital, and cars and buses make the trip in under two hours. The city is used more as a day-trip destination, with visits to the beach combined with boat trips to uninhabited islands in the Golfo de Nicoya. The best of these trips are run by **Calypso Tours** (233-3617, San José.

WHERE TO STAY

The moderately-priced **Tioga Inn** (661-0271 FAX 661-0127, across the street from the beach, Apdo 96-5400, Puntarenas, is the

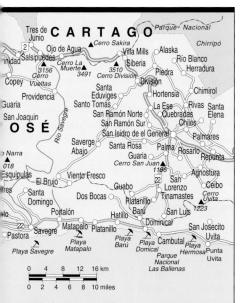

Tres de Junio
CARTAGO
Parque Nacional

2
Ojo de Agua
Cerro Sakira
Vitla Mills
Alaska
Chirripó

inidad
Salsipuedes
Cerro La
Muerte
Siberia
Río Blanco
Herradura

3156
Cerro
Vueltas
3491
3510
Cerro División
Piedra
División

Copey
Santa
Eduviges
Santo Tomás
Hortensia
Chimirol

Guaria
Providencia
San Ramón Norte
La Ese
Quebradas
Rivas
Chiles
Santa
Elena

San Joaquin
OSÉ
San Ramón Sur
San Isidro de el General
Palmares

Narra
Saverge
Abajo
Santa Rosa
Guaria
Palma
Rosario
Repunta

018
Cerro San Juan
1196
Agnostura

Esquipulas
El Brujo
Viento Fresco
22
San
Lorenzo
Tinamastes
Ceibo
Cerro
Uvita

tres
Santa
Domingo
Dos Bocas
Guabo
Platanillo
Baru
San Luis
1223

io
Portalón
Hatillo
Dominical
San Josecito
Uvita

22
Pastora
Savegre
Matapalo
Platanillo
Playa
Barú
Playa
Domical
Cambutal
Parque
Nacional
Las Ballenas
Playa
Hermosa
Punta
Uvita

Playa Savegre
Playa
Matapalo

0 4 8 12 16 km
0 2 4 6 8 10 miles

THE CENTRAL PACIFIC

traditional hangout in this neighborhood. It has 46 air-conditioned rooms and a swimming pool.

Travelers heading out on cruises who must spend a night in Puntarenas typically pick the moderately-priced **Fiesta Inn (** 293-4266 FAX 239-0217; RESERVATIONS THE U.S. TOLL-FREE (800) 662-2990, a sprawling complex with 310 rooms, three pools, a casino and several restaurants. It's a 10-minute cab ride south of town.

HOW TO GET THERE

Puntarenas is 130 km (81 miles) west of San José off the Carretera Interamericana; the drive takes about two hours. Buses run regularly throughout the day from San José to Puntarenas. Ferries to the southern Nicoya Peninsula also depart from Puntarenas.

JACÓ

If you're looking for a beach community close to San José, it's worth going the extra 60 km (37 miles) south of Puntarenas to Jacó. The long beach is immensely popular with Ticos on weekend getaways, and there are several hotels that cater to Canadian

groups on chartered, all-inclusive holidays. The small town (population: 4,000) — filled with a colorful clutter of ice cream stands, restaurants, cabinas and even a miniature golf course — feels more like a theme park than an authentic community. But there are some fine hotels on its outskirts, and Jacó's proximity to Reserva Biológica Carara and the Río Taracoles makes it a worthwhile destination.

GENERAL INFORMATION

Jacó does not have a tourist information office. It does, however, have two banks, several gas stations, markets and pharmacies, and it's is a good place to stock up on supplies when heading south. The largest tour operator in the area is **Fantasy Tours (** 643-3231 FAX 643-3383. Car rentals are available through **Elegante (** 643-3224.

WHAT TO SEE AND DO

Surfing and partying are Jacó's two biggest attractions, followed closely by the **Reserva Biológica Carara**, one of my favorite parks in the country. Until a few years back Carara was relatively unknown. I remember wandering down trails in the early Nineties with a small group and guide and encountering no other humans. Instead, we came upon a family of white-faced capuchin monkeys lounging in the forest canopy. We humans behaved in a most undignified manner, pointing binoculars and telephoto lenses at the babies clinging to their mothers, who stared back stoically, as if we were a barely tolerable intrusion. Your chances of stumbling upon such a scene are much less likely these days, since Carara has become a favorite tour for day trippers from San José and cruise ship passengers from Puerto Caldera. The rangers attempt to keep the crowds down by allowing no more than 150 people into the park at one time.

The 4,700-hectare (11,614-acre) reserve contains a large section of primary forest with a tall tree canopy spreading over a base of vines and ferns. Anteaters, armadillos, lemurs, iguanas and 850 species of birds live in the preserve, and though you can spot lots of wildlife on your own I strongly recommend hiring a guide for your trek. Carara is also the base for a long-term ecological study of the scarlet macaws who are becoming endangered due to loss of habitat and poaching. Over 200 macaw pairs (who mate for life) have been spotted in the region. The park opens at 7 AM — be there when the rangers and guides arrive for the best wildlife viewing. Late afternoon is also good. The park closes at 5 PM; entry is $6.

Crocodiles are the big attraction at the **Río Taracoles** just north of Carara. Those driving by often pull off the road at the bridge straddling the river and peer down to the banks to spot the crocs. Good luck to them. First, the bridge is notorious for automobile break-ins. Secondly, no self-respecting crocodile is going to pose in the sun for tourists' enjoyment. Those serious about spotting one of these endangered creatures should schedule a boat ride up the river, with **Jungle Crocodile Safari** (661-0455, in Taracoles, or through one of the Jacó hotels.

WHERE TO STAY

Jacó has a good range of accommodation, with inexpensive cabinas clustered in town and resort hotels sprinkled along the coast and forest north and south. I find it much nicer to stay outside town and buzz through on errands and for meals. Since Jacó is an immensely popular getaway for young Ticos, the hotels tend to fill up on weekends and general revelry takes over the pools and beaches. Try to visit during the week, if possible.

Very Expensive
A long, winding road leads uphill to **Villa Caletas** (257-3653 FAX 222-2059 E-MAIL caletas@ticonet.co.cr, Apdo 12358-1000, San José, a Victorian-style mansion high above the sea. The ambiance is quite elegant and proper, with glossy black wicker chairs, black ceiling fans, gray and white tile floors and dark antique armoires in a British colonial-empire scene. The main house has eight very formal guest rooms; white cabinas tucked under a forest of trees house 20 suites. The pool faces a

staggeringly lovely view of the jungle and an aquamarine bay. The entrance is two and a half kilometers (one and a half miles) south of Punta Leona.

Expensive
I would be delighted to return repeatedly to **Villas Lapas** (284-1418 or 293-4265 FAX 293-4104, Apdo 419-4005, Jacó, north of town, adjacent to Reserva Biologíca Carara. The Río Taracolitos runs through the 220-hectare (543-acre) private reserve where pathways lead through plush lawns to several

widely spaced one-story buildings with red-tiled roofs covered in blossoming vines during the rainy season. The 47 rooms have peaked wood ceilings and air conditioning or fans, tiled floors, big desks and powerful, hot showers. Most have front terraces and lounge chairs on the lawns, and hammocks hang between trees throughout the property. The small pool is a gathering spot for guests cooling off after hikes on trails paralleling those in Carara. In early morning tiger herons swoop down to the river, parrots and scarlet macaws screech overhead and bird watchers bearing binoculars flock to the river's edge. The hotel is sometimes filled with tour groups from Carara, who stop by to visit the butterfly garden filled with blossoming plants and fluttering mariposas extracting fruit nectars from hummingbird feeders and hanging gourds. The large restaurant and bar sometimes fills with tour groups, too, but is peaceful when left to the hotel guests at night. Tours to the Río Taracoles and a nearby waterfall are available.

Also recommended in this price range is **Punta Leona Hotel and Club** (231-3131 FAX 232-0791 RESERVATIONS IN THE U.S. TOLL-FREE (800) 554-4398, Apdo 8592-1000, San José, south of Villa Lapas. Some find the

high-security in this gated community a bit disconcerting, but no one can fault the 300-hectare (740-acre) forest, beach and grassy lawns. Part of the property is a private wildlife refuge; the rest is dotted with 118 rooms, bungalows and condominiums. This self-contained resort has three pools, six and a half kilometers (four miles) of beach, two restaurants and all the activities you could desire.

Moderate

I'm also quite fond of the friendly feeling and gorgeous beach at **Club del Mar** (643-3194, Apdo 1107-4023, Jacó, south of town. Owners Philip and Marilyn Edwardes are considered as family to many of their guests,

who return annually, claiming their favorites among the 18 rooms. Even the older, less expensive rooms have their charms; the best are in two-story pink buildings by the beach. Go for a top floor room with sea-green tiled floors, orthopedic mattresses and French doors leading to patios furnished with rocking chairs for relaxing amidst stunning views. Some guest rooms have kitchenettes and refrigerators. Fax ahead and request the room descriptions before making your choice.

Labeled plants fill the botanical gardens at Club del Mar; toucans, sloths, butterflies and birds fill the forested hills behind the property. Don't miss the horseback ride through this mini-reserve.

Las Sandalias restaurant, run by Philip, is excellent. On my last visit, I was sorely disappointed to miss the Indian curry served on Monday nights. The owners speak English, Spanish, German and a smattering of Swahili, and celebrate Guy Falks Day (November 5) with a massive party. They also represent Fantasy Tours and offer knowledgeable recommendations on touring the area.

Terraza del Pacifico (546-3222 or 643-3444 FAX 643-3424 RESERVATIONS IN THE U.S. (212) 213-2399, Apdo 168, Jacó, south of town on Playa Hermosa, has 43 rooms with views of an, indeed, beautiful beach. The open-air restaurant is right by the sea, and a small casino operates during high season.

WHERE TO EAT

Expensive

Most of the hotels mentioned above have good restaurants. Make reservations in advance for dinner at **Club del Mar** if you're craving tender chateaubriand or some spice in your grilled fish. **Terraza del Pacifico** is dependable, and a live calypso band plays on Saturday nights.

Moderate

Always packed with surfers, travelers and locals, **Killer Munchies** (643-3354, in town,

OPPOSITE: Locals beat the heat on a shady sidewalk in the port city of Puntarenas. ABOVE: A colorful café sign beckons vacationers.

serves up burritos, burgers, pizzas and pastas that satisfy gringo cravings. **La Piraña** (643-3725, in town, has an unusual menu featuring spicy blackened fish and steaks, pastas and casados. **Banana Café**, in town, is a dependable choice for huge plates of stir-fried veggies with chicken or beef.

How to Get There

Jacó is around 60 km (37 miles) south of Puntarenas on the Costanera Sur. If your flight comes in early enough to San José,

you should be able to rent a car and drive out to Jacó in the same day. The most direct car route is the Carretera Interamericana from San José, which links up with the Costanera Sur south of Puntarenas. A little bit longer drive, but so much more scenic, follows Highway 11 west from San José through Atenas and Orotina, where the road is lined with produce stands packed with homegrown cashews, watermelons, pineapples and other tropical snacks. Portions of this roadway were used by Spanish settlers in the sixteenth century; yucca trees planted as live fences cordon off the ranches and farms. Keep an eye out for the yucca's white flowers in February and March. Called the *flores itabo,* these waxy flowers are eaten alongside scrambled eggs. The highway ends at the Costanera Sur near the small town of San Jeronimo; follow the signs directing you south to Quepos.

Buses depart frequently from San José and Puntarenas; the Jacó bus station is at the north end of town.

QUEPOS AND PARQUE NACIONAL MANUEL ANTONIO

The half-moon curves of the pale yellow-brown sand against the emerald forest at **Parque Nacional Manuel Antonio** are some of the most beautiful beaches in Costa Rica. The aquamarine water shimmers in the sun and glows by the light of the moon. Sailboats, cruise ships and luxury yachts pose against the backdrop of Isla Mogote and Punta Catedral jutting upward from the sea, where whales, dolphins and flying fish frolic in calm waters.

The park sits at the south end of the Quepos–Manuel Antonio region. Quepos is the main town and site of budget hotels and residents. The curving hillside road (which I call the Corridor) south of town to the national park is lined with ever-more luxurious inns and lodges. The Corridor ends at the edge of the park in the small settlement of Manuel Antonio, where a free public beach, a few small hostelries and large parking lots are located.

On returning to Parque Manuel Antonio after several years' absence, I was fortunate to approach it from the sea. Riding a raft to shore from the *Temptress* cruise ship, I got to see the park at its best, seemingly empty of humanity. I spent the day body surfing in gentle waves, brushing iguanas off my beach towel and wandering around the forest for a glimpse of squirrel monkeys in the trees. A few weeks later, I came back via the Costanera Sur two-lane highway into Quepos, the town closest to the park. I was in for a shock.

Quepos and Manuel Antonio have grown faster than any other region in Costa Rica in the past decade. When I first visited in 1990, there were perhaps a dozen hotels in the area; now there are over 100, with over 1,000 rooms. The region has been overbuilt and nearly smothered by adoring fans. It has grown haphazardly into a congested conglomeration of tourist establishments and neighborhoods housing nearly 15,000 residents. Quepos is now a busy town with several dirt and paved streets, no street signs and little sense of organization. The twisting, tortuous Corridor road is chock-full of one-of-a-kind hotels and restaurants, many overlooking the sea. Manuel Antonio and the park are suffering from unprecedented popularity. Tourists and Ticos alike can't resist the region's natural beauty.

BACKGROUND

The original residents of Manuel Antonio were the Quepoa people, who are believed to have lived here up to 1,000 years before the conquest. The first Spanish mission in

way for a train line, constructed from the settlement of Quepos.

The banana business boomed until the 1960s, when a flood washed out the train lines and the banana trees were hit by Panamanian disease which destroyed the crop. The company switched production to African oil palms and the government began construction of a road linking Quepos to Puntarenas. When Parque Nacional Manuel Antonio was established in 1972, the area was still sparsely populated. In 1980 the government allotted

Costa Rica is said to have been established here in 1570, but it languished in isolation for centuries. Until the 1930s the lands of Quepos and Manuel Antonio were inhabited by a handful of families who subsisted on agriculture and fishing; most of these land were forested hills and mangrove swamps converging with the sea. Then in 1938 the United Fruit Company was granted the rights to develop banana plantations along the Pacific Coast. The fruit company first had to clear the virgin forest by logging miles of coastline and mountains, destroying the natural habitats of ocelots, marguays, mountain lions, jaguars, howler monkeys and scarlet macaws. Acres of wetland were drained to make

funds to pave the road to Puntarenas. Once the road was partially paved and completely graded people began arriving in droves, buying property and speculating on future tourism.

Costa Rica's financial boom in the 1980s fueled intense real estate speculation and hotel construction around the park, which became reknown throughout the international tourism grapevine as one of the most beautiful preserves in Central America. As the demand for palm oil has decreased,

OPPOSITE: Jacó, population: 4,000. ABOVE: It is possible to see capuchin monkeys swinging about in the trees that meet the beach on Playa Blanca. OVERLEAF: Roads linking beach towns travel through palm plantations and past small settlements, all with a center soccer field.

tourism has become the economic foundation for the ever-increasing population, who have witnessed a worrisome decrease in visitors in the mid-1990s. The locals who have witnessed the changes in the region over the past 15 years are justifiably concerned about the future. Manuel Antonio's reputation has been sullied as word of over-building, congestion and even the possible pollution of the sea has reached travelers. Still, it remains a special, unique place well worth exploring (but preferably during low season).

GENERAL INFORMATION

Quepos has no official tourist office. **La Buena Nota** (777-1002, at the Manuel Antonio end of the Corridor road, is the next closest thing. Anita Myketuk, who has lived in the area for over 20 years, owns this souvenir, clothing, book and map shop filled with high-quality merchandise. She and her husband Donald are the region's unofficial ambassadors of information and goodwill. Donald is a devoted student of local history, anthropology and archaeology, and he occasionally lectures at the Costa Verde Hotel (check at the hotel restaurant for schedules). He has also worked hard to bring lifeguards and services to the public beach, where drownings have been all too common. Anita stocks the shop with irresistible beach wear and a bounty of new and used books, and can answer most questions with good humor.

A guide pulls in a 11-kg (25-lb) wahoo, the highpoint of an exhilirating day on the water.

The phone number in Quepos for emergencies is (911; police (117 or 777-0196; Red Cross (777-0116; hospital (777-0020.

Car rentals can be arranged through hotels or **Elegante Rent-a-Car** (777-0115.

Given the area's popularity, it's wise to keep a close guard on your possessions: Don't not leave keys or money lying on the beach and remove your luggage from your rental car before parking in public places.

WHAT TO SEE AND DO

Parque Nacional Manuel Antonio (777-0644 FAX 777-0654 is seven kilometers (five miles) from Quepos. Though it's one of Costa Rica's smallest parks at 683 hectares (1687 acres), it's also one of the most lively. The wildlife that seems so elusive elsewhere is easily viewed here. In fact, hikers are warned to hold their packs and gear tight, since the park's monkeys are so accustomed to humans that they may try to snatch your lunch.

The entrance to the park is just a short walk from Manuel Antonio's hotels and parking lots across a shallow estuary. Trails lead to the three main beaches: Puerto Escondido, Playa Espedilla Sur and Playa Manuel Antonio. The surf and crowds are biggest at Espedilla; I prefer Playa Manuel Antonio's soft sands and tame waves. A longer, more arduous hike will bring you to the rocky beach at Puerto Escondido, accessible only at low tide. This is an agreeable hike for nature lovers even if you can not get all the way to the beach; with luck you will spot white-faced capuchin monkeys, sloths and coatis. Another trail leads to Punta Catedral, which was once an island and ceremonial site for the Quepoa Indians. The point is now linked to the beach by a *tómbolo*, a land bridge created by the accumulation of sediment and sand. Those who sweat through the 100-m (300-ft) climb up a steep trail to the point's *mirador* (lookout) are rewarded with wondrous views of the sea and Isla Mogote, another ceremonial Indian site.

The park was established in 1972 and for years visitors could camp on the beaches and underneath the trees and spot sloths, trogons coral snakes and bashful spider monkeys. Unfortunately, the animals and humans grew too familiar with each other, the beaches became too crowded and the trails overtrodden. The park is now closed on Mondays and camping is not permitted at any time. More than 50 percent of the park's territory is closed; some out-of-the-way trails are accessible if you hike with a guide. The park is open Tuesday through Sunday from 8 AM to 4 PM, and no more than 600 persons are admitted daily. The fee is $6 per day.

Refrain from feeding the monkeys and touching the giant iguanas that perch on fallen logs by the trails; though the wildlife may seem abundant and friendly at first glance, many species are threatened by human interference. Manuel Antonio is one of the few natural habitats for spider monkeys, which have become the area's mascot. Hotels and restaurants near the park advertise "monkey hours" in the late afternoon, when the creatures crash through the trees to the buildings and are rewarded with bananas and other food. Luring wild animals into civilization for human enjoyment makes the monkeys dependent on handouts.

You needn't pay the park fee to appreciate Manuel Antonio's beaches. **Playa Espedilla**, also called Playa Numero Uno, is just north of the park entrance. This public beach is immensely popular, though the surf can be very rough. Be very careful when swimming here.

Costa Rica Adventure Travel (/FAX 777-0850 E-MAIL iguana@sol.racsa.co.cr, next to Hotel Sí Como No in the Corridor, is a full-service travel agency that can arrange nature hikes, sea kayaking and canoeing, sunset sailboat rides and sport fishing along with other kinds of tours. **Horseback** riding tours to rivers, waterfalls and natural pools are available through **Brisas del Nara** (777-1889 and **Quepos Trail Rides** (777-0489. **Savegre Ranch** (/FAX 777-0528 offers six-hour tours (including three hours on horseback) through a typical Costa Rican farm and ranch, a palm oil plantation and along the banks of the Río Savegre to Playa el Rey. **Sunset cruises** and other boat excursions can be arranged through **Sunset Sails** (777-1304.

Quepos is one of the main **sport fishing** centers on the Pacific Coast. Serious anglers should reserve a boat and a captain in advance of their travels through **Pacific Coast Charters** (/FAX 777-1382, Apdo 122-6350, Quepos, Puntarenas, or **Blue Fin Sportfishing Charters** (777-1676 or 777-0674 FAX 777-0674 E-MAIL bluefin@sol.racsa.co.cr, Apdo 223-6350, Quepos, Puntarenas, IN THE U.S. SJO 1412, P.O. Box 025216, Miami, FL 33102-5216. Richard Krug, sport fishing columnist for the *Tico Times,* can also book sport fishing trips throughout the country from his desk at the Hotel del Rey (221-7272 or 257-3130 or 255-3232 FAX 221-0096, Apdo 6241-1000, San José.

An early morning or evening walk through the town of **Quepos** has its rewards. Start at the blue and purple church at the foot of the Corridor road, across from the ever busy soccer field. Stop by **La Botánica** (/FAX 777-1223, for a cup of herbal tea and browse through the enlightening array of herbs and spices gathered by owners Tey and Milo Bekins. Several small supermarkets, produce stands and sportswear shops line the main (unnamed) street from the Corridor to the waterfront, where a pathway leads past small fishing boats resting on the sand.

WHERE TO STAY

Manuel Antonio has an excess of rooms; some of its hotels are sure to fail. The room rates here are among the highest in the country, and budget travelers are relegated to small hostelries in downtown Quepos and just outside the park. The most luxurious spots are in the Corridor facing the sea. Despite the abundance of rooms, advance reservations are essential for the hotels mentioned below. Many do not accept credit cards, or may tack on a large service charge for their use.

Very Expensive
I've never had the good fortune to stay in secluded luxury at **Makanda by the Sea** (777-0442 FAX 777-1032 E-MAIL makanda @sol.racsa.co.cr WEBSITE http://www .makanda.com, Apdo 26, Quepos, Puntarenas, on a seaside road off the Corridor.

But I have toured the property and heard rave reviews from dozens of guests. The hotel's seven deluxe villas are hidden in the natural jungle and Japanese gardens and have vaulted hardwood ceilings, open-air living rooms with hammocks and cushioned couches and king-sized beds draped with mosquito-net canopies. The pool seems to flow into the blue horizon, and the silence is broken only by chattering spider monkeys and birds.

One of the area's first deluxe hotels is on the same sideroad. Competition and

age have marred the reputation of the **Hotel la Mariposa** (777-0355 FAX 777-0050, Apdo 4, Quepos, Puntarenas; RESERVATIONS IN THE U.S. TOLL-FREE (800) 223-6510. It's still one of my favorite places for a sunset drink on the terrace, and loyal guests return each year to the 10 villas with plants in the bathrooms.

Los Angeles meets the jungle at **Sí Como No** (777-1250 FAX 777-1093 E-MAIL sicomono @sol.racsa.co.cr web http://www.sicomono .com, Apdo 5, Quepos, Puntarenas; RESERVATIONS IN THE U.S. TOLL-FREE (800) 237-8201, SJO 297, P.O. Box 025216, Miami, FL 33102-5216. It is the only hotel around with a laser movie theater with a THX sound system. Hollywood stars hang out at the

hot tub, waterslide and free-form swimming pool and in the private peaked-roof villas tucked in the jungle. Stained glass windows give the roadside lobby the feeling of a Pentecostal church, while hill trails and ocean views reflect a harmony with nature. The property may well be the most ecologically responsible in the country, with solar-powered energy, recycled water systems and nontoxic resins protecting the flora and fauna.

The **Hotel Casitas Eclipse** (777-0408 FAX 777-1738 E-MAIL Eclipse@sol.racsa .co.cr, Manuel Antonio, Puntarenas, is also recommended in the Corridor, with several white villas barely visible among the trees.

Expensive

Monkeys do not need any handouts to encourage them to crash through the trees in front of the 12 villa suites terraced down a forested hillside at **Villas Nicolas** (777-0481 FAX 777-0451, Apdo 236, Quepos, Puntarenas, in the Corridor. There were only two buildings in the complex when I first stayed here many years ago, watching the monkeys and a stray scorpion from the hammock on my hardwood deck. Most of the villas now have kitchenettes, and there's a large pool at the top of the property and long stairways leading to the nearly hidden villas. I would love to stay here again.

I'm also quite fond of the traditional Tico feeling at **Costa Verde** (777-0584 FAX 777-0560 E-MAIL costaver@sol.racsa.co.cr WEBSITE http://www.gorp.com/costaverde, on the inland side of the Corridor road near the park, Apdo 6944, San José; RESERVATIONS IN THE U.S. TOLL-FREE (800) 231-RICA. The best rooms are in the rear of the property away from the highway and beside a pool. Private nature trails lead through the jungle from the rooms to the restaurant, where evening lectures on archaeological historical and anthropological aspects of the area are offered here. The restaurant is a favorite of locals.

Moderate

As soon as I climbed the tiled staircase to the open-air lobby I knew I'd found the friendliest accommodation in the Corridor at the **Hotel las Tres Banderas** (777-1871 or 777-1521 FAX 777-1478, P.O. Box 258-6350, Quepos, Puntarenas. I'd been hearing about this newcomer from travelers all over the country, and quickly got the scoop from the guests sipping gin and tonics by the front desk. One couple had returned three times in two months to their favorite room after finding other beach towns and hotels lacking. The compact building is tastefully designed with white arches and wooden railings on the balconies of each of the

good deal. Three miles of trails lead uphill to clearings with great views of the forest and sea. The restaurant is one of the best around.

No longer a budget property, the **Aparto-tel el Colibrí** (777-0432, Apdo 94, Quepos, on the Corridor road, now has rates comparable with those of its neighbors. Still, the 10 rooms with fans and private hot water baths are quite desirable, thanks to the French doors opening to terraces with hammocks. Some rooms have kitchenettes, and the small pool is surrounded by a tropical garden.

14 rooms, all with air conditioning. The swimming pool and hot tub are backed by the jungle behind the property, where the presence of sloths, monkeys and birds make up for the lack of a sea view. The chef whips up gourmet breakfasts and dinners for the guest, who find little reason to leave the property.

The guests are a polyglot crew at the **Plinio Hotel** (777-0055 FAX 777-0558 E-MAIL Plinio@sol.racsa.co.cr, Apdo 71, Quepos, Puntarenas, near Quepos on the Corridor road. A pool, restaurant and wide variety of rooms, suites and apartments are staggered up a hillside (lots of stairs here), and the three-story suites with roof-top decks and room for four persons are a

The standout among the modest (and overpriced) selections in downtown Quepos is the **Hotel Sirena** (/FAX 777-0528, one block from the bridge into Quepos. Anglers fill most of the 14 rooms, which have air conditioning, small refrigerators and powerful showers but no televisions or telephones. The rooms face the swimming pool and restaurant, secluded from the street noise by exterior walls. An acceptable alternative is the **Hotel Kamuk** (777-0379 FAX 777-0258, across the street from the Quepos waterfront. The best

OPPOSITE: A baby monkey clings to its mother's back as she travels from tree to tree. ABOVE: The terrace at the El Parador is a favorite sunset hangout for the well-heeled.

rooms, if you don't mind street noise, are those on the third floor with balconies overlooking the sea. There's a pool and restaurant.

Inexpensive

Budget-priced options are extremely limited during high season. The most desirable option in the Corridor is **El Mono Azul** (777-1548 (/FAX 777-1954. The eight rooms all have private bathrooms; some have air conditioning. There's a pool and the best healthfood restaurant around.

Most other inexpensive places are closer to the beach and park entrance in Manuel Antonio. **Hotel Cabinas Vela-Bar** (777-0413 FAX 777-1071 is next to the park and has 10 rooms of varying prices and comfort with hammocks on the front porches. **Cabinas Piscis** (777-0046, located on the beach side of the road, Apdo 219, Quepos, Puntarenas, has small, basic rooms with shared baths.

WHERE TO EAT

Manuel Antonio has the best selection of gringo-style restaurants outside San José, with comparably pricey pasta, seafood and steaks. Many of the best places are in the hotels. Don't miss the monkey visitors and extensive menu at **Costa Verde**, the inexpensive fish and sandwiches at the **Vela-Bar** by the park, and **Plinio's** outstanding spinach lasagna, eggplant parmegiano and *mano de piedra*, a pot roast with mustard and herb sauce. **Mono Azul** in the Corridor has the best selection of vegetarian meals. There are precious few budget sodas in the Corridor and only a few overpriced markets and delis. Stock up on snacks at the grocery stores in Quepos.

Moderate

Barba Roja (777-0331, midway along the Corridor road, is a traditional standby serving bountiful sandwiches, salads and piles of French fries at lunch and more expensive grilled fish and steaks at dinner. The wooden deck dining area and outside terrace are gathering spots for locals and travelers, and you'll pick up some great travel tips from the crowd gathered at the bar. Located at the end of a steep dirt drive beside Barba Roja, **Karolas** (777-0424, has become my favorite breakfast spot. Tables covered with pastel cloths are set amidst flowers and trees, and on clear mornings there's a view of the ocean shimmering below the forest. Try the French toast, fresh fruit plate and huevos rancheros. Fruit daiquiris are served by the pitcher to accompany lunches and dinners of grilled yellowfin tuna with wasabi and brochettes of tenderloin with onions and peppers. **Pickles**, next door to Sí Como No in the Corridor, is a wonderful deli that serves pastrami and reuben sandwiches, grilled ahi on foccacio, rosemary lemon chicken, an assortment of salads and sinful ice cream sundaes. Eat at the outside tables or take your lunch to the beach.

Inexpensive

Early risers sip espresso while reading the *International Herald Tribune* at the bright yellow and purple **Café Milagro**. The original branch of this coffee shop is located in Quepos across from the waterfront, and is a great spot for thumbing through used magazines, playing chess and meeting local expatriates; the second branch is in the Corridor.

Most inexpensive sodas are located in Quepos, where locals feast on huge breakfasts of gallo pinto and eggs at **El Pueblo** and **Restaurant Isabel**. Fishermen favor the United States-style **El Gran Escape**, both for the inspirational photos of huge marlin and sailfish on the walls and the reliable menu of salsa and chips, fajitas, spicy chicken wings and burgers. A few other sodas are located by the beach in Manuel Antonio village. The most popular is **Mar y Sombra** serving casados, fresh fish and cheap rice plates under the shade of palm trees.

HOW TO GET THERE

Both SANSA and TravelAir have daily flights to the Quepos airstrip (which just happens to be next door to the hospital), about a 15-minute drive from town. Taxis meet all flights.

Drivers from San José arrive via the Costanera Sur, which meets the Carretera Interamericana at Puntarenas; the drive takes about four hours. The road is paved through stretches north of Quepos, but it is still quite rough in other places. From the south, the Costanera Sur travels through palm plantations from Dominical, 42 km (26 miles) south of Quepos. There is frequent bus service from San José and

Puntarenas; the bus station is two blocks north of the Corridor road to Manuel Antonio, near the soccer field. Buses travel hourly from dawn until 10 PM from the Quepos bus station along the Corridor to Manuel Antonio. Ask the driver to let you off at your hotel.

DOMINICAL

When I'm overwhelmed by the throb and pulse of Manuel Antonio, I head south to the secluded beachside community of Dominical. The 200 or so residents here all seem to know each other and have a vested interest in keeping their town small and sedate. Gentrification by foreign residents has brought about a modern mini-mall which features a small supermarket, a real estate office and the Mercado del Mundo gift shop. One developer is handing out glossy brochures seeking investors for a beachfront hotel–condominium project.

But for now, the small town of Dominical is a tranquil place with one main street, or two if you count the sandy beach road. Small cabina hotels and informal restaurants in town and along outlying beaches cater to the surf and budget crowd. Others are clustered in Escaleras (Stairsteps), a steep hilltop overlooking the ocean. The road to Escaleras is rough and rutted, more suited to a four-wheel-drive vehicle than a sedan (which might suffice in dry season).

WHAT TO SEE AND DO

Dominical's waves have long been popular with surfers. Swimmers are best off at **Playa Hermosa**, south of Jacó, where the water is calmer.

Escaleras is a great area for horseback riding. Bella Vista hotel and ranch has both spirited and gentle native *crillo* horses for long rides up and down hillsides and onto the beach where the horses gallop with utter abandon and riders whoop and scream with glee. Most riders

OPPOSITE: The beach can be utterly mesmerizing. ABOVE: A fresh coconut is essential for a day on the sand.

stop by **Cascada Dominicalito** for a brisk splash in small natural pools before heading back to the ranch. Full-day rides take in the hilltops and **Cascadas Nauyaca and Pozo Azul.**

Shopping choices are limited in Dominical, though there is a good selection of Latin American folk art and clothing at **Mercado del Mundo**, located at the Plaza Pacífica Dominical.

Few vistas can beat the treetop view from the forest canopy at **Hacienda Baru**. The 336-hectare (830-acre) private nature

GENERAL INFORMATION

Dominical is so remote it doesn't have phone service; locals communicate by radio and the grapevine. Electricity is also scarce and sporadic; many hotels have generators or use solar power.

WHERE TO STAY

Dominical has a wide range of accommodation, including luxurious small inns,

reserve encompasses beach, the Río Barú valley, forests and highland fields with pre-Columbian petroglyphs hidden in the rocks. Hikes, horseback rides and a 30-m (100-ft)-high observation platform in the trees keep day trippers busy. Overnight guests choose from tents in the forest or cabins by the beach.

There are more humpbacked whales than tourists at **Parque Nacional Ballena**, 16 km (10 miles) south of Dominical. The whales migrate to the marine preserve from December to March, while dolphins, pelicans and frigate birds are visible year round. The park is not developed for tourism, but you can arrange boat tours through hotels in Dominical.

cabinas on the beach and nature preserves. Make advance reservations by faxing the properties or **Selva Mar (** 771-4582 FAX 771-1903, a tour company with an office in San Isidro de el General. The staff at Selva Mar will radio your reservation request to the hotel and fax a confirmation.

Expensive

Guests are asked to take off their shoes before walking across the gorgeous purpleheart wood floor in the main dining room and deck at Dominical's most elegant property, the **Escaleras Inn (**/FAX 771-5247, Suite 2277; RESERVATIONS IN THE U.S. SJO, P.O. Box 025216, Miami, FL 33102-5216. Three guest rooms in the main lodge are decked out with Guatemalan textiles, Boruca Indian masks and tropical plants and have huge bathrooms with powerful showers. A separate 100-sq-m (1,100-sq-ft) guest house is the ultimate retreat with a blue-and-white tiled kitchen stocked with handpainted dishes, a large bedroom with king-sized bed and a long deck amidst the trees 360 m (1,200 ft) above the beach. I'll always remember floating in the inn's hilltop pool to the sound of the Gypsy Kings, watching shooting stars in the midnight sky. Nor will I ever forget the dinner that

mature landscaping backed by forest. A large pool sits in the center of the complex, which also includes a tennis court, a restaurant suitable for large groups, a hot tub and exercise equipment. The only drawback here is the 20-minute walk to the sea. As one local wag put it, "The owners came 10,000 km (6,000 miles) from Holland to build a hotel. You'd think they would have gone the extra mile to the beach."

South of town, a small road twists to the end of a rocky point to **Cabinas Punta Dominical** (/FAX 787-0016 or 787-0017.

preceded this reverie: pasta with sun-dried tomatoes and California wine. Make reservations for dinner if you're not staying at the inn. Children over 12 are welcome.

Moderate

The largest resort in the area is the **Villas Río Mar** (/FAX 224-2053 or 283-5013, north of town on the Río Barú, P.O. Box 1350-2050, San Pedro Montes de Oca. Each of the 40 large rooms has an outdoor living area with a wet bar, small refrigerator and cushioned bamboo chairs; white gauze curtains can be pulled aside or draped around the terrace for privacy. Constructed with interior bamboo walls and thatched roofs, the buildings are set amidst

Four older hardwood cabins (each housing up to six people) are set under huge mango trees with water on both sides of the buildings. Air filters in through screened and louvered walls; the hammocks hanging on each porch are perfect perches for watching the sea. The restaurant here serves good seafood.

Camping and cabinas with hot showers are both available at **Hacienda Barú** (787-0003 FAX 787-0004, just north of Dominical en route to Quepos.

OPPOSITE: Found on Isla de Caño, stone spheres weighing several thousand pounds are Costa Rica's archaeological wonders. ABOVE: Stone metates have been used for grinding corn since pre-Hispanic times.

Inexpensive

The modest **Bella Vista Ranch and Guest Lodge** (771-1903; RESERVATIONS IN THE U.S. (305) 254-7592 is surrounded by forest on a hilltop in Escaleras, and has three guest rooms in a converted farmhouse on a working cattle ranch. The deck along one side of the house overlooks the ocean; meals are available on request. The ranch also offers horseback riding lessons and excursions. Across the dirt road from Bella Vista is **Finca Brian y Milena** (/FAX 771-1903, a working tropical fruit and nut farm

with day and overnight tours. Guests stay in rooms with shared baths. The unusual wood-fire heated hot tub is the perfect star gazing spot. Also in Escaleras is **Pacific Edge** (/FAX 787-0031 or 771-1903, Apdo 531-8000, San José which has four cabins on a forested hillside, each with an outdoor living area, a kitchenette and solar-heated water.

Cabinas Nayarit (787-0033 is my favorite budget restaurant and hotel right on the beach in town. The white buildings with blue trim are well maintained; the more expensive buildings have air conditioning. Aromas from the restaurant keep guests in a constant state of hunger, easily sated with a big plate of crisp French fries and grilled fish. The tables under fans within the restaurant are the coolest place to eat, but I prefer the cement tables with umbrellas right on the sand.

WHERE TO EAT

The hotel restaurants mentioned above serve some of the best meals in the area. **Roca Verde** south of town is popular on Saturday nights when the *disco movil* (mobile discotheque, which travels from town to town) plays a regular gig of dance tunes. **Thrusters**, right in town, is a wave riders hangout serving burgers, sandwiches, espresso and brownies. The **San Clemente Bar and Grill**, across from Playa Dominical, is a Mexican-American home-style restaurant serving inexpensive breakfasts and full meals.

HOW TO GET THERE

Dominical is 45 km (28 miles) south of Quepos on the Costanera Sur. The road is an alternate to the Carretera Interamericana south of San José and is partially paved. The drive past palm plantations and small workers' villages takes at least 90 minutes. The alternate route, if coming from San José, is to take the Carretera Interamericana south from the city through Cerro de la Muerte to San Isidro de el General. An unnamed road leads west from the main intersection in San Isidro to Dominical; the drive takes about 60 minutes. There is frequent bus service from San José to Quepos or San Isidro de el General with connections in both towns for Dominical.

ABOVE and OPPOSITE: Relaxation is a 24-hour affair at Sí Como No resort hotel.

The Zona Sur

UNTOUCHED FOR CENTURIES, the Zona Sur is the last great Costa Rican wilderness for travelers to explore in relative isolation. The Cordillera Talamanca divides the two coasts of southern Costa Rica, providing a landscape of high peaks, rushing rivers, cloud forests and fertile valleys. At the far south, the Pacific Coast curves along the wild Osa Peninsula and Burica Peninsula, where tiny settlements are bordered by seemingly endless rain forest. Few roads pass along the mountains into the southern zone; in fact, the best route is the rough and risky Carretera Interamericana. Buses, huge logging and tractor-trailer trucks and puny sedans power along the highway's twists and turns, providing a thrilling, albeit frightening, rush.

The highway runs south from San José and the Meseta Central, then quickly climbs the mountain foothills to a series of peaks, called *cerros*, many bordered by national parks and reserves. The most famous, and most aptly named, is Cerro de la Muerte — the Hill of Death. Though the name precedes the highway, which was completed in the 1950s, most drivers agree that this is indeed a deadly stretch of potholes, rough pavement and steep cliffs often shrouded in rain and fog. When the skies are clear the views are astonishing — some days it's possible to see both coasts and the snow-shrouded Cerro el Chirripó, the highest peak in the country. Small lodges tucked in valleys and hills provide their guests with some of the best bird watching and hiking in the country. Comparable to the wildly popular Monteverde region in northern Guanacaste, this untrammeled area harbors hundreds of reclusive resplendent quetzals, the sacred bird of the ancient Maya.

The highway continues on south to San Isidro de el General, where a sideroad meanders to the Central Pacific Coast and Dominical. Farther south at Palmar Sur, another sideroad travels north along the coast, past tiny beach communities popular with diehard surfers. The land becomes more rugged and unpopulated from Palmar south, as rivers carve the coastline into lagoons and mangrove swamps framing the sea. Those who brave tiny byways to the Golfo Dulce and two southern peninsulas,

the Osa and the Burrica, are rewarded with sublime isolation and superb natural settings. The nature lodges here have been built at great physical and financial expense. Owners talk of arriving via dugout canoe, slogging through knee-deep red mud, hacking trails with machetes and laying gravel roads by shovel load after shovel load of rock. Guests are similarly awed by nature's grasp on the area, and become accustomed to wearing knee-high boots on mud trails, accepting red clay stains on their socks, dodging and ducking

through thrashing branches and clinging vines. Having traveled both coasts extensively, I can say this outpost of civilization is my favorite coastal region, filled with the morning growls of howler monkeys, the evening screeches of scarlet macaws and an overall sense of true wilderness.

CERRO DE LA MUERTE

Several small towns dot the highway around Cerro de la Muerte, some bordering the Parque Nacional Tapantí. The park is one of the more difficult ones to access; the best entry is from **Orosí** (see OROSÍ TO CACHÍ DAM in SAN JOSÉ AND THE MESETA CENTRAL, page 97). The region sits 2,100 to 2,500 m (7,000 to 8,000 ft) above sea level,

PRECEEDING PAGES: An iguana LEFT poses in the trees in a coastal rain forest. Villagers, such as this girl RIGHT, in the Bahía Drake must travel by foot, boat or horseback to leave their idyllic settlements. OPPOSITE: Burros transport milk through the highlands. ABOVE: Dining companions provide much entertainment at remote lodges on the Osa Peninsula.

and some peaks poke into the cloud forests while valleys are often shrouded in mist. Easily accessed from San José, which is only about 80 km (50 miles) north, the region has become a popular day tour from the city.

GENERAL INFORMATION

There are no sources for tourist information outside the hotels; telephones are few and electricity is sparse.

WHAT TO SEE AND DO

This is an area for hiking, bird watching and for relaxing in isolated lodges. Some lodges offer trout fishing in the Río Savegre, and mountain bikers who bring their own gear delight in the maze of dirt trails running through the forest. If you have a four-wheel-drive vehicle you can explore the small villages of Santa María de Dota and Copey by turning west off the highway at Empalme. San Gerardo de Dota, several kilometers south, is set in a valley at the foot of a narrow, twisting road, and has a few lodging options.

WHERE TO STAY

Small family-run lodges are nestled in forest and valleys off the highway. Most offer hot water and some have fireplaces or wood stoves to cut the evening chill which can be penetrating, especially during rainy season. Bring a warm jacket or sweater, heavy socks and a durable rain poncho. It's best to make reservations in advance through fax or phone; mail service is almost nonexistent here.

Expensive

A rough road leads east from the church in Cañon (look for the sign handpainted with birds and bromeliads) to **Genesis II** (381-0739 FAX 225-6055 E-MAIL ctocjso@racsa .sol.co.cr, Apdo 10303, San José. Settled into the cloud forest almost 2,500 m (8,000 ft) above sea level, this private reserve and lodge are run by Steve and Paula Friedman with the help of a cadre of volunteers. At least 150 species of birds have been spotted in the 38-hectare (95-acre) reserve, including

rare three-wattled bellbirds with their distinctive folds of skin hanging from their beaks and throats. Genesis has five guest rooms in a central lodge with two shared hot water baths. Meals are served family style.

Moderate

Don Efraín Chacón and his multigenerational family operate **Cabinas Chacón** (771-1732 or 284-1444 FAX 551-0070, in San Gerardo de Dota, at the KM 80 turnoff from the highway. Don Efraín's name has long been synonymous with quetzals, and his property is filled with laurel trees that keep the birds happy year round. Hummingbirds, trogons, toucanettes and at least 100 other species keep bird watchers occupied, while anglers delight in fishing for trout in the Río Savegre, which runs through the property. The complex includes 15 basic cabins with private baths and a restaurant that serves overnight guests and day trippers. Also in San Gerardo is the **Trogon Lodge** (223-2421 FAX 255-4039, Apdo 10980 1000, San José. Cabins spread around the gardens house 10 rooms with private baths and wood stoves.

Inexpensive

Turn off the highway at KM 107 in División to reach **Avalon Private Reserve** (380-2107 (/FAX 771-7226. One of the newest properties in the area, Avalon has 150 hectares (375 acres) of cloud, primary and secondary forest, with portions of land that were cleared in the past for pastures and are now home to Guinevere the resident white horse. The best lodgings are in a private hardwood cabin with two beds downstairs and an upper sleeping loft, powerful hot showers and a back porch nearly buried in the forest. A second cabin has private and communal rooms with shared baths; camping is also allowed. A wood-heated hot tub was under construction when I last visited. You can stay here quite cheaply, and eat good inexpensive meals in the main lodge. Trails and old dirt roads run through the property — some are great for mountain biking. Arrange bird-watching or bicycling tours in advance.

Quetzal seekers are delighted with **Finca de Serrano** (454-4746 or 534-4415 CELLULAR

381-8456, at KM 70 off the Carretera Inter-americana, where Don Eddie Serrano and his family have lived for nearly three decades. Two hardwood cabins have separate toilet and shower rooms, bunks, queen beds and private porches. The main lodge has seven rooms with shared bath, and a dining room serving Tico meals. Don Eddie is a master at spotting quetzals, who nest in the giant laurel trees throughout the property; they're easiest to see from November to May. The property is also known as Albergue y Cabinas Mirador de Quetzales.

SAN ISIDRO DE EL GENERAL

The Cerro División, just south of Cerro de la Muerte, is the highest stretch of the Careterra Interamericana, at 3,510 m (11,500 ft). From here the road descends into the Valle de San Isidro, a rich agricultural area that has grown steadily since the 1950s. If traveling this stretch of the highway in February and March you'll see roadside stands selling huge white flowers called the *flor de itabo*, a delicacy when mixed

Cabinas del Quetzal (771-2376, San Gerardo de Dota, near the Cabinas Chacón, is operated by Rodolfo Chacón. It's a good option for those on a budget. Two communal cabins with baths are available.

HOW TO GET THERE

By car, exit San José through the southeastern suburb of San Pedro and follow signs to Cartago and San Isidro de el General. Though a short distance, the trip can take two hours or more. Buses run from San José to San Isidro, with stops in between. Most lodges will arrange transport from the bus stop if you call ahead. Don't expect to find phones or taxis along the road.

with scrambled eggs. The flowers bloom on the yucca hedge, which is often used as a live fence because it is easy to reproduce from wood cuttings and protects the soil from erosion. The entire landscape changes quickly here with the decrease in altitude as the road slides down into the valley; watch for mud, rocks and trucks with bad brakes.

San Isidro de el General, with a population of 41,000, is the largest town in the Zona Sur. A relatively new town, San Isidro has become popular with Ticos and foreign residents seeking a favorable climate, clean air and uncrowded surroundings. The town makes a good rest stop when en route to Dominical and the Central Pacific, 29 km

(18 miles) southwest of San Isidro on Highway 22. It also serves as a base for visiting the Parque Nacional Chirripó and other nearby sights.

GENERAL INFORMATION

There are plenty of gas stations, markets, pharmacies and public phones along the highway through town.

WHERE TO STAY

Several small hotels in San Isidro cater to truck drivers and business people; none are particularly noteworthy but it's good to know you can probably find a room if you're running late on your drive south or just need a break.

Moderate

The resort-like **Hotel del Sur** (771-3033 or 234-8871 FAX 771-0527 is located four kilometers (two and a half miles) south of San Isidro. A popular weekend getaway for Josefinos, the resort has 47 rooms and 10 cabins set in a grove of trees and gardens just off the highway. The large pool is a blissful place to work out driving kinks, and facilities include a restaurant, volleyball and tennis courts and transportation to nearby sights.

WHERE TO EAT

Moderate

I've been tempted to go far out of my way when touring the Zona Sur just for another meal at **Mirador Vista del Valle** (284-4685, located at KM 119 on the Interamericana Sur, a 20-minute drive north of San Isidro. I first discovered the restaurant one early morning after a night in División, and devoured a huge breakfast that satisfied my hunger throughout the day. Owners Flor and Roger Calderón Vega have created such a delightful spot that weekend visitors from the capital linger for hours watching hummingbirds dip their beaks into feeders and flowers encircling the rustic wooden building. The best seats are along the counter that runs the length of a back deck with mesmerizing views over the treetops

into the valley. My breakfast consisted of an enormous fruit plate with fresh papaya, bananas and pineapple, moist, flavorful gallo pinto with eggs, and fried plantains smothered in melted cheese. I longed to return for a lunch of trout fresh from the Río Chirripó or *olla de carne*, a typical stew made with lean beef and fresh vegetables from nearby farms. The menu is translated into English and makes a great souvenir for anyone interested in Costa Rican cuisine. The family raises gorgeous orchids that brighten the dining room. Don't you dare drive by without stopping.

CERRO EL CHIRRIPO

I've yet to climb Cerro el Chirripó, though its looming presence is nearly irresistible. Chirripó is the highest peak in Central America south of Guatemala, and stands 3,819 m (12,529 ft) above sea level in the Parque Nacional Chirripó. Glacial lakes shimmer at the highest points, and the hike up the peak passes through swamps, fern groves, the stunted trees of Andean-like páramos, oak and cloud forests and hawks gliding on whistling winds. Steady hikers can make the 14-km (eight-and-a-half-mile) ascent to the refuge huts below the summit in about 10 hours, though it helps to start out acclimated to the base altitude at 1,219 m (4,000 ft). In all, the ascent is 2,600 m (8,500 ft) to the peak. Most hikers make it as far as the refuges in one day, and crash on the foam mattresses, grimace in cold water showers and recover beside wood-burning stoves. The next day is devoted to the relatively easy two-hour climb to the summit and a bit of exploring, with the third day spent climbing and sliding back down. To ensure entrance (only 40 hikers are allowed in the park per day), you must make advance reservations through the National Parks Office (257-0922 FAX 223-6963, in San José. During the rainy season it may be possible for you to get a reservation and permit after you arrive in San José, but during high season you should contact them well in advance

OPPOSITE: Spotting the plaintive white faces of capuchin monkeys can make or break a rain forest hike.

of your visit. When climbing the peak, remember that temperatures can drop to 4°C (40°F); carry warm clothing, water, a flashlight and food. The San Gerardo de Rivas ranger station and park entrance is 15 km (9 miles) northeast of San Isidro.

SAN VITO

South of San Isidro the Interamericana runs through farms and pineapple plantations and the small town of Buenos Aires, then begins curving west to Palmar and several

sideroads to Golfito and the southern coast. Before Palmar, at Paso Real, an unnamed, but paved, road runs southeast to San Vito, a small ranching and farming settlement largely populated in the 1950s by Italian immigrants. This town is reknown for its Italian restaurants, fresh produce and cheese. A road leads from here to the edges of the **Parque Internacional la Amistad**, named for the *amistad* (friendship) between Costa Rica and Panama. The Costa Rica portion of the park is enormous, spread over 193,929 hectares (479,199 acres) of rain forest, watershed and páramo along the Talamanca range. Large portions of the park have yet to be explored except by jaguars and puma, which thrive in these wild ranges. The park is most easily accessed through **La Amistad Lodge** (773-3193 or (290-3030 FAX 232-1913, within **Hacienda la Amistad** private biological reserve. The large wooden lodge has 10 guest rooms, some with private bath, and

is mecca for botanists and biologists specializing in arthropods, mammals and birds. The hacienda includes acres of coffee, citrus, spice, sugar cane fields and produces organic products for export. Tour packages, including transportation from San José, overnight stays, meals and guided hikes are available.

Equally fascinating for plant lovers is the **Wilson Botanical Gardens** inside the **Las Cruces Biological Station** (240-6696 FAX 240-6783 E-MAIL reservas@ns.ots.ac.cr, five and a half kilometers (three and a half miles) south of San Vito, which is operated by the Organization for Tropical Studies, Apdo 676-2050, San José. The 10-hectare (25-acre) gardens were created by Robert and Catherine Wilson, former owners of a tropical nursery in Florida. The Wilsons, with the help of Brazilian landscape designer Roberto Burle-Marx, started creating their showplace in 1962; ever since, it's been a magnet for those who love heliconia, ferns, bromeliads, orchids, ginger, bamboo and idyllic landscaping. Over 7,000 species of tropical plants, including 700 species of palms, create a gorgeous setting in the mist which attracts hummingbirds, tanagers, toucans, trogons and a bounty of butterflies. A 235-hectare (580-acre) forest surrounds the gardens. After a disastrous fire destroyed the former lodge, library and laboratories in 1994, a new lodge opened in 1996. It contains 12 high-ceilinged rooms with private baths and balconies overlooking the gardens. Day and overnight guests wander along paths with alluring names — Tree Fern Hill Trail, Heliconia Loop Trail, Bromeliad Walk, Orchid Walk, the Hummingbird Garden and Fern Gully — and hike farther into the forest preserve. Reservations for day visits and overnights must be arranged through the **Organization of Tropical Studies** (240-6696 FAX 240-6783 E-MAIL oet@cro.ots.ac.cr, Apdo 676-2050, San Pedro, San José.

PALMAR

The Carretera Interamericana twists in hairpin curves south from Paso Real to Palmar Norte and Palmar Sur, where some travelers, on the way to the south coast, arrive at

A tiny rain forest fern clings to a tree trunk in the Parque Nacional la Amistad.

The Zona Sur

the airstrip via SANSA or TravelAir. Gas stations, markets and public phones line the intersection of the Interamericana and Highway 18 leading west to the tiny town of Cortés and the central Pacific Coast. Boats depart from near here to travel the Río Sierpe to Bahía Drake (see below). South of Palmar another sideroad leads to Golfito, while the Interamericana continues south to the Panamanian border at Canoas.

GOLFITO

Golfito, the main port on the Golfo Dulce between the mainland and the Osa Peninsula, was a critical port for the United Fruit Company from the mid 1930s to the 1980s, when the Panamanian disease destroyed the banana crops. Many of the plantations were replanted with African oil palms, but the international market for palm oil has dwindled, as has Golfito's fortunes. But Costa Ricans maintain a certain fondness for Golfito due to its status as a duty-free port, established in 1990. Most visitors to the port city of some 14,000 residents come in search of relatively inexpensive washers, dryers, refrigerators and compact disc players (import taxes in the rest of the country are prohibitively high). There's little reason for tourists to pass through town unless they're headed to private reserves north of town or across the gulf on the Osa Peninsula.

WHAT TO SEE AND DO

The town of Golfito is bordered by **Refugio Nacional de Fauna Silvestre Golfito**, a 2,300-hectare (5,683-acre) wildlife refuge protecting virgin tropical hardwood trees (including the precious purple-heart wood), a community watershed and many species of birds, monkeys and wild cats. Some hotels in Golfito and lodges in the area offer tours to the refuge.

Tours from Golfito are also available to **Casa Orquideas**, where the McAllister family has lived on Playa San Josecito, north of town, for nearly two decades. Though not as spectacular as the Wilson Gardens, Orquideas has a lovely selection of 100 species of orchids, unusual tropicals

and citrus, spices and vegetables — all grown organically. You can arrange a tour of Orquideas through an area hotel.

Caña Blanca (735-5043, in Puerto Jiménez, is a private nature reserve on the Golfo Dulce and one of the most secluded inns you can find on the coast (see WHERE TO STAY below). **Rainbow Adventures** (755-0220, Golfito, a 45-minute boat ride north of Golfito on Playa Cativo is a 486-hectare (1,200-acre) private reserve beginning at a perfect beach and continuing into primary and secondary forest harboring macaws, toucans and plenty of monkeys.

WHERE TO STAY

Expensive

I yearn for a long term stay some day at this reserve! **Caña Blanca** (/FAX 735-5062 E-MAIL osatrex@sol.racsa.co.cr, Apdo 48, Puerto Jimenez, RESERVATIONS IN THE U.S. Mariah Wilderness Expeditions ((510) 233-2303 TOLL-FREE (800) 4-MARIAH FAX (510) 233-0956, P.O. Box 248, Point Richmond, CA 94807.

Owner Carol Crews summed up my feelings when she described an English lady visiting the remote hotel who fretted about missing the boat back to Puerto Jiménez and the plane to San José. "But dearest," her husband said, "who cares? We've found paradise." Privacy is ensured at this small property with only two wooden cabins set on stilts above the sand, with hammocks hanging high on the decks. Beds draped in mosquito nets sit in the center of spacious rooms with hardwood dressers and chairs; solar panels provide electricity and hot water. Two smaller rooms above the kitchen are available at lower rates than the cabins. Guests awaken to coffee and juice delivered to their doors; meals of poached fish with peppers and chilies, heaps of fresh papaya and pineapples, home baked ginger cake and other delights are served in an open-air dining room. Kayaking, hiking and horseback riding tours are available, though you can easily pass the day in a hammock reading a book from the well-stocked shelves. Caña Blanca is 16 miles west of Golfito and nine miles north of Puerto Jimenez. The lodge provides transport from either point. Most guests arrive at the Puerto Jiménez airstrip and then take a 20-minute boat ride past dolphins and turtles in the Golfo Dulce to the hotel on Playa Josecito.

Larger, but still delightfully secluded, is **Rainbow Adventures** (775-0220; RESERVATIONS IN THE U.S. ((503) 690-7750 FAX (503) 690-7735, a 45-minute boat ride north from Golfito to **Playa Cativo**. On a beach amidst an abundance of wildlife, the lodge is an extraordinary three-story structure filled with antiques and handmade furnishings.

SOUTH OF GOLFITO

BURICA PENINSULA

Small pristine beaches dot the coast south of Golfito, past the marshlands around the Río Coto flowing into the Golfo Dulce. Be forewarned that traveling this far south has its disadvantages and a four-wheel-drive vehicle is essential year round. My instructions for driving to **Tiskita Lodge** near the Panamanian border were four pages long,

The rooms are luxurious and the meals of gourmet quality.

Moderate

In Golfito the options include **Las Gaviotas Hotel** (775-0062 FAX 775-0544 (also called the Yacht Club), Apdo 12-8201, Golfito, with 18 rooms, a restaurant and pool. **Hotel Sierra** (775-0666 FAX 775-0087, near the airport, has 72 air-conditioned rooms, pools, restaurants and a tour desk that arranges trips to the Wilson Botanical Gardens and nearby beaches.

ABOVE: A secluded beach at Bahía Drake on the remote southern Pacific Coast. OPPOSITE: A boy wears a make-shift life preserver for a swim in the placid waters of Bahía Drake.

and I've never been so traumatized behind the wheel in all my life. But the road (loosely speaking) led to what may be my favorite part of Costa Rica, along the edge of the snaking Burica Peninsula, which is largely a part of Panama.

Costa Rica retains ownership of the peninsula's Pacific Coast, a strip of white-sand beaches beloved by surfers and reclusive souls. Swimmers and sunbathers hang out at **Playa Zancudo**, where the waters of Golfo Dulce are protected by the southern tip of the the Osa Peninsula. Surfers head further south to **Bahía Pavon** and **Playa Pavones,** where raging surf is juxtaposed with tranquil coves. There's little to do in this region but play in the water, hike forest trails and mingle with the other tourists and the few locals who maintain permanent residence in outpost settlements.

GENERAL INFORMATION

Forget about phones, faxes, hot water and electrical currents. The Burica Peninsula is as isolated as you can get, and if it weren't for the airstrip at Tiskita Lodge, civilization would be far away indeed. Basic supplies can be purchased at pulperías in **Pavones** and **Zancudo**. Bring all the colónes you

think you'll need; don't expect to be able to change money.

WHERE TO STAY

Small cabinas, bed and breakfasts and rooms for rent dot the sandy road around Zancudo and Pavones. None has a phone and the surfers who hole up for as long as possible by the beach tend to wander from place to place until they get the best deal. I liked the look and name of **Siempre Domingo B&B** on the road just north of Tiskita.

As far as I'm concerned, one of the top five lodges in the country is **Tiskita Lodge** (233-6890 or 255-2011 FAX 255-3529 or 255-4410 (expensive), just to the south of Playa

Pavones, Apdo 1195-1250, Escazú; BOOK THROUGH Costa Rica Sun Tours (255-3418 FAX 255-4410, Avenida 4 at Calle 36, Apdo 1195-1002, San José.

A note from 12-year-old Tim in the Tiskita Lodge guest book sums it up well: "Chiggers, scorpions in my bathroom, scraped my back, stomach and chest, burnt my back, burnt my feet. I loved it! I got to see so many animals and ate so many different fruits. Thanks for a great time!" Helen from England wrote "On a cold winter's night in England I shall close my

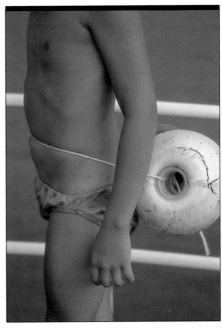

eyes and remember this place with a smile." I overheard and experienced similar lofty sentiments during my two-night stay. I stared out the screen by my bed the first morning listening for rustling leaves, then ran to the outdoor bathroom and shower to watch squirrel monkeys lope hand over hand through the trees, tails stretching and looping around branches. Chestnut-mandibled toucans chattered nearly out of sight, while smaller tanagers, motmots and parakeets twittered. Keeping my eyes turned downward in fear of disturbing a boa, I walked from my cabin-on-stilts to the main lodge, grabbed a mug of coffee and settled on a lawn chair to watch for white hawks and glistening emerald-throated hummingbirds. Around 7 AM a group of diehard *pajareros* (bird watchers) emerged from the forest in search of sustenance.

Peter Aspinall, the fascinating and somewhat obsessed owner of Tiskita, led a group of us on a tour of his fruit orchards after breakfast. He clambered up trees, disappeared down slippery slopes and generally went far out if his way to make sure we sampled both bitter and sweet star fruit, wax jambu, custard apples, mangosteens, bitter arazau and sweet slimy cacao. We hefted a 25-pound jackfruit (similar to breadfruit) and learned all about the difficulties of growing guanábanas. Aspinall has planted some 115 varieties of tropical fruit trees using seeds and cutting from Australia, Asia, the Amazon and other regions within the equatorial belt.

Trails range far and wide through the 100-hectare (247-acre) private reserve and down a hill from the cabins, over the airstrip and onto the beach at Punta Banco. There's a safe swimming beach about a 10-minute walk from the lodge, and there are world famous surfing beaches a few kilometers up the road. Horseback riding, bird watching and tours to Parque Nacional Corcovado and Wilson Botanical Gardens are available. Advance bookings are advised for these activities and to reserve one of the 14 cabins separated by secondary forest, fruit trees (of course) and giant heliconia and ferns. Basic, hearty meals are served buffet style in the main lodge and there is an honor-system bar; if you crave snacks, smokes and sodas, bring them with you or purchase them at the pulpería in Pavones. Many of Tiskita's guests arrive via air charter from San José; transportation is included in some packages.

HOW TO GET THERE

Wonderful challenges face the driver tackling the road to Pavones and Tiskita. First there's the ferry across the Río Coto, which runs from 6 AM to 7 PM. The restaurant next to the ferry is a great place to stop for a bracing cup of coffee or meal of fresh fish while studying the river.

Once you've driven onto the metal ferry platform and been guided via pulleys across the water, the fun begins. I counted at least 13 cement, dirt and rock bridges between the river and Tiskita, and I quickly developed an abiding respect for their deathtrap potential. I managed to hang our rental car off the edge of the first bridge we encountered, a skinny strip of cement which lacks guardrails at the top of a sandy rise in the rutted road. Onward we drove, past cows grazing beside bridges, kids snorkeling under them and even an occasional paved stretch of road. People have died trying to do this drive during the rainy season; unless you've got loads of time and temerity I suggest flying in over the astonishingly beautiful coastline and vast marshlands.

Buses travel from Golfito to Zancudo in the dry season, but shut down when it rains. Boatmen in Golfito will shuttle you to the settlements at Zancudo and Pavones; from there you must rely on foot power and the kindness of strangers to get you to your destination.

PARQUE NACIONAL ISLA DEL COCO

Remember the scene in *Jurassic Park* where a helicopter hovers over a solitary mountainous island surrounded by rough seas? That fantastic landscape is **Isla del Coco**, a 22-sq-km (14-sq-mile) volcanic island, part of the Cocos chain of underwater volcanoes that runs almost to the Galápagos Islands off Ecuador. Only five kilometers (three miles) wide, the island rises to Cerro Iglesias, at 634 m (2,080 ft). Waterfalls cascade down moss-green hillsides; caves and underground passageways dot the coast; and forests of healthy coral are visible through the turquoise sea. Dedicated SCUBA divers dream of the hammerhead sharks, manta rays and huge pelagic fish in the waters around Isla del Coco, about 480 km (300 miles) off the southern coast of Costa Rica. Natural scientists delight in spotting the endemic plant, animal and bird species that have been discovered on scientific expeditions over the past century. Isla del Coco was included in the national park system in 1978, and access to the fragile

Childhood in rural coastal settlement has its advantages.

ecosystem has been greatly limited since then. Only members of scientific research teams and those with permits arranged in advance through the National Parks Office are allowed on the island, where a ranger station keeps contact with the mainland via radio.

BACKGROUND

Pirates and buccaneers have been stashing their treasures on Isla del Coco since the late 1600s, when the English pirate Captain Edward Davis made the island his base camp for looting expeditions along the coast of New Spain from Baja California to Guayaquil. Wilson and his companions, William Dampier and Lionel Wafer, buried their treasures on the island and wrote journals of their expeditions that were best sellers in England. Davis eventually left much of his booty on the island and retired to Virginia. He made one last trip to retrieve his treasures, but stopped off along the Caribbean Coast of Central America for a bit more looting and was never seen again. For a fascinating rendition of Davis' expeditions, read *Cocos Island — Old Pirate's Haven* by J. Christopher Weston Knight (San José: Imprenta y Litografía).

Naturally, the rumored buried gold has entranced treasure hunters ever since, and several expeditions have been launched over the centuries. Fishing boats have also found a wealth of billfish in the waters off the island. United States President Franklin Delano Roosevelt stopped by in 1935 on a fishing excursion; one of the endemic palms on the island is named after him. Jean-Michael Cousteau led an expedition in 1987 for an oceanographic survey of hammerheads and is now involved in an international consortium of nature organizations attempting to protect the island and nearby waters.

HOW TO GET THERE

Visiting Isla del Coco is an expensive proposition, usually limited to serious SCUBA divers who arrive via the *Okeanos Aggressor* TOLL-FREE IN THE U.S. (800) 348-2628. The 36.5-m (120-ft) live-aboard dive

boat travels from Puntarenas to Coco on nine and 10-night cruises throughout the year. The boat trip takes 36 hours each way; in between, divers spend six or seven days amidst hammerheads, white-tipped sharks, whale sharks, rays and over 200 species of fish.

OSA PENINSULA

One of the last truly wild places in Costa Rica, the Osa Peninsula juts into the Pacific at the southern tip of the country. Much of the peninsula is protected within the **Parque Nacional Corcovado**, established in the 1970s. Several conservation groups and individuals have created private reserves around the park, thereby increasing the amount of protected land. Difficult to get to (and equally difficult to leave) the peninsula captivates wanderers with its isolation, beauty and abundance of wildlife. It's one of the few areas where scarlet macaws still thrive, giving bird watchers the once-in-a-lifetime thrill of spotting a screeching flock of macaws soaring above the seaside rain forest canopy. Howler monkeys growl their wake-up call much like roosters crowing in farm communities, and keel-billed toucans lay claim to the fruit of papaya and mango trees. Tourists are gradually discovering this remote paradise, and a few luxury hotels, campgrounds and bed and breakfasts have opened to meet the demand. Some fear Osa will suffer from its increasing popularity, and rumors of planned resorts abound.

BACKGROUND

The first known residents of the Osa Peninsula were the Diquis, who discovered a plentiful supply of gold in the rivers and streams. In the early twentieth century the peninsula was home to escaped prisoners and criminals fleeing the law, and the area was known as a Wild West-style frontier with dangerous terrain and even more dangerous residents. A frenzied gold rush struck the region in the 1960s when word spread that gold could still be panned and mined in the peninsula's rivers. Fortunes were built in those days by the *oreros* (miners), their suppliers and customers. Prospectors, outcasts and hermits claimed their territory as squatters; land titles, as such, have always been a matter of great dispute. In 1968 the government began the controversial task of clearing the land of squatters, and in the mid 1970s, claimed a enormous chunk of the Osa Peninsula as the Parque Nacional Corcovado. By 1986 oreros were banned from within the park's boundaries.

Fortune seekers of a different kind have since staked their claims to pieces of land

bring all the colónes you think you might need. There is also an Osa Conservation area office in town ℭ 735-5036, where you can arrange last-minute permits to camp in the park (though it's best to get permits in San José or from abroad before your travels).

The town nearest to the park is **Carate**, 43 km (27 miles) southwest of Jiménez. Four-wheel-drive vehicles are always best for this trip, though I've heard many a boastful tale from travelers who forded riverbeds and mud ruts in rented sedans.

outside the park, where a series of private reserves and lodges create a buffer zone for the region's abundant wildlife.

GENERAL INFORMATION

There are few settlements, telephones or roads on the Osa Peninsula, and no central source of information. The largest town here is **Puerto Jiménez** (population: 7,000), where the airstrip is conveniently located next to the town cemetery. Puerto Jiménez has grown steadily with the growth of tourism to the area, and the services are improving. A few pulperías have public telephones. There is a very small branch of the Banco Nacional, though it's better to

WHAT TO SEE AND DO

Much like the oreros of the past, birders and naturalists flock to the Osa Peninsula for its natural wealth. Though much of their attention is focused on the **Parque Nacional Corcovado**, the surrounding areas are filled with the same abundance of wildlife — marguays, ocelots, keel- and chestnut-billed toucans, peccaries, tapirs and anteaters — to name just a few of the 100 or more species of mammals and 360 species of birds found in and around the park. The peninsula's land mass ranges

Hikers arrive by boat to access Parque Nacional Corcovado's remote trails.

The Zona Sur

through eight different habitats from coastal beaches to cloud forests, and a coral reef attracts tropical fish off Punta Salsipuedes. Visitors to the park and nearby lodges fill their days with hikes, horseback rides and boat rides, and their nights with star gazing.

The park includes over 54,000 hectares (133,380 acres) of land and 2,000 hectares (4,940 acres) of marine habitat, and it is controlled from ranger stations (called *puestos*) in Sirena, San Pedrillo, La Leona, El Tigre and Los Patos.

atop of a hill overlooking a canopy of trees and a deserted beach. The 14 enchanting bungalows are scattered down the hillside (it's a bit of a climb down to the lower ones). When I first walked into my room, a haughty toucan gazed disapprovingly from the railing of my private deck, then withdrew only as far as the nearest tree. Gauzy white netting draped around the carved wood bed kept me protected from mosquitos, as I slept with bamboo screens open to the breeze. Tropical hardwoods (from trees already felled) were used for

WHERE TO STAY

Rooms are limited and best reserved far in advance, especially for visits during the dry season.

Very Expensive

Like Quixotes tilting at windmills, John and Karen Lewis have created an extraordinary hotel in the middle of the wilderness and named it **Lapa Ríos** (735-5281 FAX 735-5179 E-MAIL laparios@sol.racsa.co.cr, Apdo 100, Puerto Jiménez, 16 km (10 miles) south of Puerto Jiménez, RESERVATIONS IN THE U.S. P.O. Box 0252116, SJO 706, Miami, FL 33102-5216. Set in the midst of a 400-hectare (988-acres) private preserve, the hotel sits

the floors and furnishings; the shower is screened so you can watch finches and parakeets play in the trees. A 15-m (50-ft)-high thatched palm A-frame roof covers the main lodge where guests dine on fresh fish and fruits, sip tropical drinks and sign up for forest trail, beach and night walks. Don't miss the medicinal plant forest walk led by Augusto, the resident shaman. Part of the hotel's proceeds go towards maintaining a small school for children in the area, and for reforestation of the region. Meals are included in the rates; transport from Puerto Jiménez and hikes are extra.

On the edge of Corcovado above Playa San Josecito is **Marenco** (221-1594 FAX 255-1346 E-MAIL marenco@sol.racsa.co.cr,

Apdo 4025-1000, San José. A private rain forest reserve with rustic cabins housing up to 50 people each, Marenco's holdings extend the corridor protecting the park's wildlife. Boat tours to Corcovado and Isla de Caño are available.

Expensive

Michael Kaye, the founder of Costa Rica Expeditions and a leader in ecotourism, walked the Osa Peninsula for 12 days back in 1979 to find the right piece of land for his dream camp. It took until 1990 for him to purchase the land and construct the **Corcovado Lodge Tent Camp** (257-0766 FAX 257-1665 E-MAIL crexped@sol.racsa .co.cr, the perfect base for hardy wilderness explorers. Guests hike for 45 minutes along the beach to reach the cluster of 18 tents sheltered by palms. The tents cover wooden platforms and two sturdy bamboo cots; cold water showers are located in two shared bathrooms. Electricity is provided a few hours a day by generator, and meals are served family style in a thatched-roof lodge. One of the biggest attractions here is being hoisted atop a forest canopy platform in a 60-m- (200 ft-)-high ajo tree; try it early in the day when you're most likely to spot monkeys and birds, or pay an additional fee to spend the night in the trees. Park hikes, both easy and difficult, are offered through the park for an extra fee or as part of a package including lodging, meals and activities. The camp is located near the small town of Carate at the southern edge of Corcovado.

Creature comforts in a rustic setting bring guests back many times to **Bosque del Cabo** (/FAX 735-5206, hidden on a hilltop above **Playa Matapalo** at the southern tip of the peninsula. Mosquito netting over comfy beds, outdoor showers with a view of toucans in the trees, and solar-powered electric lighting provide the necessities to live amidst hummingbirds, howlers and sloths.

Moderate

A rustic alternative in a clearing atop Punta San Pedrillo is the **Casa Corcovado Jungle Lodge** (256-3181 FAX 256-7409 E-MAIL corcovado@sol.racsa.co.cr, Apdo 1482-1250,

Escazú, RESERVATIONS IN THE U.S. Casa Corcovado, Interlink #253, P.O. Box 526770, Miami, FL 33152. Bungalows are spread about a clearing adjacent to the national park; tours to the park, Isla de Caño and nearby waterfalls are available. Guests arrive via boat down the Río Sierpe.

Inexpensive

There are a few small cabina hotels in Puerto Jiménez, many operating illegally in private homes. Few have phones, but you may be able to make advance reservations

through the **Osa Peninsula realty office** (735-5138 FAX 735-5073. The standard favorite in town is **Cabinas Manglares** (735-5002, near the airstrip.

Camping is allowed within the national park, but you must have reservations and a permit arranged through the **National Parks Office** (257-0922 FAX 223-6963, in San José. Facilities are beside the ranger stations, and you can dine with the rangers if you reserve and pay in advance. Otherwise, you'll need to pack your food along with a tent, bedding, mosquito netting, water,

OPPOSITE: Macaws mate for life and depend on each other for beak cleaning and other essential matters. ABOVE: Bamboo trunks clatter in the rain like wind chimes.

first-aid supplies and clothing. Hiking trails connect the stations, and dedicated explorers can spend days and even weeks exploring the park. The terrain is difficult, however, and you must be vigilant about snakes, insects and trail accidents.

HOW TO GET THERE

TravelAir and SANSA have flights from San José to Puerto Jiménez. Buses run from San José via San Isidro de el General. A paved road runs from the Carretera

bears his name. Arched into the rain forest between the Río Sierpe and Parque Nacional Corcovado, Bahía Drake. It is one of the most isolated places on the coast, yet five settlements of hardy Costa Ricans reside on the hillsides, river banks and beach, living quite happily on the gifts from the sea, small vegetable and cattle farms and, increasingly, on the benefits of tourism. A few nature lodges, cabinas and vacation houses offer luxurious wilderness experiences. Visitors to Bahía Drake have the advantage of being able to explore the

Interamericana at Chacarita to Rincón; from there on you face ridges, ruts, bridges and mud en route to Jiménez. The road (actually barely a path) continues on from town paralleling the coastline to Carate; a four-wheel drive is essential for this stretch.

You can also reach the Osa Peninsula via boat from Golfito, where captains in Puerto Jiménez will ferry you to Carate and the puesto at Playa Sirena.

BAHÍA DRAKE

Sir Francis Drake spotted a sheltered bay two kilometers (one and a quarter miles) wide on the northern Osa Peninsula in 1579; that bowl of warm, calm water now

sea, the river and traditional Costa Rican towns from a single base.

WHAT TO SEE AND DO

I once had the privilege of touring the largest town in the area, **Aguajitas**, with a resident nature guide who was working on the *Temptress* cruise ship. Tony had lived in the town for 18 years, and evidenced a tremendous pride and fondness for his community. What's not to like? Resident scarlet macaws, oblivious to the blare of reggae from a nearby radio and our camera-laden group, munched on fruits from an almond tree spreading its shade over the beach. People paused to chat and stare from their porch chairs; children posed proudly before their new school. As we reached the river the housing improved considerably, and signs for rental rooms and horseback rides began to appear. We crossed the freshly painted red, blue and yellow hanging bridge swaying over the Río Aguajitas, and entered the tourist zone at the mouth of the river. If you stay in any of the lodges in the area be sure to make at least one trip to town, buy a few essentials (or nonessentials) at the neighborhood pulpería and practice your Spanish with the locals.

Sport fishing, boat rides up the river (great for bird watching), trips to Isla de Caño, horseback riding, kayaking — the opportunities to eat up a week's time are abundant. Corcovado is just 13 km (eight miles) south. Some visitors walk the beach and mountain trails from the river to the park's San Pedrillo entrance. Naturally, you should allot a bit of time for lounging in a hammock at the edge of the river or sea or on a private deck in the trees.

GENERAL INFORMATION

There is one public telephone run by solar power in **Aguajitas** at the **pulpería** (771-2336. According to locals, the government says the area will have electricity by the turn of the century. The clinic in town is sporadically staffed by a nurse; she rides a circuit of the five local settlements on horseback then returns to what some call "the capital of Drake Bay" at Aguajitas, which has about 200 residents. Everybody in town knows how to find the local supply of snake bite antivenin, which is typically needed by farmers and cattle ranchers who disturb the resident snakes. The local lodges use solar power, generators and radios to provide creature comforts, and they count on phones and faxes in San José for contact with the outside world.

WHERE TO STAY

Expensive
Rock and roll booms over the roar of the river from the deck of the **Aquila de Osa Inn** (296-2190 FAX 232-7722 E-MAIL aguilar @sol.racsa.co.cr, RESERVATIONS IN THE U.S.

P.O. Box 02-5635, Miami, FL 33102. The fanciest hotel in the area, it has 13 rooms in cabins planted up a hillside with great views of the sea; all have hardwood floors, peaked ceilings, fans and hot showers. The hotel offers fishing, diving, hiking and river trips.

Moderate
More tranquil and environmentally conscious is the **Drake Bay Wilderness Camp** (/FAX 771-2436 E-MAIL hdrake@ticonet.co.cr, Apdo 98-8150, Palmar Norte, Osa, on the

river. Herbert and Marleny Michaud began the camp in the 1980s on a point of land between the river and the sea. Today they have 20 comfortable rooms in cabins separated by long stretches of lawn and palm groves. The rooms have white walls with stenciled flowers, firm mattresses, tiled bathrooms with solar and gas powered water heaters and reading lamps over the beds. Windows have good screens, though bugs are not a major problem. Guests gather for meals in a large peaked-roof dining room where the walls and shelves are covered with fine balsa wood masks and animal carvings made by local Boruca Indians. Meals here include homemade breads and biscuits, piles of tropical fruits, and fish caught daily in local waters. The best accommodations for nature lovers are five spacious tents on platforms in isolated spots along the water. The tents have cement floors, fans and lights; a table and

OPPOSITE: Young Ticas share a popular refreshment near Bahía Drake. ABOVE: Tapirs snuffle and shuffle along the rain forest floor.

chair sit outside, offering a perfect spot for reading, writing or gazing at the turquoise sea. Facilities and activities include sport fishing, a professional SCUBA diving operation, kayaking, canoeing, horseback riding, river rafting trips and mountain biking. The best bargains are the four- and seven-day packages, which include chartered air transport from San José.

Also recommended are **La Paloma Lodge** (/FAX 239-0954, between the river and town, **Cocalito Lodge** (/FAX 786-6150, and **Cabinas Ceclia** (771-2336, in town.

HOW TO GET THERE

Most visitors arrive by boat from the town of Sierpe down the river of the same name; the trip of 30 km (18 miles) takes about two hours. The surge and surf can be rough when the river meets the open sea; most captains know the tides and best times for the trip. Once the boat enter Bahía Drake, the water is usually placid, but be prepared for a wet landing in the small waves lapping the beach. Most lodges offer transportation from Sierpe; some have docks on Rio Aguajitas for dry landings. You can reach Sierpe by plane from San José to Palmar, by car from the Palmar intersection on the Carretera Interamericana and by

bus or taxi from Palmar. If you haven't arranged transport in advance, negotiate with the boat captains in Sierpe for your trip.

ISLA DE CAÑO

Isla de Caño is one of the most important archaeological sites in Costa Rica — believed to be a burial ground for the Diquis peoples. The tiny island, only three kilometers (under two miles) long by two kilometers (one and a quarter miles) wide, is also a prime snorkeling and diving spot, where lobsters, octopus, sea urchins and sea turtles can be seen when the waters are calm. Isla de Caño is now part of the Parque Nacional Corcovado and both the land and water are protected, but this designation came too late to preserve the Diquis burial grounds. Many of the graves have been looted; however, visitors can still see bits of pottery that date back to the first century. More exciting to archaeologists is the abundance of lithic spheres — huge, perfectly round stone balls found throughout the Diquis region. Little is known of their origin and meaning, but the presence of the spheres on the island suggests that the Diquis transported them across the sea to the island, a considerable feat. The island is 20 km (12 miles) west of Bahía Drake and has a small ranger station. Only 20 visitors are allowed on the island trails at one time; tours can be arranged through hotels in Bahía Drake, Dominical and Quepos.

OPPOSITE: Keel-billed toucans are among the forest's more amusing characters, and can be spotted in lodges on the Osa and Burica peninsulas. OPPOSITE: Rewards such as this cascade await those who trudge through Corcovado's red mud.

The Caribbean Coast

THOUGH NOT SPECIFICALLY part of the legendary Moskito Coast, the province of Limón has all its steamy mystique. Jungles and mangrove swamps border the sandy strip between Nicaragua and Panama, creeping into the turbulent sea, which doesn't really seems Caribbean with its gray waves and log-strewn shores. Long separated from the rest of the country by rain forests and tall mountains, the Caribbean Coast is bordered by the Cordillera Central to the west and the formidable Cordillera Talamanca in the south. Only two roads make their winding way from the capital to the coast; boats and planes are, thus far, the only transport north.

Such isolation has preserved the Caribbean's cultural attributes. Most of the population is Afro-Caribeño, and the food, music and language all have a spicy Caribbean flare. English is more common than Spanish among the residents, while a few Indians still speak only the indigenous Bribrí and Cabécar tongues. Long stretches of the land mass and adjacent waters are protected in nature preserves, and explorers seeking the wilder side of the country find much to enjoy.

To the north, murky canals form a maze of waterways leading to the settlements of **Parismina**, **Tortuguero** and **Barra del Colorado**, where sea turtles nest in the sand and anglers ply the waters for tarpon and snook. Paul Theroux described **Puerto Limón**, at the center of the province, in *The Old Patagonian Express* as "…a beachhead of steaming trees and sea stinks." Much has improved since Theroux made his crabby way through Latin America by train, but similar impressions stick. Limón has little of the beauty of the towns to the south. **Cahuita**, **Puerto Viejo de Limón** and **Manzanillo** — all popular destinations for surfers, bird watchers and naturalists — are cleaner, friendlier and far more accommodating than their capital city.

PUERTO LIMÓN

Though disparagements are common, those who linger in Limón are quick to defend the city's character. Judy Arroyo zips up to Limón at least three times a week

from Aviarios del Caribe (see below), near Cahuita. She points out the improvements, saying, "The pavement's better. We've got curbs and good sewage."

Arroyo, who is constantly fixing meals for her guests, justifiably praises Limón's central market, a cornucopia of tropical fruits from the land and sea. She swears she's never been accosted, robbed or hassled in the street.

But then Arroyo, though obviously a gringo, doesn't stick out like a tourist with a camera and suitcase. Rumors abound

when it comes to issues of safety in Limón, and I would never leave a packed rental car parked on the street. Like other backwater Caribbean ports, the city attracts drug dealers, scammers, schemers and desperate souls. Displays of wealth and abundance are targets for trouble. It's not wise to wander alone after dark; always practice your street smarts.

PRECEEDING PAGES: Fine sand, clear waters and trails of seashells LEFT are among the southern Caribbean's natural attributes. An egret RIGHT balances above the marsh in the Refugio Silvestre Gandoca-Manzanillo. OPPOSITE: Gandoca-Manzanillo, at the south end of the coastal road — where travelers find the Almonds and Corals Tent Camp hidden among the trees. ABOVE: The jungle grows dense and fetid near Caribbean shores.

I prefer Limón in the morning, when Limónenses escape the heat along shaded streets, visiting neighbors, running errands and following their languorous daily routines. If possible, treat Limón as a day trip from your hotel on the beach outside of the city unless you're looking for a bit of debauchery. If so, don't miss Carnaval, which is celebrated on Día de las Culturas (Columbus Day) in October.

BACKGROUND

Christopher Columbus first discovered Costa Rica when he landed at Isla Uvita just off present-day Limón city in 1502. But the region was inhabited by only a few sparsely populated indigenous groups scattered along the coast and in the Cordillera Talamanca, and the Spaniards looked elsewhere for their booty and slaves. In the 1800s English-speaking African Caribbean workers were imported from Jamaica and other islands to work on cacao plantations along the coast. English pirates stopped by occasionally to raid the plantations and take refuge in sheltered bays.

Coffee put Puerto Limón on the global shipping map. In 1871, coffee barons from the central region sought an eastern port for shipping the *grano de oro* (grain of gold) to Europe. They chose a small fishing village called El Limón as their port and began constructing a railway through uncharted mountains and jungles from San José to the coast. Workers from China, Italy and Caribbean islands provided the manpower. At least 4,000 lost their lives to the rail line, which took over 20 years to construct. Minor Keith, an American who oversaw the construction, gained possession of some 324,000 hectares (800,000 acres) of land along the railway and coast and began planting bananas as a second export crop. Eventually Keith joined with the Boston Fruit Company to create the United Fruit Company, which ruled the economy, coastal lands and labor force of much of Central America, well into the twentieth century.

Coffee, bananas and shipping shaped the fortunes of the Caribbean Coast through booms and busts. The black residents, who these days make up 30 percent of the population of Limón province, were virtually cut off from the rest of Costa Rica. They were denied citizenship and prohibited from traveling into the highlands until 1949. Even today many Ticos look down on the Caribbean and its residents being as inferior and dangerous.

The Jungle Train was the main form of transportation to the capital (and a tourism highlight) for nearly a century. Then the amazingly engineered Carretera Guápiles (Highway 32) through Parque Nacional Braulio Carrillo was completed in 1987. Suddenly the coast was open to explorers and a new wave of settlers seeking inexpensive property and business opportunities by the sea. The earthquake of 1991 brought everything to a halt, blocking the highway and completely destroying the rail line.

The earthquake shaped the future of the Caribbean Coast, bringing both devastation and restoration. It struck during the international celebrations of Earth Day on April 22, 1991 at 3:57 PM. Registering 7.4 on the Richter scale, it was centered just south of Limón.

More than 3,000 buildings were destroyed in Limón province. The Las Olas Hotel — a longtime favorite of mine with rooms built over the waves — dropped into the sea. Limón's streets rose one and a half meters (five feet); oil refinery tanks burst into flames. Over 400 people were injured; at least 25 died. Coral reefs rose above water level and dried into calcified skeletons. More than 40 km (25 miles) of roads were destroyed; trees torn from the Talamanca foothills tumbled in mud slides and floods to the sea. Canals leading to Tortuguero were left high and dry.

Years later you can still see the results of the quake's destructive force, along with its mixed blessings. Limón city is much more pleasant looking than it was in the late 1980s, and a modern suspension bridge now straddles the Río Estrella north of Cahuita. Many houses and businesses have here been rebuilt, and foreigners are moving in to open upscale hotels and restaurants. The area's largely black population is now augmented by immigrants

CARIBBEAN COAST

from Nicaragua, El Salvador, Honduras and Panama seeking peace and prosperity. The Indians who used to live in the lowlands have been driven into reserves in the hills, and are most evident in the southern Talamanca area.

All of the indigenous peoples of Costa Rica were finally granted full citizenship rights in 1992. Despite lingering prejudice on the part of Costa Rican and foreign inlanders against the region, tourism and local activism are both booming along the Caribbean Coast.

FESTIVALS

Even those who shun Limón the rest of the year can't resist **Carnaval**, which takes place (strangely enough), in mid-October. Scheduled around the October 12 national holiday of Día de las Culturas, celebrating the cultures of the country and Columbus Day, Carnaval attracts some 200,000 people to the port city. This week-long debacle shuts down businesses and all civic functions and brings everyone into the street, dressed in spangles, glitter, beads and glow in the dark colors. The festivities culminate in an hours-long riotous parade. Gorgeous teenage girls in ruffled yellow miniskirts and skimpy tops carry giant plastic bananas with the Chiquita label. Men glistening with sweat wear ruffles as well, on their pants, on their shirt sleeves, even crowning their heads. The music is downright cacophonous with an underlying steel-drum beat luring everyone to shimmy, shake, shuffle and swing. Calypso, reggae, rap, merengue, cumbia — all forms of tropical music fill the air for the entire week, when sleep is abandoned for revelry. Hotels are booked months in advance, and buses are added to carry passengers from the interior to the coast.

WHAT TO SEE AND DO

Limon's waterfront sidewalk, the *malecón,* is worth a stroll in the daylight; but, don't walk it alone at night. **Parque Vargas**, the main square, sits at the waterfront end of Avenida 2, the main drag through town. A sidewalk runs along the waterfront from

here, past some restored classic Caribbean residences alongside those still in ruins from the quake. Guide books and a few locals swear there are sloths in the park's banyan trees and Royal Palms — I'm not convinced. Artist Guadalupe Alvarea's mural of Limón's peoples and history covers a wall sheltering the park, which faces town hall and the justice building.

The **Mercado Central** at the north side of Parque Vargas is one of Costa Rica's finest, with a grand array of regional produce. Purple and blue cacao fruit, bananas, plantains, pejibayes, mangoes and herbs compete in the stands with bundles of drab yucca, cabbage and chayote; naturally, fish is a staple of the market's aromas.

Surfers and history buffs hire captains with small skiffs to ferry them to **Isla Uvita**, a national landmark one kilometer (just over half a mile) offshore. Hikers enjoy the small island's sandy trails and caves; surfers come for the waves in December and January and during hurricane season (roughly August to November).

WHERE TO STAY

Limón's inner-city hotels are a sorry lot — I've never found one fit for vacationing. Ticos seeking a weekend getaway head for the more scenic establishments a few kilometers north of town at Playa Bonita (a misnomer, since it's not all that pretty) and Portete, a bay favored by surfers. Advance reservations are essential during Carnaval week and on national holidays.

Moderate

An old-time survivor of the quake, the **Hotel Maribu Caribe** (758-4543 FAX 758-3541, Apdo 623, Portete, Limón, has 52 rooms in thatched-roof bungalows, a good restaurant, a pool and transportation from San José for an additional fee. **Hotel Jardín Tropical Azul** (798-1244 FAX 798-1259, Playa Bonita, Limón, is more upscale, with 32 air-conditioned rooms in white buildings across the street from Playa Bonita.

Inexpensive

The budget traveler's favorite in downtown Limón is the 39-room **Hotel Acón** (758-1010

FAX 758-2924, Apdo 528, Limón, which also has one of the town's most popular discotheques. Choose your room accordingly, and be thankful for the air conditioning, which will allow you to close your windows and escape the noise.

WHERE TO EAT

All of Limón's restaurants are inexpensive, but only a few give you the opportunity to sample the region's best cuisine. The best Creole–Caribe restaurant in town is

Drivers usually take the Guápiles Highway, a 148-km (92-mile) drive from San José. This drive takes about two and a half hours, and cuts through Parque Nacional Braulio Carrillo. Modern and relatively smooth as the highway is, it is also one of the most dangerous in the country. Its steep hills are often shrouded in mist and fog; rock and mud slides are common. Passing lanes are usually provided on the uphill stretches; drivers going both ways use them recklessly. Speed traps are often set on the flat stretch from Siquirres to Limón, where truck drivers

Springfield's at the north end of the malecón. **Mares,** on Avenida 2 between Calles 3 and 4, is where expats head for burgers, sandwiches and clean surroundings. There is an abundance of cheap , mediocre Chinese cafés thanks to the descendants of the Chinese laborers who helped build the Jungle Train. Try the cleanest of them all: **Restaurant Sien Kong** or **Restaurant Chon Kong**, by the market.

HOW TO GET THERE

Buses depart from San José for Limón (about a three-hour trip) from 5 AM to 7 PM; try to arrive during daylight as the city can be intimidating and threatening at night.

gleefully pass each other without regard for tiny rental cars.

An alternate route from San José through Cartago and Turrialba takes about four hours and joins the main highway at Siquirres.

Those headed north to Tortuguero will likely avoid the city altogether by departing by boat from Moín just northwest of Limón, where cruise ships on day stops put in. Those headed south who wish to avoid Limón should look for the small road sign for a bypass route headed for Cahuita.

Banana plantations form the economic foundation of east coast villages, where descendants of Afro-Caribeño settlers live a tropical, laid-back lifestyle.

THE NORTHERN CARIBBEAN

About as isolated as any place can be, the Northern Caribbean Coast is made up of a sweltering maze of canals (both natural and man-made), swamps and beaches, all havens for nature. Canoes, small engine-driven skiffs and ferries are still the main modes of transportation in the region, bordered by the Mar Caribe and the Cordillera Central. Nicaragua's border undulates through the northern Río San Juan just above Costa Rica's Río Colorado and the natural seaport at Barra del Colorado. This region has long been studied as an alternative to the Panama Canal, since the Río San Juan flows nicely west into Lake Nicaragua and on to the Pacific Coast.

Travelers, naturalists and pregnant sea turtles are drawn to the settlements of **Tortuguero, Parismina** and **Barra del Colorado** — all classically reminiscent of the Moskito Coast. Fishing, bird watching, culture and escape are the region's biggest draws year round. From May through September, turtle watchers pack the lodges and research camps.

TORTUGUERO

As its name implies, Tortuguero is devoted to turtles. Archie Carr, of near-godlike status to turtle-watchers, began documenting the annual green turtle migration to Tortuguero's strip of coastline in the 1950s. Conservation groups from all over the world are now involved in research and preservation of the turtle's nesting grounds. The largest settlement in the northern Caribbean, Tortuguero village has some 500 residents, double the number who lived here in the early 1980s. When all guest rooms, dorms and camp sites are full, the population swells to over 1,000.

Tourism a catalyst for both the rise in population and for concerns over Tortuguero's future. Some hotel owners would like their customers and supplies to arrive via a road; the only opposition to such "progress" are local protests and the boundaries of **Parque Nacional Tortuguero.**

Spread over 18,600 hectares (46,000 acres) of land and 52,000 hectares (129,000 acres) of marine habitat, the park shelters West Indian manatees, crocodiles, howler monkeys and over 450 species of birds. Endangered mammals, including jaguars and cougars, are relatively safe in the mystifying melange of water and land; most of the guides I've talked to have yet to spot the cats.

Rain drips and pours through the heavy air almost 365 days a year. They say an Englishman visiting the region years back grew overwhelmed with the incessant downpours. One day, he asked a boy in the village "When does it stop raining here?"

"*No se, señor*," the boy replied, "I don't know. I'm only 12."

With all the moisture, steam and tumescent air, Tortuguero feels surrealistic, like something from a Gabriel Garcia Márquez dream. Everything moves slower than the speed of a hand-paddled canoe — at least it seems that way sometimes. Flights are unpredictable and you can get damned uncomfortable sitting by the airstrip as the afternoon sun melts the asphalt. And the region is buggy, to say the least. All those frogs hanging about have quite a lot to eat. But these drawbacks only increase the region's mystique — if you're in the proper mood. For me, Tortuguero is absolutely captivating.

General Information

Telephones, electricity and other modern creature comforts are sparse in these parts. The best places to gather information on the area are at the lodges, the park's ranger station and the Caribbean Conservation Corporation turtle museum (see WHAT TO SEE AND DO, below). When you are feeling adventurous, keep in mind that the rural doctor pays visits to the town only every few weeks, and anyone who needs major medical care will need to be airlifted to San José. Naturalist Rafael Robles González has published a small *Field Guide to Plants of the Caribbean Coast of Costa Rica*, which helps amateurs understand what they're looking at. You can find it at hotels and pulperías.

What to See and Do

One of the most popular destinations in the national park system, **Parque Nacional Tortuguero** is worth exploring for days on end. After three successive early morning boat rides through the park's canals, I still craved more — more howler monkeys, more skinny-legged, yellow-beaked northern jacanas perched on blue water hyacinths, Jesus Christ lizards walking on water, giant iguanas (nicknamed *gallena de palo* or chicken of the tree), chestnut-bellied herons, kingfishers, blue anhinga

Tortuguero's lodges, for the most part, line the Río Tortuguero between the Caribbean and the jungle. To term the strip along the sea a Caribbean beach is stretching the point — though some enjoy sunbathing and rain showers amidst driftwood, sea grapes and sargasum seaweed on mud-brown sand. Ghost crabs skitter about, dodging hook-billed brown whimbrels feeding upon crustacea, and butterflies and moths of all stripes hover about wild ginger and morning glories. The best beach lies between the lodges and the village; wear a

snake birds. Accompanied by three guides well-versed in local lore, we floated down the spooky black water canals, which mirror palms on the shore. We stopped at the **Estacion Biológica Caño Palma**, a lonely outpost opened in 1990 to pursue nonprofit research on birds and butterflies. I grew utterly mesmerized by the sensations, not caring about sunburn, bug bites and a soaking T-shirt. I was oblivious to all but the boat's chugging engine, the flash of wings as birds stalked bugs like cats chasing mice and the sudden splashes in turgid waters. Next time I'll travel the canals in a kayak or canoe. The daily fee to enter the park is $6, payable at the ranger station south of the village.

hat and sweat-proof sunblock. Swimming in the sea is discouraged because of rip tides, high surf and occasional shark sightings.

It's a pleasure to take a leisurely walk around **Tortuguero Village**. Men of all ages loiter about the **Super Morpho pulpería (** 710-6716, where lines assemble before the public phone. The pulpería sells basic consumables, insect repellent, piñatas and blond dolls. The women prefer the front porch of Miss Rosie's and other informal home businesses selling clothing and basic necessities ferried up

Green turtles migrate to the beaches of Tortuguero every spring to lay their eggs.

from Limón. The bright pink and green **Paraíso Tropical**, at the end of the ramp where tour boats arrive, sells handcrafts, T-shirts, postcards, books and print film.

The center of village social life is the playground and park on the sea side of town. The well-maintained kiosk at the plaza contains information on turtles; nightly tours depart from here during nesting season. When you spend time visiting the village, it seems as if everyone is related. The *union libre* (free marriage) concept is widespred here; some men

boast of numerous children mothered by many local women and girls. More Nicaraguan and Honduran immigrants are settling here amidst the longtime Afro-Caribeño families; many of them find the area's agriculture, fishing and tourism businesses far more prosperous than those in their homelands.

Tortuguero Natural History Visitor Center, just north of the village, is headquarters for the oldest sea turtle conservation organization in the world: the **Caribbean Conservation Corporation** or **CCC** ((904) 373-6441 E-MAIL ccc@cccturtle.org; TOLL-FREE IN THE U.S. (800) 678-7853, P.O. Box 2866, Gainesville, FL 32602. The visitor center is a remarkable establishment, with

displays on the region's history and the interwoven story of sea turtle preservation. Carr's classic books on turtles, along with other informational materials, T-shirts and postcards are sold here. Donations are requested, and the center is open daily during daylight hours; closed for lunch.

Green, loggerhead and hawksbill turtles nest on the 35-km (22-mile)-long beach between Tortuguero and Parismina. **Turtle tours** are available through the lodges, the CCC and the independent guides operating from the kiosk in town. Only 200 people are allowed on the beach at any given time when the turtles are nesting, and everyone must be accompanied by a guide (10 persons per guide). If you are seriously interested, arrange your tour through the CCC or your lodge; the merely curious might be satisfied with the kiosk guides. The CCC enlists paying students volunteers, and researchers to assist with tagging sea turtles and other conservation efforts.

The only decent **hike** in the area is to the top of **Cerro de Tortuguero**, 119 m (390 ft) above sea level, where, on a clear day, you can see the outlying areas of the park.

Fishing for snook and tarpon is also a big draw at Tortuguero, though the dedicated tend to favor the fishing lodges at Barra del Colorado and Parismina.

Where to Stay and Eat

Tortuguero's lodges are surprisingly well-outfitted and comfortable, and are becoming increasingly fancy. One has added a massive pool with a waterfall; others are following suit. Purists find such amenities pretentious, but the growth of comfort-based tourism seems inevitable. The CCC has sponsored a proposal to regulate development, which seems to have spurred local businesses to build in a flurry before the codes are passed.

Bar la Culebra, the biggest night spot in town, hangs over water at the south end of the village; unfortunately, its canned music echoes in the canals here. **Restaurante Pacana** and **Restaurante Sabina** are your better choices for seafood and Caribbean fare.

Consider location when choosing a lodge — those on the sea side of the river have the advantage of proximity to the beach and may be within walking distance of the village. Those on the jungle side have more wildlife and will ferry you over to the village by boat. Most places offer morning and night canal tours and transport from San José; rates are typically based on packages including transport, a two- or three-night stay, meals and tours. These extras mean that most rates are in the expensive range. Meals are usually served family or

wildlife watching. Flocks of white egrets skim across the river, spider monkeys swing in the trees, crickets and red poison-arrow frogs provide background chirping. The newest rooms have screened French doors which open onto the back verandah; all have ceiling fans and hot water. Bountiful meals are served family style in the main lodge. Rubber boots and ponchos are available. The croton and heliconia gardens are being expanded, and there's talk of adding a pool behind the buildings, with native plants and fish.

buffet style and have set menus; if notified in advance, some lodges will accommodate vegetarians and those with special dietary. Reservations are essential during turtle nestings; most can be arranged through offices in San José. Budget travelers are best off at the small cabinas in town.

EXPENSIVE TO MODERATE

I'm partial to the staff and ambiance at the **Tortuga Lodge** (257-0766 FAX 257-1665 E-MAIL crexped@sol.racsa.co.cr, Apdo 6941, San José. Set amidst 20 hectares (50 acres) of private property on the outskirts of civilization, the lodge has wood and leather rocking chairs outside the front and back doors of each room, beckoning guests to

Also on the jungle side is the aptly named **Jungle Lodge** (233-0133 FAX 233-0778 E-MAIL cotour@sol.racsa.co.cr, Apdo 26-1017, San José, marked by a red, white and blue tire-like sign visible above the trees. Somewhat worn down, the lodge has 45 rooms with ceiling fans and hot water; meals are served family style.

Architecturally distinct, the **Pachira Lodge** (256-7080 FAX 223-1119, Apdo 18118-1002, San José, is set back from the river amidst palms and heliconia. The 28 rooms are in wooden cabins spread about the grounds and interconnected with thatch-

OPPOSITE: A Tortuguero nature guide describes the local flora. ABOVE: Surf-watching Caribbean style in Tortuguero.

roof plank pathways. A floor-to-ceiling window offers unobstructed vistas of the jungle from the coffee bar where espresso and cappuccino are served in late afternoon. Meals are served buffet style. The facilities are indeed lovely, but some guests report indifferent service.

The friendly staff and management make the **Laguna Lodge** IN SAN JOSÉ (225-3740 FAX 283-8031 one of the best choices on the sea side of the river. The 26 rooms in wood cabins on stilts with thatched roofs are set within gorgeous hibiscus, orchid and heliconia gardens; a long trail leads to the village — a steamy 45-minute walk. Meals are served family style in a large dining room decorated with hanging oropendula nests.

A three-hectare (seven-acre) private reserve adjoins **Mawamba Lodge** (223-2421 FAX 222-4932, Apdo 6618, 1000 San José, perhaps the fanciest place in the region. The 39 rooms in wooden cabins are surrounded by blooming ginger plants. A big restaurant and swimming pool with waterfall were nearing completion when I last visited. Hammocks hang under thatch umbrellas close to the river, where tour groups load and unload at the hotel's two docks.

INEXPENSIVE

A few small cabina operations offer rooms on the sea side of town, none have phones but you may be able to make reservations through the **Super Morpho pulpería** (710-6716. Try **Cabinas Sabrina** or **Cabinas Merry Scar. Camping** is permitted by the park entrance south of town; at most times of the year you'll need a tent to protect you from the rain.

BARRA DEL COLORADO

Reserva Biológica Barra del Colorado sits at the far northeastern corner of the country. The 98,000-hectare (242,000-acre) refuge is a top sport fishing destination, and it also serves as a hideaway for nesting sea turtles. Birds abound; even the scarce, endangered green macaws can be spotted above the treetops. Small settlements and farms lie within the park's boundaries, connected by a web of waterways.

Where to Stay
EXPENSIVE

The most famous building in the area is the **Río Colorado Lodge** (232-4063 FAX 231-5987 E-MAIL tarpon4u@cyberspy.com, Apdo 5094, San José, RESERVATIONS IN THE U.S. TOLL-FREE (800) 243-9777 FAX (813) 933-3280. The lodge sits at the mouth of the Río Colorado and the Caribbean Sea, prime fishing grounds for tarpon and snook. The entire complex is roofed and built on stilts above the muddy ground; the 18 wood-paneled rooms have ceiling fans and hot showers. Meals with generous portions are served family style. Air transfers from San José are available. Better yet are the boat transfers down the Río Sarapiquí to the Río San Juan and the Colorado.

Luxurious by fishing outpost standards, the **Silver King Lodge** (381-0849 FAX 381-1403; RESERVATIONS IN THE U.S. TOLL-FREE (800) 847-3474 FAX (813) 943-8783, P.O. Box 025216, Department 1597, Miami, FL 33102, has large rooms with hardwood floors, bamboo ceilings, in-room coffee makers, ceiling fans, and firm mattresses. Fishing, nature tours, air transfers and boat transport are available, and there is a large hot tub to soothe muscles strained by fighting the big ones.

PARISMINA

Just south of Tortuguero on the Caribbean Coast, Parismina is a tiny village that devotees prefer to keep secret. A favorite spot for anglers, the **Río Parismina Lodge** RESERVATIONS IN THE U.S. TOLL-FREE (800) 338-5688 FAX (210) 824-0151 (expensive), 1800 N.E., Loop 410, Suite 310, San Antonio, TX 78217, is five kilometers (a bit more than three miles) south of Parque Nacional Tortuguero, the rooms and dining room are housed in red-roofed, white stucco buildings raised above the lawns. Both river and deep sea fishing are available, along with a swimming pool, hot tub and nature tours; closed in July.

HOW TO GET THERE

Small airlines and boat tour companies compete for the tourist traffic through the region. TravelAir, SANSA and several air charter companies fly small prop planes for two to 20 passengers into small airstrips at **Tortuguero**, **Barra del Colorado** and **Parismina**. You should fly at least once, in spite of the size of these airplanes and their undependable flying schedules. The 20- to 30-minute fight from San José heads northeast over the fog-shrouded peaks of the Cordillera Central, the outer regions of Parque Nacional Braulio Carrillo and some of the wildest land in Costa Rica. Most lodges in the three areas can arrange air transportation. Passengers are restricted to 11 kg (25 lbs) of luggage.

Day trippers and travelers with time, cruise the northern passage in boats, spotting howler monkeys, herons and crocodiles en route. Tour, ferry and private boats depart from Moín (near Limón) for the three- to four-hour ride to Tortuguero; go in early morning or evening when the canals and wildlife appear much as they would from the village's lodges. Most tour companies in San José and the lodges in Tortuguero offer bus or van transfers to Moín and scheduled boat transport.

CAHUITA

Marking the start of the southern Caribbean Talamanca Coast (named for the Cordillera Talamanca), Cahuita didn't even have a road to Limón until 1979. The first major town 44 km (27 miles) south of Limón, Cahuita has less than 1,500 residents and one of only two protected coral reefs on the Caribbean at the **Parque Nacional de Cahuita.** It's an established community with several generations of family living side by side in faded green and pink wooden houses raised on stilts above sandy streets. Clusters of handpainted signs point the way to small cabina hostelries in the village, and to more luxurious hotels and bed and breakfasts on sideroads along the beach.

Bright orange, yellow, green and red stripes adorn the main businesses as if boasting their Jamaican rasta roots; Bob Marley is practically a god in these parts. Long the province of dropouts, surfers and budget travelers, the village is relaxed and

laid-back. The tourist crowd is young and parsimonious, willing to spend a few colónes to obtain the rasta look by hiring a local woman to plait their hair into dozens of tiny *trencitas* (braids).

Cahuita has its down side, largely due to drugs. Ganja has long been readily available here (some of the pulperías sell rolling papers). Lately cocaine and crack have added an ugly edge to the scene here. Reports of thefts are common. Though the majority of residents and travelers are friendly and trustworthy, a few persistent

thieves give this area a bad reputation. Keep a close eye on your possessions at all times, and don't leave cameras and keys lying on the beach. Lock your doors and windows at night.

The pickup scene between local rasta boys and young blonde tourists is intense, and the girls seem happy to supply their short-term Caribbean boyfriends with beer, food and companionship. As a result, some of the guys can be quite persistent. Women travelers should take sensible precautions. The pickup scene grows at the central park and bus stop in the evenings, when locals and tourists perched upon backpacks size up new arrivals.

Cahuita village has achieved a sense of order after years of haphazard building, and it's now relatively easy to navigate the two main roads and several sidestreets that make up the village proper. Street addresses are nonexistent and unnecessary; everything you need is either in the village

Caimans slither up river banks in search of unwary birds.

or on the one road running north of town along Playa Negra (Black Beach). A few lodges and inns attract a more upscale clientele who stick to the hotel pools and beaches at Playa Negra and venture into town for a meal.

BACKGROUND

Until the road south from Limón was bull-dozed through and a bridge built over the Río Estrella in the 1970s, Cahuita and other Caribbean settlements were virtually cut off

from the rest of the country. A few families worked fishing and farming, enjoying the solitude of Cahuita's forest-sheltered bay. Most residents were Afro-Caribeño settlers brought in to work on the Jungle Train and banana plantations; today's population is comprised of their offspring, and of United States and European émigrés banking on the tourist trade.

The completion of the Guápiles highway from San José to Limón in 1987 drastically changed Cahuita's peaceful scene, bringing Ticos curious about this untrammeled part of their country. Tourism was on a steady incline until the earthquake of 1991 tossed half the village, along with its bridges and roads, into the sea. The quake's destruction is still evident. Bridges leading nowhere have been replaced but not removed, and piles of fallen trees litter the beaches.

GENERAL INFORMATION

Until December, 1995, the entire village of Cahuita had only one phone number (758-

1515) and businesses and residences were accessed through extension lines. Now phones and faxes ring all over town, making it much easier to arrange reservations and tours. **Cahuita Tours and Adventure Centre (** 755-0232 FAX 755-0082, Apdo 1, Cahuita, Talamanca, is headquarters for information, changing money, sending mail and faxes and making public phone calls. They also set up tours to jungles and Indian reserves, arrange glass-bottom boat rides and rent gear. Several other tour companies have popped up along the main drag; ask other travelers about their experiences before forking over cash.

Buses from Limón and points south stop at the park across from Salón Vaz; tour agencies and hotels post the latest schedules. If you're driving, be sure to unload and lock up your gear at your hotel before cruising the town. There are no banks in town; change money at tour agencies or hotels.

WHAT TO SEE AND DO

The biggest attraction and best beaches in the area are at the **Parque Nacional de Cahuita** (no phone), with 1,068 hectares (2,639 acres) of beaches and jungle and 22,409 hectares (55,350 acres) of ocean preserve. Though brochures make the park sound idyllic, the beaches are actually tan rather than white and the aquamarine sea is sometimes murky with sediment, depending on the season.

Several factors have endangered the reef and darkened the waters at Cahuita. Deforestation in the Cordillera Talamanca and the banana plantations creates sediment that runs down the foothills into the sea. The 1991 earthquake caused more problems when buildings close to the sea crumbled and debris floated in the currents. Several environmental groups are working to clean up the beaches; you can help by carrying along a plastic bag and picking up any trash and cigarette butts you see.

Nature trails wind through the tropical forest fringing the beach; early morning hikers may spot howler monkeys, sloths and green parrots in the trees. There are two entrances to the park; one at the south end of Cahuita town, and one further south at Puerto Vargas, with camping facilities, picnic tables and toilets. Admission to the park is $6.

From December to May, when the coast's persistent rains are less torrential, divers and snorkelers have the best view of tropical fish around the **Punta Cahuita reef** and a sunken eighteenth-century slave ship. Sea urchins, parrotfish, lobsters and green turtles are protected in these waters and can be spotted in abundance. But this is not Cozumel or the Cayman Islands, and dedicated divers may be disappointed.

north of Cahuita off the main coastal highway. Much of the 8,910-hectare (22,000-acre) park is virtually unexplored. A few rugged trails run under the forest canopy along rivers and waterfalls, and wildlife is abundant. Guides are essential; arrange for one through hotels and tour agencies in Limón, Cahuita or Puerto Viejo.

Far more accessible and quite delightful is **Reserva Biológica Aviarios del Caribe**, on the Estrella River, 10 km (six and a quarter miles) north of Cahuita. Though not directly on the ocean, the reserve has its

Tour companies and hotels can arrange boat trips to the reef, 500 m (1,640 ft) from shore.

North of town is **Playa Negra**, a long stretch of black sand and blue waves. Strong surf and rip tides make swimming dangerous here, but it's a lovely spot for walk.

Local agencies offer tours to the **Indian reserves** in the area, though if you're truly interested in the culture you're better off taking a tour from the ATEC office in Puerto Viejo (see below).

The seldom-visited **Reserva Biológica Hitoy-Cereré**, in the hills of the Cordillera Talamanca, is 60 km (37 miles) southwest of Limón; a road to the park is located just

own water attractions — a river island where caimans, river otters and herons have free range in a private wildlife refuge. Owners Luís and Judy Arroyo have a way with nature's injured creatures, who thrive under their care. Buttercup, the resident three-toed sloth whose mother was killed in an auto accident, has her own swinging chair and an album of photos sent by guests (she also stars on a greeting card from the Nature Conservancy). Three toucans thrive in large wire buildings beside the reserve's

OPPOSITE: Dugout canoes glide peacefully through lagoons at Cahuita without disturbing herons, kingfishers and other birds feeding on shore. ABOVE: Lovable three-toed sloths get mildly curious between naps on their favorite limbs.

lodge. When I last visited, Judy was caring for two newborn sloths whose mother had been killed by a logger.

Day visitors are treated to languid canoe trips down the river through canals and lagoons, where guides easily spot herons, kingfishers, manakíns, northern jacanas, warblers and sloths high above the canopy in cecropia trees. Binoculars, rain ponchos and umbrellas are provided. Back at the lodge, a trail leads through tropical forest; watch out for hundreds of frogs hopping about in the rainy season.

Tours can be arranged through Cahuita and Limón hotels and travel agencies, or by the Arroyos (382-1335. Day trippers typically envy those spending the night.

WHERE TO STAY

Small, rundown cabinas and hotels are the norm in Cahuita. If the hotels below are all full and you must stay elsewhere, be sure your room has a good lock on the door, and put your valuables in the hotel's safe. It can be difficult to make reservations since few places have faxes or post office boxes. When writing for reservations, address your letter to the hotel's name, Cahuita, Limón, Costa Rica. Start the process a couple of months before your visit. Cahuita Tours and Adventure Centre (see GENERAL INFORMATION, page 228) acts as a booking agent for many of the area's hotels.

Moderate
I took up residence at **Aviarios del Caribe** (/FAX 382-1335, Apdo 569-7300, Limón, on a whim while traveling the coast and ended up canceling other reservations in order to extend my stay. While my companion dozed in a womb-like waterbed, I woke up every morning with the howler monkeys and sipped coffee on the verandah, watching herons, kingfishers and egrets slowly swooping up from their sleeping perches along the lagoon. Aviarios has six comfortable guest rooms with private baths and hot showers (one room has a tub); all rooms and public spaces are decorated with imaginative wildlife paintings by Mindy Lighthip. Breakfast is served on the deck; guests drive into Cahuita for other meals. The huge

enclosed lounge area is packed with books. Guests can catch the latest soccer games and satellite movies with Luís on the color television. Tours to the Reserva Hitoy-Cereré, Punta Uva and Bribrí are available, along with fresh and saltwater fishing and endless bird watching (the Arroyos have counted 312 species from their verandah, thus far). Best of all is the night frog walk, where guests wear headlamps to spot these tiny, elusive creatures who proliferate during the rainy season.

I didn't expect to see oriental rugs, wood and glass French doors, tropical wood desks and clipper-ship prints in a six-room Cahuita hotel. But the **Magellan Inn** (/FAX 755-0035, Apdo 1132, Limón, has all that, plus a coral reef left exposed by the receding sea 10,000 years ago. A bougainvillea-covered path leads through the fossilized reef alongside a small swimming pool; some heliconia, hibiscus and citrus trees are artfully planted around the lawns. There's a distinct sense of refined comfort here. As owner Elizabeth Newton says, "We chose to build in Cahuita because there was no place we would have wanted to stay here." Now there is a place for those in search of luxury.

El Encanto (/FAX 755-0113, just south of the village at Playa Negra, is a pleasant bed and breakfast with three comfortable bungalows with hot showers. The El Canto will also arrange tours. **Chalet and Cabinas Hibiscus** (755-0021 FAX 755-0015, Apdo 943, Limón, has an ideal location beside the pounding waves at Playa Negra; swimming is not advised, but you can splash about in the small pool while listening to the sounds of the sea. Three bungalows and three houses are scattered about the lawns.

The principle attraction at the **Atlantida Lodge** (755-0115 FAX 755-0213, Playa Negra, Cahuita, Limón, is the freshwater swimming pool. The 30 rooms with ceiling fans and hot water baths are in ochre-colored buildings. Facilities include a full-service restaurant, a gymnasium with free-weights, and a tour desk.

Inexpensive
An exception to the rundown accommodations in Cahuita village is **Kelly Creek**

Hotel (755-0007, right next to the national park between the jungle and the sea. The four rooms are in a varnished laurel-wood building reminiscent of a New England beach house, with high sloping roofs and wood railings on the front porch. All rooms are unusually large, with two double beds, ceiling fans, wood tables and chairs and louvered windows looking out to sea. The adjacent restaurant serves Spanish and Caribbean dishes, with the seasonings influenced by the French and Spanish owners. Advance reservations are

Steak au gingembre? Lobster with vanilla oil and ginger vinaigrette? That pretty pink house with white gingerbread trim and the table set with white linens, crystal and candlelight had to be an hallucination, and the aromas drifting from the kitchen just a fantasy for undernourished senses. But no, Casa Creole is for real, thanks to Hervé and Terry Kerinec's ambitious dreams. Using the finest ingredients from local gardens (including their well-tended herb patch), meat markets and the sea, the couple proves that the ingredients for fine dining

essential and must be made by phone. A three-room addition was in the planning stages when I last visited.

WHERE TO EAT

Cahuita dining spots are limited but the menus are varied thanks to many Caribe and European restaurateurs. Some of the best places are open for dinner only and few accept credit cards.

Expensive

After weeks of eating greasy eggs, dry gallo pinto and bland casados, I nearly fainted at the astonishing menu at **Casa Creole** (755-0104. Paté, blue cheese, spicy fish beignets?

do exist in Costa Rica, even if you have to drive all the way to Cahuita to find them. Don't miss dinner here — and save room for the astonishing profiteroles. The Casa is located on the road along Playa Negra; closed Sundays.

Moderate

The hours are erratic , but locals rave about the homebaked breads, seafood and salads at **Margaritaville**, on Playa Negra. Just down the road is **Sobre la Olas**, where Tex-Mex style fajitas and steaks are served beside the sea.

Poison dart frogs, barely the size of a child's fingernail, hide under jungle leaves and sing in the night.

Inexpensive

Several small restaurants in Cahuita village offer typical fish and Caribe fare, heavy on the rice and beans. The best of the lot is **Tipico Cahuita** (try their seafood soup or lobster); other popular spots are **Restaurant National Park** and **Restaurant Vaz** (not to be confused with Salón Vaz down the street, which happens to be Cahuita's hottest dance spot). **Miss Edith's** at the north end of the village has long been acclaimed for its Creole food, but the service has become downright rude; as one customer said, "You know it's bad when you have to bring along a deck of cards to keep you busy while you're waiting." For oily yet yummy pizza try **Mamma Mia's** or **Cactus**.

HOW TO GET THERE

The 43-km (27-mile) dirt road from Limón to Cahuita was completed in 1979 and destroyed by the quake of 1991. It took many months to repair the road, which is now paved in most places. Bus travelers can avoid changing buses in Limón by taking the Sixaola-bound (Panama border) line from San José; the ride takes about four hours.

Drivers can make it from Limón to Cahuita in 45 minutes; look for road signs pointing the way into the village.

PUERTO VIEJO DE LIMÓN

The road bumps along south of Cahuita past wood-stilt houses to **Hone Creek** (also called Home Creek) and the turnoff to **Puerto Viejo de Limón**. Less than a decade ago Puerto Viejo could barely be called a town. My enduring image of it, from a trip in 1990, is the sight of an old man sleeping on his folded arms in the glassless window of a faded green house. The town has changed considerably since then, but the beaches are still free (no park fees here), the surf can be downright awesome, and everyone appears to be in a state of tropical bliss, enjoying the hammock culture in full swing.

The 1991 earthquake was, perversely enough, the catalyst for Puerto Viejo's growth. It devastated the area. As one

witness wrote: "Call it exquisite timing. I'd been in the southern Atlantic town of Puerto Viejo a bare 25 minutes when my friend Ana's house began to shake… Ana, who is Salvadorian and something of a connoisseur of earthquakes, dove for the kitchen table and yelled at me to get under it with her. 'What are you waiting for, a bus? Get down here.'

"The reef was totally exposed. Stranded fish flopped in the sunlight. The obvious question, 'Where has the water gone?' immediately led to the scarier 'What if it comes back all at once?' A few people with knapsacks and bedding started heading for higher ground in the jungly hills west of the village." Andrew Wilson who wrote about the event for the *Tico Times* (May 10, 1991) described helicopters shuttling the injured to San José and the aftermath of crumbled buildings and shattered lives.

Then, it seemed that all 1,500 residents of Puerto Viejo cried in unison, "If I'm gonna to stay here, I'm gonna make money." Now Puerto Viejo is hot, booming, echoing with the sounds of wailing saws and pounding hammers. It seems everyone who owns a home has turned it into a café or rooming house along a maze of halfway-bulldozed streets. Electric wires twine around tree trunks like vines from a strangler fig, and the scents of ganja, coconut oil and frying fish fill the air. Vendors sell beaded jewelry, incense, candles and bongs along the road closest to the black sand beach, which starts at the entrance to town across from a rusted, waterlogged barge sprouting trees. Puerto Viejo is rapidly displacing Cahuita as the budget destination of choice.

GENERAL INFORMATION

Asociación Talamanqueña de Ecoturismo y Conservación (/FAX 750-0188 (Talamanca Association for Ecotourism and Conservation, or ATEC) operates a general information and tour office in town. Pick up a copy of the *Coastal Talamanca Cultural and Ecological Guide* for background and touring possibilities.

The association does its best to promote ecologically sound tourism, encouraging local culture and business; their pro-environment stance is evidenced in the "Stumps Don't Lie" bumper sticker over the front door.

Some nights it seems everyone in town is lined up on the benches by ATEC's public phone. They also have a fax service and sell stamps, postcards and printed information on the region. Notices of events and causes are posted on the bulletin board.

Buses stop at the edge of the beachfront road past the entrance to town, across from

June and July; the Salsa Brava is a mecca for surfers from South America, Australia and the United States who add their distinct character to the village when surf's up.

Tours to **KëköLdi Indigenous Reserve** (/FAX 750-0119, home to about 200 Bribrí and Cabécar peoples are a must for the culturally curious; both ATEC (see above) and Mauricio Salazar (see CABINAS CHIMURI below), offer culture and nature tours to the reserve. ATEC also offers educational tours to Indian towns, nature preserves, a banana plantation, and some turtle nesting sites;

the Taberna Popo where the street vendors and tourists converge.

with advance reservations you may be able to arrange a trip to the remote Cordillera Talamanca or to Panama.

WHAT TO SEE AND DO

Puerto Viejo's windswept, log cluttered, black sand beaches are its biggest draw. They don't invite lounging, *per se*; the combination of jungle fauna, skittering crabs, ruthless no-see-ums and sand flies discourage the uninitiated. The cleanest sands and prettiest vistas are at **Punta Uva** south of the village; farther south, **Punta Uvita** has big waves, and the best surfing of all is at the notorious **Salsa Brava**, where massive waves break over a reef. The best surfing months are from December to May and in

WHERE TO STAY

Ever-increasing options now include everything from rustic cabinas to a sprinkling of higher quality accommodations. Reservations for the best places are essential during surfing season and Tico holidays, and they are a hassle to arrange. Start at least three months in advance faxing or writing to the properties at Puerto Viejo, Limón, Costa Rica, and follow up frequently.

A white-tailed deer pauses in a lowland rain forest near Limón.

Expensive

If you must have air conditioning and a swimming pool, your best choice is south of town at **Hotel Punta Cocles** (234-8055 FAX 234-8033, Apdo 11020-1000, San José. The 60 rooms are in white cabins spread along lawns with play equipment for kids; the beach is across the street. Some rooms have kitchenettes.

Moderate

El Pizote Lodge (/FAX IN TOWN 299-1428 AT THE LODGE (798-1938, just north of the bridge leading into town, has several wood cabins set far apart on lawns interspersed with large trees. Rooms with shared baths are in a long building at the end of the grounds; the six private bungalows have cold showers and somewhat ineffectual ceiling fans (beware of termites in the old wooden bedframes). Parrots, oropendulas and other birds twitter about the grounds; monkeys and frogs stay hidden in the forest behind the property. Breakfast is available for an additional charge, and there is a full bar, complete with darts, billiards and a ping pong table. The prices are high for what you get (especially since some nearby properties have pools and hot water), but the place has a desirable wilderness feeling. Hire a guide to lead you into the adjoining jungle.

A place of dreams for architect Julian Grae and his wife Marlena, a decorator, **La Perla Negra** (/FAX 381-4047 is crafted from tropical hardwoods and bordered by forest. The 24 spacious rooms have bathrooms with separate toilet areas and hot water, ceiling fans, and balconies or terraces. Guests mingle at the swimming pool, leaving only to explore Puerto Viejo's restaurants.

Inexpensive

Cabins built in the Bribrí style (A-frame roofs covered in cane thatch) house guests at **Cabinas Chimuri** (/FAX 798-1844, set in a 20-hectare (49-acres) private reserve near the sea. Shared baths and cooking facilities allow guests to mingle as if they are family, boasting together about sightings of boa, kingfishers, armadillos and bats. Owner Mauricio Salazar guides morning and night hikes through the reserve's trails

and a full-day hiking tour (for the hardy) to an Indian reserve.

Casa Verde (750-0015 (/FAX 750-0047, Apdo 1115, Puerto Viejo, is by a long shot the most pleasant budget hotel in town, with immaculate rooms set in gardens on a quiet residential street. The 14 rooms have hammocks in front and two single or one double bed; rooms with shared baths are the least expensive. It's the first in-town spot to fill up, so reserve well in advance.

Ceiling fans, hot showers and large, clean rooms make **Cabinas Tropical** (/FAX 750-0012 a stand-out among its neighbors. The proprietors were adding rooms when I last visited, but advance reservations are still a good idea in the high season.

WHERE TO EAT

Moderate

Some say it's worth traveling the rutted road to Puerto Viejo to dine at **The Garden Restaurant**, where the Trinidadian chef prepares Caribbean, Thai and Indian dishes served in a candlelit dining room. Pizzas, pastas and *postres* (desserts) bring crowds to **Restaurant Coral** at dinner; breakfasts of whole-wheat pancakes, Mexican omelets and baskets of muffins fuel surfers before they hit the waves.

Inexpensive

Gallo pinto prepared with coconut milk is the standard side dish at **Restaurant Tamara**, though you can have French fries or *patacones* (refried plantains) with your fish, chicken or beef. Across from the beach, **El Parquecito** is a favorite for lobster and fish, while **Stanford's** stokes a young crowd with rice and beans before they hit the reggae dance floor.

MANZANILLO

More a settlement than a town, Manzanillo sits within the **Refugio Silvestre Gandoca-Manzanillo**, which extends south to the Panama border. This remote region with few roads comes the closest to fulfilling television-inspired images of white-sand beaches and swaying palms, and residents are committed to keeping it that way. The Federación de Organizaciones de Corridor Talamanca-Caribe is comprised of at least 13 groups creating a conservation corridor connecting the Refugio Gandoca-Manzanillo with Parque Internacional la Amistad. They hope to extend the corridor into Panama's Parque del Boca Verde.

GENERAL INFORMATION

The nearest telephones and tourist services are at Puerto Viejo. Buses are infrequent;

area. Offshore, a coral reef spreads for about 200 m (650 ft); the best snorkeling is at Punta Uva and just south of the Almonds and Coral Tent Camp (see below). Trails lead from the beach into forested foothills and along mangrove lagoons, where manatees, crocodiles and caimans are protected from human predators. There are several turtle nesting sites in the area, and howler monkeys, sloths and ocelots find shelter in the forest. Explorers can arrange boat trips along the shore and lagoons or hikes into the forest through hotels in the area.

buses to Sixaola at the Panamanian border drop passengers at the edge of Manzanillo. If you're driving, go slowly. The roads are rutted and sandy, with narrow bridges that appear suddenly.

WHAT TO SEE AND DO

Beaches and a small coral reef are Manzanillo's biggest draw. The **Refugio Silvestre Gandoca-Manzanillo** spreads along the coastline from Punta Uva south; a wooden sign near the Hotel Punta Cocles marks the beginning of the refuge. Classified as a mixed-management preserve, the park contains a few ecolodges and camps, which aim to stabilize the economic base of the

WHERE TO STAY AND EAT

Expensive

My favorite accommodations are the net-covered tents on stilts at **Almonds and Corals Tent Camp** (272-2024 or 272-4175 FAX 272-2220. Platforms built a few feet above the jungle undergrowth house big white hammocks, private bathrooms with cold showers, single beds inside a water-proof green tent (you can close the flaps for privacy), and electric lamps and portable fans. The camp is often cited as a leader in the ecolodge movement, and it serves as a model for similar projects underway on

A four-wheel-drive vehicle maneuvers the rocky road to the Panama border.

both coasts. The 18 units are camouflaged under tall trees and thick foliage. At night it's easy to imagine you've struck out alone like a modern-day Robinson Crusoe. Raised wooden boardwalks connect the tents with the large dining room where fixed-menu meals are served to the beat of cumbia tunes. Howler monkeys greet the morning with rumbling roars; answer their call and walk along the long beach to spot toucans, parrots and trogons in the trees. The best swimming is 100 m (110 yards) south of the camp near the solitary

Talamanca. The only bank in the region, a branch of the Banco Nacional, is located here. The village sits at the edge of **Parque Internacional la Amistad**, which covers 194,00 hectares (479,200 acres) of mountains, cloud forests and watershed. Entrance to the park is at the west side near San Vito (see SAN VITO in ZONA SUR, page 200).

Indian reserves for the KéköLdi, Bribrí and Cabécar groups are located in the area. You must have prior permission to visit the settlements; contact the ATEC office in Puerto Viejo (see above) for information.

Maxi's restaurant, the only nearby option for meals. The camp is in a private reserve surrounded by the Refugio Silvestre Gandoca-Manzanillo. Tours include snorkeling, kayaking, and visits to a nearby Bribrí Indian village. Owner Aurora Gamaz handles reservations through her agency **Geo Expediciones (** 272-2024 FAX 272-2220, which specializes in out-of-the-way tours to the Caribbean and Sarapiquí regions.

MOVING ON TO PANAMA

Sixty kilometers (37 miles) south of Limón, the road to Manzanillo passes through **Bribrí**, a small village and management center for Indian reserves in the Cordillera

Many foreigners on long-term stays in Costa Rica use the Sixaola border crossing as a quick way to enter another country (Panama) to renew their Costa Rican visas. Buses run to the border from Limón and San José. Geo Expediciones (see ALMONDS AND CORALS above) offers tours farther into Panama, and there is talk of creating a circuit tour running down Costa Rica's Caribbean Coast, along Panama's northern area and back into Costa Rica at the Pacific Coast border crossing at Paso Canoas.

ABOVE: Snorkelers find clear waters in the marine refuge off Cahuita. OPPOSITE: Caribbean Coast transportation ranges from light aircraft TOP to traditional dugout canoes BOTTOM.

The Caribbean Coast

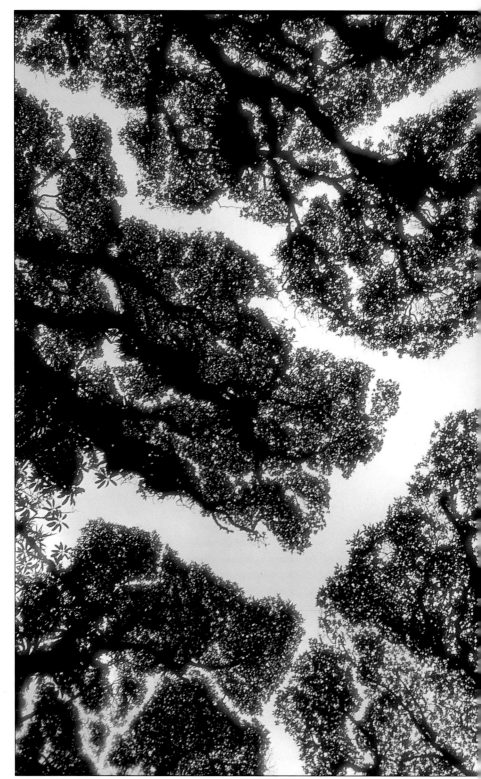

Travelers'
Tips

GETTING TO COSTA RICA

BY AIR

Most flights come in to the **Aeropuerto Internacional Juan Santamaría** (443-2682, located 10 miles northwest of downtown San José in Alajuela. During high season some charters arrive at the **Aeropuerto Daniel Obudar** in the northwest province of Guanacaste.

Most airlines from Canada and Europe make connections through Miami, Dallas, Houston, Los Angeles or Mexico City en route to San José. Airlines with daily flights include Continental, American, Lacsa, Air Canada, Aviateca, Iberia, Mexicana and United. European travelers usually pass through Miami or Houston; KLM and Iberia have direct flights. Fares are highest from December through April and in August.

Once you've passed the immigration desk in the lower level of the San José airport, you must haul your bags up a steep flight of steps. A gauntlet of ticket sellers hawk a confusing array of transportation options atop the steps. They'll grab for your bags — possession being half the sale. Ignore them until you've got your bearings. *Colectivos* (mini-vans to several destinations) are the least expensive option, but they may take a circuitous route to your lodgings. Taxis park in an isolated lot past the car rental stands. Enterprising drivers will chat you up regarding fares and hotels; some are not licensed cabbies but rather individuals hoping to make a few extra colónes on the side. Some outlying hotels offer airport transfers, which must be arranged in advance.

BY INTERNATIONAL BUS LINE

There is good bus service between Costa Rica and Panama, Nicaragua, Honduras and Guatemala, though the trip can be long and rough. Cost Rica's international bus company, Ticabus, has direct service from Guatemala City and Managua, Nicaragua. Since peace has broken out in Central America, bus travel is far safer than in the past.

BY SHIP

Several cruise lines stops in Costa Rica's Caribbean port at Moín and the Pacific port at Puntarenas. You might be able to arrange to debark at these points.

BY CAR

Inveterate travelers with plenty of time to spend driving on the Carretera Interamericana through Central America can

cross the border from **Nicaragua** into Costa Rica at **Peñas Blancas**, or from **Panama** at **Paso Canoas**. These border crossings are open only during daylight hours; check with the Costa Rican embassy regarding current red tape. Once you have entered Costa Rica, the Pan-American is called the Carretera Interamericana, or Highway 1.

PRECEEDING PAGES: The rain forest canopy LEFT etches a lacy pattern on the sky. The blue morpho butterfly RIGHT is found in abundance throughout the lowland rain forests. OPPOSITE: Sailors find shelter in several remote bays along the Pacific Coast. ABOVE: Coatis sometimes rattle trash cans around lakeside hotels.

VISAS

International travelers need a valid passport stamped at the airport immigration desk or border crossing. The stamp is good for 30 to 90 days; in theory (though rarely in practice at the airport), you are required to possess a ticket out of the country and sufficient funds (around $400) for the duration of your stay. Once your passport has been stamped, copy the photo and immigration stamp page. Keep it with you at all times. Traffic police and even museum guards can ask to see your passport whenever they wish. A copy usually suffices.

CONSULATES AND EMBASSIES

Canada (296-4149 FAX 231-4783, Oficentro Ejecutivo la Sábana, Sábana Sur (Building 5, 3rd Floor).
France (225-0733 or 225-0933, Road to Curridabat, 200 m (585 feet) south and 25 m (24 yds) east of Indoor Club.
Germany (232-5533 or 232-5450, Rohrmoser.
Great Britain (221-5566 or 221-5816, Edificio Centro Colón, 11th Floor, Avenida Colón, Calle 38.
Holland (296-1490, Oficentro Ejecutivo, La Sábana Sur (Building 3, 3rd Floor).
Italy (224-6574 or 234-2326, Los Yoses, Avenida 10 between Calles 33 and 35.
Japan (232-1255, Residencial Rohrmoser, 400 m (437 yds) west, 100 m (110 yards) north of La Nunciatura.
Spain (222-1933 or 222-5745, Calle 32 between Paseo Colón and Avenida 2.
Switzerland (221-4829, Centro Colón, 10th Floor, Paseo Colón, Calle 38.
United States (220-3939, in Rohrmoser on the road to Pavas in front of Centro Comercial.

TOURIST INFORMATION

The Instituto Costarricense de Turismo (Costa Rican Tourism Institute or ICT) has become ineffectual and virtually useless for travelers with specific questions. There are rumors of ICT's imminent demise or major overhaul. Costa Rica has closed all

its international tourism offices and the once valuable ICT information office at the Plaza de la Cultura in San José is also closed. The main **ICT office (** 223-1733 FAX 223-5452 is in the gray Caja building, on Avenida 4 between Calles 5 and 7. This office does operate a TOLL-FREE NUMBER FOR THE U.S. AND CANADA (800) 343-6332; they'll send a color tourist brochure on the country's highlights with no useful service information. Travel agencies and tour companies are much better sources for practical information.

TRAVEL AGENCIES

Fortunately, Costa Rica has many excellent travel agencies, some with Internet sites and e-mail addresses. Most will work with individual travelers, as well as international travel organizations. The following companies are particularly professional and knowledgeable.

Costa Rica Expeditions (257-0766 FAX 257-1665 E-MAIL crexped@sol.racsa.co.cr WEBSITE http://www.cool.co.cr/crexped.html, Apdo 6941, 1000 San José, Calle Central at Avenida 3, was one of the first to offer adventure travel arrangements in the country. It's still one of the best, with lodges in Tortuguero and Monteverde and an exciting tent camp in Corcovado. The company's nature guides are excellent, and their web site contains a wealth of information.

Costa Rica Sun Tours (255-3418 FAX 255-4410, Apdo 1195-1002, San José, Avenida 4 at Calle 36, represents two excellent private nature reserves — Tiskita Jungle Lodge on the southwest coast and Arenal Observatory Lodge by the Volcán Arenal. Many international tour operators use Sun Tours for their in-country services and guides, and the company offers several unusual itineraries.

Horizontes Nature Adventures (222-2022 FAX 255-4513, Apdo 1780-1002, San José, Calle 28 between Avenidas 1 and 3, is known for its superb multilingual guides and individualized itineraries, and it frequently works with French travel agencies.

Camino Travel (257-0107 or 234-2530 FAX 257-0243, Calle 1 at Avenida Central, is conveniently located in downtown San José; its agents are quite adept at arranging on-the-spot itineraries for any budget, and they work well with undecided travelers. Your options are greater if you contact them well in advance.

Geo Expediciones (272-2024 FAX 272-2220 operates two nature reserves in less-traveled parts of the country — Quinta

Sarapiquí in the northeast and Almonds and Corals Tent Camp on the southern Caribbean Coast. The company specializes in travel to remote regions, including trips into Panama.

TRAVEL AGENCIES IN THE UNITED STATES

Several United States companies specialize in travel to Costa Rica and work directly with in-country operators and guides. Most have arrangements with European and Canadian travel agents:

Costa Rica Connection ((805) 543-8823 TOLL-FREE (800) 345-7422 FAX (805) 543-3626, 975 Osos Street, San Luis Obispo, CA 93401, is linked by family and business ties to some of the country's best nature lodges. They do a great job with individual itineraries, suggesting unusual options.

Holbrook Travel ((800) 451-7111 FAX (352)371-3710 WEBSITE http://www.holbrooktravel.com, 3540 NW 13th Street, Gainesville, FL 32609, is connected with the

OPPOSITE : Most churches, such as this one in Quepos, are functional and simple. ABOVE: Dairy ranchers use many modes of transportation LEFT to get their product to town. A park sign RIGHT points the way to one of Costa Rica's most popular destinations.

Selva Verde Lodge in Sarapiquí, and offers nature and adventure tours of the country.

Euro-Global ((213) 525-3232 TOLL-FREE (800) 235-5222 FAX (213) 525-3234 E-MAIL euroglobal@aol.com, 5670 Wilshire Boulevard, Los Angeles, CA 90036, offers a fly–drive–hotel voucher program that allows you to design your own itinerary as you travel. You save money on the air and car package alone, especially in high season. The agents know Costa Rica inside out and work well with resourceful, independent travelers.

Overseas Adventure Travel TOLL-FREE (800) 221-0814, 625 Mount Auburn Street, Cambridge, MA 02138, offers off-the-beaten path itineraries for small groups (maximum, 16 people).

GETTING AROUND COSTA RICA

By Air

Two regional airlines serve the many small airstrips located in the remote regions of the country. Weather conditions often hamper flight schedules; it's not unusual to sit around for hours waiting for the clouds to clear. Fares are reasonable when compared with the cost of rental cars. Passengers are usually limited to 11 kg (25 pounds) of luggage. **TravelAir (** 232-7883 or 220-3054 FAX 220-0413 is relatively reliable and has flights from San José's Tobias Bolano Airport, seven kilometers (four and a third miles) west of downtown San José in the suburb of Pavas, to most airstrips. **SANSA (** 233-5330 or 233-0397 or 233-3258

FAX 255-2176, Calle 24 between Paseo Colón and Avenida 1, is the government-subsidized line. It flies nearly everywhere out of San José's Aeropuerto Internacional Juan Santamaría.

Always book your flight far in advance and reserve your seat with a credit card deposit. Be sure to confirm and reconfirm your reservation, know which airport you're flying from, and arrive at least one hour before the scheduled departure. Overbookings are common. Some hotels in outlying areas offer air transportation on private or charter flights.

By Bus

Bus travel is cheap, easy and fairly comfortable. Intercity buses currently depart from downtown San José's terminals and bus stops (*paradas*) clustered in the Coca-Cola area (named for a long-gone bottling plant). The government is considering building several terminals outside downtown for intercity travel, thus relieving some of the inner-city traffic congestion.

By Rental Car

Many travelers prefer to see Costa Rica at their own pace in the comfort of a car. Sedans and four-wheel-drive vehicles are both available; air conditioning is optional. If you plan to leave the few major highways, you're best off in a four-wheel-drive vehicle with high suspension and durable tires. International and national car rental agencies barely meet the demand for cars in the dry season (November to March) and rates seem to climb constantly. Always reserve far in advance of your travels, and be specific about your requirements. You may get a better rate renting ahead with Budget, Hertz or National (Europe-Car) in your home country.

Costa Rican agencies have competitive rates. You can rent in advance by faxing or calling the company; most have English-speaking clerks. You may be able to talk them into a bargain during low season. Try **Prego Rent-a-Car (** 221-8680 FAX 255-4492 TOLL-FREE FROM THE U.S. (800) 949-5520 or **Adobe (** 221-5425.

All the car rental companies have offices in San José. It's difficult to rent a car outside the city, though there are small agency branches in Quepos, Jacó, Liberia and Limón. Some companies will deliver your car to Puntarenas, Heredia and other outlying areas for an additional fee.

DRIVING TIPS

Conquering Costa Rica's roads is a rite of passage and certainly as exciting as spotting a two-toed sloth. Travelers tell stories, with surprising equanimity, of Volkswagen-sized potholes, flooded river beds, flat tires and busted suspensions. Range Rovers, Suzukis and Toyotas are vehicles of choice for those with unlimited budgets and time. But even a short cruise through the countryside in a Nissan sedan has its rewards.

Part of the adventure is the very real danger inherent in driving in Costa Rica. For all their amiability, Ticos are deadly on the road. Costa Rica has one of the highest auto fatality rates in the world (18 deaths per 100,000 km or 60,000 miles, compared to 2.7 per 100,000 km in the United States), due to horrendous weather, road conditions and the native pursuit of reckless driving. Don't drive in San José unless you've already conquered Buenos Aires, Quito or Mexico City. First-timers are best off renting cars at the airport or at their hotel.

Outside San José the few main highways quickly access the full spectrum of landscapes: forested ocean cliffs; barren, fog-shrouded volcano peaks; vast, rolling cattle ranges; banana, coconut, coffee and macadamia plantations; and all the irreplaceable snapshot scenes of village life. Most highways are two-lane affairs with few directional signs and plenty of holes, ruts and ridges. Rain run-off causes *derrumbes* (rock slides) in the mountain ranges. Pavement dissolves into ruts in an instant.

Local drivers may try to intimidate you by riding your tail and flashing their lights. All drivers pass with impunity, impervious to like-minded suicidal souls coming toward them. Drive slowly until you've

grown accustomed to the roadways and your vehicle's limitations.

Speed limits

Speed limits are 80 kph (50 mph) on all primary roads and 60 kph (37 mph) on secondary roads, dropping down to 40 kph (25 mph) around towns and schools. Traffic police use radar, and speed limits are enforced by handing out moving violations (pay them through your rental company). Beware of the speed trap between Guápiles and Limón.

Road Rules

- A foreign driver's license is valid for the first three months you are in Costa Rica.
- Seat belts are mandatory.
- Motorcyclists must wear helmets.
- It is illegal to make a right turn on a red light unless a white painted arrow on the road indicates otherwise.
- It is illegal to enter an intersection unless you can also leave it.
- At unmarked intersections, yield to the car on your right.
- Drive on the right side of the road; pass on the left.

HITCHHIKING

Hitching is relatively uncommon in Costa Rica, even among budget travelers. The frequency and range of public buses make it unnecessary. If you do hitch, make it an

OPPOSITE: Bicycles are a preferred mode of transport throughout the country, despite the steep and rutted roads. ABOVE: Four-wheel-drive vehicles come in handy in mountainous areas.

active, friendly affair. Smile and wave at passing drivers, dress neatly and try to look nonthreatening. Ticos consider many budget travelers to be an unruly lot, ill-mannered and shabbily dressed. Once you get a ride, practice your Spanish and converse with the drivers and passengers. Offer to pay for the ride by asking, *"Cuanto le debo?"* (How much do I owe you?).

Use discretion when accepting a ride; if possible, try to hitch with a companion at a store, restaurant or gas station. Avoid

reserves or amidst macadamia, coffee and fruit plantations.

Large chain-operated resorts are mostly found in San José's suburbs and along the Pacific Coast, and are becoming grander in scale. Marriott, Meliá, Holiday Inn and Radisson all own or manage San José properties, and Meliá and Marriott have luxury resorts on the northern coast of Guanacaste.

The ICT does not have an official star rating for hotels; and few hoteliers take the ICT's list of inspected and approved hotels

hitchhiking on major roadways or in urban areas and bear in mind that if a bus does not go to your destination, few cars will either.

One of the great pleasures in driving through rural areas is the opportunity to offer a ride to locals accustomed to walking for hours to work or school. It's a good way to learn more about the country, the people and the language.

ACCOMMODATION

Costa Rica is blessed with hundreds of one-of-a-kind small hotels sprinkled around the main tourist attractions. Many outlying lodges are set in private nature

seriously. Most hoteliers operate independently, working with national and international travel agencies and independent guests. The majority of hotels spread throughout the country have less than 100 rooms. Some have developed a fervid following. Advance reservations for all the hotels mentioned in this book are absolutely necessary in the high season, though you might stumble upon an unclaimed room at the last minute. Make your reservation through the fax numbers or e-mail addresses listed. The postal system is notoriously unreliable; some hotels have postal drops in Miami, Florida with courier air service to Costa Rica, which seems to be reliable.

HOTEL PRICES

Room rates in Costa Rica are higher than those in neighboring countries, and an expensive room does not mean you'll get air conditioning, television, telephones — even hot water, in some cases. Within San José and the surrounding regions such amenities are common in most hotels. In remote areas, the expense of building, maintaining and transporting supplies causes rates to rise.

Showers in some inexpensive places may have an electric unit in the shower head that heats the water. These "suicide showers" can be quite disconcerting at first. To get hot water, turn on the heating switch while the water is off (wear rubber-soled shoes), then turn the water on.

Nature lodges typically include meals in their rates and offer packages for several nights' stay. Some include transport from San José via small plane or van. In such cases the flat room rate may be deceptive, since the cost of setting up your own transport may be much higher than what the hotel offers.

Our categories for hotel room prices are calculated at the cost of a standard double room during high season (November through April and again in August). Many establishments drop their rates by about one-third in the low, or green, season. Most hotels post their rates in United States dollars. A 15 percent sales tax is added to the bill; often, there is a 10 percent service charge added as well.

Very Expensive	Over $100 (20,000 colónes)
Expensive	$75 to $100 (15,000 to 20,000 colónes)
Moderate	$50 to $75 (10,000 to 15,000 colónes)
Inexpensive	$50 and under (less than 10,000 colónes)

BED AND BREAKFASTS

Many small hotels offer breakfast with their room rates though they are not bed and breakfasts, per se. There are more officially termed bed and breakfasts springing up around San José and small coastal towns, though the network is informal.

YOUTH HOSTELS AND CAMPING

There are a few official youth hostels such as the Toruma in San José that are affiliated with international organizations. For information contact **Red Costarricense de Alburgues Juveniles (RECAJ)** (/FAX 224-4085, Apdo 1355-1002, San José, Paseo de los Estudiantes, Avenida Central between Calles 29 and 31.

For information about camping see BACKPACKING/BUDGET TRAVEL in YOUR CHOICE (page 27).

HOMESTAYS

Given the abundance of foreign students, many private homes accommodate guests. If you're a student, get a list of homes from your school. If you're a traveler, contact **Bell's Home Hospitality** (225-4752 FAX 224-5884 E-MAIL homestay@sol. racsa.co.cr, Apdo 185, 1000, San José, which represents dozens of homes.

Lavish resorts such as the Meliá Playa Conchal continue to rise in the northern Pacific.

RESTAURANTS

For information on Costa Rican cuisine see GALLOPING GOURMET in YOUR CHOICE (page 34). For information on the top restaurants in the country see LIVING IT UP in YOUR CHOICE (page 28).

PRICES

Our restaurant prices are based on the average cost of a meal per person, not including drinks.

Expensive $10 or more (2,000 colónes)

Moderate $5 to $10 (1,000 to 2,000 colónes)

Inexpensive $5 (1,000 colónes)

TIPPING

Tips are generally not expected. Taxi drivers aren't tipped unless they provide an additional service like carrying luggage. A 10-percent service charge is added to all restaurant (and some hotel) bills and is supposed to be distributed among the servers. Unfortunately, this often is not the case, and waiters are beginning to realize that American tourists are accustomed to tipping. If the service is exceptional, leave a few extra colónes (about five percent of the bill). Tour guides and drivers do expect tips, about 10 percent of the tour's cost.

BANKING

Banks are generally open weekdays from 9 AM to 3 PM, but are best avoided. You'll spend time waiting in one line to have your cash or travelers' checks approved, then in another for the actual exchange. It is no exaggeration to say that a transaction can last two hours or more. Exchange rates offered by hotels are usually competitive with those at the bank. If you're traveling to outlying regions carry enough colónes for your entire stay (some lodges will allow you to pay your bill with travelers' checks). Automated teller machines are difficult to find in San José and essentially nonexistent outside the capital.

BASICS

TIME

Costa Rica time is six hours behind Greenwich mean time, one hour behind New York and two hours ahead of the United States west coast. It is the equivalent of United States standard time.

ELECTRICITY

Costa Rica operates on 110 volts AC (60-cycle) nationwide. Some remote lodges are not connected to power lines and generate their own electricity. Check in advance to see if they run on direct current (DC) or a nonstandard voltage. Two types of United States plugs are used: flat, parallel two-prong plugs and rectangular three-prong pins. A two-prong adaptor (found at most hardware stores or *ferreterias*) is useful.

WATER

I used to say it is safe to drink the tap water throughout Costa Rica, but times have changed. San José's environment has been so severely affected by development and overpopulation that I hesitate to recommend drinking tap water in older hotels. The same goes for the overbuilt coastal regions such as Manuel Antonio and for the Caribbean Coast. When in doubt, don't drink the water. Hotels usually do not provide bottled water, but you can buy it in small markets nearly everywhere.

WEIGHTS AND MEASURES

Costa Rica operates on the metric system. Liquids are sold in liters, vegetables and fruits by the kilogram.

Distance   1 km = .625 (5/8) mile
1 meter = 3.28 feet

Weight   1 gram = .035 ounces
1 kilogram (kilo) = 2.2 pounds

Volume   1 liter = 2.1 United States pints = 1.76 United Kingdom pints

Temperature To convert Fahrenheit to centigrade, subtract 32 and multiply by $5/9$. To convert centigrade to Fahrenheit, multiply by 1.8 and add 32.

CLIMATE

Costa Rica lies about eight to 11 degrees north of the equator, right in the middle of the tropics. Although it is a small country without a lot of variation in latitude, the climate varies greatly depending on the

terrain (mountain, rain forest, beach). The temperature can drop over short distances because of the rugged mountain chains that affect weather patterns. Costa Rica has over a dozen microclimates; temperatures are based more on elevation and location than on the season. They range from tropical on the coastal plains to temperate in the interior highlands. Mean temperatures on the central plateau are 22°C (72°F), and 27°C (82°F) on the Caribbean Coast.

Most regions have a rainy season between May and October. The intense rains hamper road conditions and flight timetables, but they also provide rushing rivers and waterfalls, fresh, clean air — even in San José — and a pleasant dearth of

large tourist groups. It's a great time to travel if you're flexible. Prices are generally lower for hotels and car rentals (though you'll definitely need a four-wheel drive for extensive exploring). Dry season usually lasts from November through April, and is called summer.

COMMUNICATION AND MEDIA

TELEPHONES

The area code for the entire country is 506, which is followed by a seven-digit local number. Local numbers are listed throughout this book.

The Directory Assistance number is 113.

In 1996, local numbers were changed from six digits to seven; if you're given a six digit number call information at 113 for the correct number. Calls within the country are fairly inexpensive; dial only the local number from anywhere in the country.

To call Costa Rica from the United States dial 011-506 and the local number. Several international phone cards can be used in Costa Rica; contact your provider for the access code. To call collect from private or public phones dial 09 or 116. Prepaid phone cards are starting to appear, but their use is not universal. Two companies offer these cards. Dial the number as instructed on the card to connect with the system.

Public phones accept five-, 10- and 20-colónes coins. In remote areas, the public phone is typically located in the neighborhood market or pulpería. Give the operator the number; he or she will dial it and signal you to pick up the phone when the connection is made. When done, pay the operator. Ask in advance how much it will cost per minute to call your number. Long lines often form at these public phones, and the caller ahead of you may stay on the phone interminably.

Many businesses use the same number for phone and fax lines. If you're trying to send a fax and someone answers the

Bus stops advertise local products in the countryside.

phone say, "Necesito enviar un fax, por favor." (I need to send a fax, please.) and they'll turn on the machine.

THE INTERNET

Costa Rica is surprisingly well connected to the Internet through RACSA, the country's telecommunications company. Its main Internet web address is www.racsa.co.cr. Many businesses have e-mail and websites which are included in listings throughout this book.

MAIL

Postal service in Costa Rica is abysmally poor, and many businesses prefer to not give postal addresses for reservations. Some hotels have postal drops in Miami with courier air service to Costa Rica. Postal codes (zip codes) are not used outside San José. In many places the mailing address is simply the business name, town, province and country. Post offices (*correos*) are open weekdays from 8 AM to 5 PM, *más o menos* (more or less). In small towns the *correo* may be in a small market or private home.

NEWSPAPERS AND MAGAZINES

Costa Rica has a relatively free press able to investigate scandals and corruption. *La Nación* is the leading daily newspaper; *La República* is a bit more lowbrow, while *Al Día* tends toward sensationalism. The English-language *Tico Times*, P.O. Box 145450, Coral Gables, FL 33114, comes out every Friday and is greeted with much joy by expats craving news. Subscriptions are available for international readers. The paper does a good job of summarizing national news and has an informative entertainment section with articles on cultural events, new hotels and restaurants, and tourism destinations. The entertainment listings are invaluable and the letters section usually controversial. *Costa Rica Today* is geared more toward tourists and tends to reflect its advertising. International newspapers are available at several hotels and book shops in San José.

Several newsletters are available for those seeking information on traveling or living in Costa Rica. The best of these is the *Costa Rica Outlook,* Away From It All Press (/FAX 619-421-6002 or 800-365-2342, P.O. Box 5573, Chula Vista, CA 91912.

ETIQUETTE

Ticos are extraordinarily polite (except when driving), and they expect the same treatment from visitors. The Costa Rican character is based on peace making and

negotiation rather than confrontation; Ticos turn stubborn and cold when facing enraged, shouting tourists. Services may not be as efficient as you are accustomed to at home, but direct anger will rarely solve the problem.

HEALTH AND EMERGENCIES

EMERGENCY PHONE NUMBERS

Emergencies in San José
  and Central Plateau (119
Fire (118
Police (222-1365 or 221-5337
Transit Police (222-9330 or 222-9245
Red Cross Ambulance (128

HEALTH CONCERNS

There are few health risks for the tourist in Costa Rica. The water supply is relatively unpolluted though this may be changing. There have been reports of unsafe levels of bacteria in San José's water supply. It is no longer safe to drink water from mountain streams or springs; campers should carry their own. As a rule, food in restaurants and hotels is prepared hygienically. I've never gotten a case of "Montezuma's

Social Security health care is available to all employed Costa Ricans and their families, and private health care is quite good. Travelers and foreign residents tend to rely on the private Clinica Biblica (257-0466, in San José, for medical treatment. Pharmacies (*farmacias*) sell antibiotics and other non-narcotic drugs without prescriptions and pharmacists are usually able to help diagnosis and care for minor ailments.

Most rural areas have medical clinics. Doctors and nurses travel a circuit within a

Revenge" here, just the occasional stomach upsets from too much fresh fruit, beer and sunshine. If you do get a case of diarrhea, try treating it first with over-the-counter products such as Pepto Bismol. Don't take more potent medications such as Lomotil for long; they can prevent the bacteria from leaving your system and make you far sicker.

Infectious diseases such as cholera, hepatitis, dengue fever and malaria are rare but do occur, particularly on the Caribbean Coast. Inoculations are not required, though it's always a good idea to make sure your tetanus shot is current. Some travelers prefer to get hepatitis A and B vaccinations before visiting Latin America.

region, seeing patients in each village one day a week or so. Most outlying lodges have access to doctors and are able to airlift emergency cases to San José.

Snake bites are a major risk to farmers and field workers, and nearly every small town has a readily available supply of antivenin. As for travelers, many never encounter a snake, try as they might. But, take precautions, nevertheless. Always wear hiking boots and socks when walk-

OPPOSITE: Many small towns have only one or two public phones where residents line up in the cool evenings to make calls. ABOVE LEFT: The promise of tourists' colónes brings out the entrepreneurs who offer tours led by local guides. RIGHT: San José attracts Ticos from around the country.

ing through rain forest and high grass, and watch where you step. Don't grab trees and vines without looking at them closely first. If you are bitten try to study your attacker's features so that first-aid workers can give you the correct anti-venin. Scorpions abound, but their sting is not deadly. Chiggers can leave a nasty itch that lasts for days. If you're doing a lot of hiking in grassy areas such as Guanacaste, sprinkle sulfur powder on your legs and socks. Mosquitoes, no-see-ums and other irritating wildlife are

SAFETY AND SECURITY

Sad to say, Costa Rica is no longer as free of crime as it was even five years ago. Thefts and muggings are common in parts of San José and some coastal towns. These crimes horrify peaceful Costa Ricans who tend to exaggerate rumors of tragic occurrences. Travelers accustomed to the street crime scenes of Manhattan, Buenos Aires or Jakarta will not be fazed. Use the same precautions you would in any large city.

common nearly everywhere. Nature guides suggest you carry bug repellent but not use it until necessary. Though Deet is the best repellent it can cause skin irritations. Use it sparingly.

Sexually transmitted diseases, including AIDS (SIDA), are a definite concern if you're sexually active during your travels. Bring condoms and use them; don't depend on the low-quality condoms sold in the country.

TOILETS

Public toilets, even in gas stations, are usually fairly clean. Carry your own tissues or toilet paper, however.

Hold on tight to your cameras, wallets and purses; don't flash money or jewelry; don't wander down deserted streets late at night. Stash your passport, plane ticket and extra money in your hotel's safe; carry a photocopy of your passport in a money belt, since the police can ask you for identification at any time.

Rental cars are easy targets for thieves more interested in the contents than the vehicle itself. Resist the temptation to leave your packed car by the side of the road while exploring. There have been several reports of automobile break-ins at car lots by parks, reserves and beaches (including Braulio Carrillo, Carara and Jacó). Leave your gear at your hotel before parking in remote areas. Don't stroll too far along deserted beaches at night. And don't park on the street in San José, Limón, Puntarenas, or other big towns. Guarded parking lots are common and inexpensive. Use them.

WHEN TO GO

The waves of tourism peak during Costa Rica's summer dry season (November to April), when prices soar and room availability is limited. Advance reservations for

with siestas. The southern coastal areas, which can be unbearably hot in February, are cooler in the winter months. All in all, the rain isn't that bad until you get on the road. You must rent a four-wheel-drive vehicle if heading toward dirt or sand roads, and you must take flooding, rock and mud slides and slippery surfaces seriously. I once hung my Suzuki Samurai off the side of a bridge with no guardrails en route to the far southern Pacific Coast. Several strangers helped me push it back onto the road; only after we finished did

the best lodges and inns are essential during high season, and again in August when many European travelers come for vacations. Though big crowds can be a deterrent, August is certainly the easiest time of year to reach outlying destinations. Once the rains begin in May, the roads start disintegrating into muddy, impassable messes.

Costa Rica's tourism industry promotes the rainy winter season as the "green season," definitely an appropriate moniker. The country becomes lush and wet and everything shimmers in the sporadic sunlight. The rains are not constant, except in the northern Caribbean; instead, there are afternoon showers timed nicely to coincide

they inform me that four German tourists had died in the same place when the river was high.

Air, car rental and hotel rates typically drop about 20 to 30 percent when tourism is at its lowest; ask about special "green season" rates.

WHAT TO TAKE

Though travel gear, clothing and books are available in San José, you're best off bringing what ever you'll need with you.

OPPOSITE: Farmers haul their produce to busy roadsides where passersby pick up great deals. ABOVE: Small towns with simple houses and shops dot the countryside.

Prices for toiletries and all imported goods are elevated, and quality is often questionable. Bring lightweight, comfortable long pants, shorts, skirts and shirts, and one warm jacket or sweater for the mountain climates. A waterproof, breathable poncho is essential at almost any time of year; rain and cloud forests have no dry season. A lightweight umbrella will come in handy as well. You will need at least two pairs of sturdy walking shoes. Pack twice as many pairs of socks as you think you'll need, and throw in

French (depending on the clientele). San José has a couple of shops devoted to selling used books, and other stores that carry a range of titles on Costa Rica. Guidebooks published outside the country are difficult to come by, but there are a few excellent English-language nature and history books published in the country.

WOMEN ALONE

Women operate businesses, hold political office, pay their taxes and are generally

one knee-high pair to wear under rubber boots.

Camera buffs should bring all the film and batteries they'll need, since supplies are scarce and expensive. Disposable waterproof cameras come in handy for boat trips. You'll be sorry if you don't bring binoculars for wildlife sightings.

Bug bites, scratches and bruises are a part of any Costa Rican adventure; your first-aid kit should include strong insect repellent, calamine lotion for itches and stings, an antiseptic such as Bactine and gauze or bandages for covering wounds.

Foreign language books are expensive; many hotels have book exchanges with selections in English, German, Italian and

respected — though a certain kind of Latin machismo still lingers. Women travelers are usually treated with courtesy and respect, though even women who might consider themselves immune to casual come-ons will find themselves dealing with *piropos* (flirtatious comments). Younger women, particularly those who dress scantily, will quickly become all too familiar with the snake-like hisses that follow them when they walk alone down the street or beach. Costa Rican men seem to believe that a woman traveling by herself is almost pitiful — a lost soul to be rescued, guided, coddled and fondled (if possible). Direct assault is not a common occurance, however.

COSTA RICAN SPANISH FOR TRAVELERS

Costa Ricans speak a more formal version of Latin Spanish, as opposed to Castillian Spanish with its lisping c- and z-sounds. Unlike their neighbors in Honduras and Panama, Costa Ricans speak slowly and clearly as a rule, making it easier for beginners to follow a conversation. But they also have a wide range of regional expressions and words that can confuse travelers accustomed to the Spanish of Mexico or South America. Costa Ricans are extraordinarily patient with travelers who mangle their language, and appreciate all attempts regardless of their content. Practice your Spanish everywhere, using basic phrases to show your respect for the country.

Ticos (as Costa Ricans are informally called) are quite fond of the diminutive, changing *un momento* (one moment) into *un momentito, mi amigo* (my friend) into *mi amigito, un café* (a coffee) into *un cafecito*. Terms of endearment are common and sometimes amusing; girlfriends are fond of calling each other *gordita* (little fatty) and all friends refer to each other as *mi amor* (my love).

Below are some common Costa Rican words and phrases, called *tiquismos*, followed by basic Spanish for travelers in Latin America.

Tiquismos

hello, good-bye, see you later   *¡adios!*
Is anyone home? I'm here   *¡Upe!*
   (typically used when approaching
   someone's home.)
great, terrific, life is good   *¡Pura vida!*
cool, okay, great   *tuanis*
uncool, bad   *mala nota* or *furris*
That's wonderful!   *¡Qué bruto! Qué bárbaro!*
That's horrible!   *¡Qué horror!*
         ¡Qué fatal! ¡Qué maje!
buddy   *maje* (used by males
         among their peers)
Costa Rican   *Tico*
San José resident   *Josefino*
San José   *Chepe*
coffee shop   *soda*

small store   *pulpería*
taxi meter   *maría*
carbonated soda   *gaseosa*

Places and Things

bakery   *panadería*
beach   *playa*
boarding house   *pensión*
book shop   *librería*
bridge   *puente*
bus station   *estación de autobus*
bus stop   *parada de autobus*
butcher   *carnicería*

cake shop   *pastelería*
cathedral   *catedral*
church   *iglesia*
cigarette   *cigarrillo*
cigar   *puro*
city   *ciudad*
dry cleaner   *tintorería*
grocer   *pulpería*
supermarket   *supermercado*
harbor   *puerto*
lane or alley   *callejón*
market   *mercado*
mountain   *montaña*
pharmacy   *farmacia*

OPPOSITE: Outdoor markets display seasonal produce. ABOVE: Travelers and guides alike delight in spotting birds at Monteverde.

police station   *delegación*
post office   *oficina de correo*
restaurant   *restaurante*
river   *río*
street   *calle*
square   *manzana*
tourist office   *oficina de turismo*
viewpoint   *mirador*

On the Road
bus   *autobus*
super gas   *gasolina super*
regular gas   *gasolina regular*
fill it up   *lleno*
oil   *aceite*
pothole   *hueco*
diesel   *diesel*
water   *agua*
petrol station   *gasolinera*
tire   *llanta*
lights   *luces*
brakes   *frenos*
accident   *accidente*

Road Signs
detour   *desvio*
stop   *alto*
slow down   *despacio*
rock slides   *derrumbes*

Key Words and Phrases
yes   *sí*
no   *no*
none   *ningun(o)*
much, very, a lot (of)   *mucho/a*
please   *por favor*
thank you (very much)   *(muchas) gracias*
you're welcome   *de nada*
okay, fine, I agree   *está bien*
hello   *hola*
good morning   *buenos días*
good afternoon   *buenas tardes*
good evening/night   *buenas noches*
good-bye   *adios*
welcome   *bienvendios*
excuse me   *con permiso, desculpe*
get in line   *haga fila*
I'm sorry   *desculpe, lo siento*
see you later   *hasta luego*
see you soon   *hasta pronto*
well, good   *bien, bueno*
beautiful   *bello(a), hermoso(a)*
how?   *¿cómo?*

how are you?   *¿cómo está?*
how many?   *¿cuánto(a)s?*
what?   *¿qué?*
who?   *¿quién?*
why?   *¿por qué?*
where is?   *¿dónde está?*
how much is it?   *¿cuánto vale,*
   ¿cuánto cuesta?
I understand   *entiendo*
I don't understand   *no entiendo*
I don't know   *no sé*
can/may I...?   *¿puedo...?*
I would like   *quisiera*
do you have...?   *¿tiene...?*
do you sell...?   *¿hay...?*
I don't speak Spanish   *no hablo español*
do you speak English?   *¿Habla usted inglés?*
he/she/it is/you are   *está*
there is/are   *hay*
this/this one   *éste(a)*
that   *ese(a)*
here   *aquí*
there   *allá*
right there   *allí*
near   *cerca*
far   *lejos*
left   *izquierda*
right   *derecha*
straight on, straight ahead   *derecho*
hot   *caliente*
cold   *frío(a)*
big   *grande*
small   *pequeño(a)*
open   *abierto(a)*
closed   *cerrado(a)*
new   *nuevo(a)*
old   *viejo(a)*
cheap   *barato(a)*
expensive   *caro(a)*
money   *dinero*

In the Hotel
room   *habitación, cuarto*
single room   *habitación sencilla*
double room   *habitación doble*
with a double bed   *con cama matrimonial*
with a bathroom   *con baño*
without a bathroom   *sin baño*
shower   *ducha*
soap   *jabón*

The Scarlet Macaw is a rare and beautiful member of the parrot family.

towel   *toalla*
toilet paper   *papel higénico*
laundry   *lavandería*
key   *llave*
registration form   *papel de inscripción*

At the Post Office
stamp   *timbre*
letter   *carta*
postcard   *tarjeta postal*
parcel   *paquete*
air mail   *por avión*
general delivery, poste restante
   lista de correos

In Emergencies
doctor   *médico*
nurse   *enfermera*
sick, ill   *enfermo*
pain, ache   *dolor*
fever   *fiebre*
I am allergic to   *tengo alergia a*
I have a toothache   *tengo dolor de muela*
help   *ayuda*
I am diabetic   *soy diabética*

In Restaurants
breakfast   *desayuno*
lunch   *almuerzo*
tea   *té*
dinner   *cena*
menu   *menú*
fixed-price menu   *plato el día*
wine list   *lista de vinos*
bill, check   *cuenta*
glass   *vaso*
pepper   *pimienta*
salt   *sal*
sugar   *azúcar*
bread   *pan*
butter   *mantequilla*
sandwich   *emparedado*
mineral water   *agua mineral*
carbonated water   *agua con gas*
still water   *agua natural*
fruit juice   *jugo de fruta*
milk   *leche*
ice   *hielo*
coffee with milk   *café con leche*
beer   *cerveza*
red wine   *vino tinto*
white wine   *vino blanco*
rosé wine   *vino rosa*

cheese   *queso*
olives   *aceitunas*
salad   *ensalada*
green salad   *ensalada verde*
meat   *carne*
beef   *carne de res*
goat   *cabra*
ham   *jamón*
beans   *frijoles*
rice   *arroz*
hot sauce   *salsa picante*
beefsteak   *bistek, lomito*
rare   *poco hecho*
medium   *tres cuartos*
well done   *bien cocido, entero*
boiled   *hervido*
baked   *al horno*
grilled   *a la plancha*
smoked   *ahumado*
fish   *pescado*
crayfish   *langostina*
shrimp   *camarones*
clams   *almejas*
tuna   *atún*
lobster   *langosta*
sea bass   *corvina*
red snapper   *pargo colorado*
mahi mahi   *dorado*
swordfish   *pez espada*
crab   *jaiba*
octopus   *pulpo*
squid   *calamar*
vegetables   *repollo*
potatoes   *papas*
mushroom   *champiñón*
onion   *cebolla*
garlic   *ajo*
fruit   *fruta*
pineapple   *piña*
orange   *naranja*
watermelon   *sandía*
strawberry   *fresa*
blackberry   *mora*
dessert   *postre*
ice cream   *helado*
cake   *queque*
rice pudding   *arroz de leche*

Animals
agouti   *tepezcuintle* (in CR), *guatusa*
armadillo   *cusuco*
bat   *murciélago*
bird   *ave, pájaro*

butterfly *mariposa*
coati *pizote*
cougar, mountain lion *puma, león*
crocodile *cocodrilo*
deer *venado*
frog *rana*
howler monkey *mono congo*
jaguar *jaguar, tigre*
jaguarundi *león breñero*
kinkajou *martilla*
lesser anteater *oso hormiguero*
ocelot *manigordo*
opossum *zorro*
parrot *loro*
peccary *pecarí*
raccoon *mapache*
river otter *nutria*
scarlet macaw *lapa*
sloth *perezoso, perica*
snake *culebra, serpiente*
spider monkey *mono araña, mono colorado*
squirrel monkey *mono ardilla, mono tití*
tapir *danta*
toad *sapo*
turtle *tortuga*
white-faced capuchin monkey
  mono cara blanca

Numbers
1 *uno*
2 *dos*
3 *tres*
4 *cuatro*
5 *cinco*
6 *seis*
7 *siete*
8 *ocho*
9 *nueve*
10 *diez*
11 *once*
12 *doce*
13 *trece*
14 *catorce*
15 *quince*
16 *diez y seis*
17 *diecisiete*
18 *dieciocho*
19 *diecinueve*
20 *veinte*
21 *veintiuno*
30 *treinta*
40 *cuarenta*
50 *cincuenta*

60 *sesenta*
70 *setenta*
80 *ochenta*
90 *noventa*
100 *cien*
200 *doscientos*
500 *quinientos*
1,000 *mil*
2,000 *dos mil*
100,000 *cien mil*
1,000,000 *millón*
2,000,000 *dos millones*

Calendar
Sunday *domingo*
Monday *lunes*
Tuesday *martes*
Wednesday *miércoles*
Thursday *jueves*
Friday *viernes*
Saturday *sábado*
January *enero*
February *febrero*
March *marzo*
April *abril*
May *mayo*
June *junio*
July *julio*
August *agosto*
September *septiembre*
October *octubre*
November *noviembre*
December *diciembre*
spring *primavera*
summer *verano*
autumn *otoño*
winter *invierno*
day *día*
week *semana*
month *mes*
year *año*

Time
morning *mañana*
noon *mediodía*
afternoon, evening *tarde*
night *noche*
today *hoy*
yesterday *ayer*
tomorrow *mañana*
What time is it? *¿Qué hora es?*
now *ahora, ahorita*
later *más tarde*

Recommended Reading

AMERINGER, CHARLES D. *Democracy in Costa Rica,* New York: Praeger, 1982.

BAKER, BILL. *Essential Road Guide for Costa Rica,* San José: Editorial Incafo, 1992.

BIESANZ, RICHARD *et al. The Costa Ricans,* Englewood Cliffs, NJ: Prentice-Hall, 1987.

BOZA, MARIO AND A. BONILLA. *The National Parks of Costa Rica,* Madrid: INCAFO, 1981.

CAUFIELD, CATHERINE. *In the Rainforest,* United States: Knopf, 1984.

DEVRIES, PHILLIP J. *The Butterflies of Costa Rica and Their Natural History,* Princeton University Press, 1987.

DRESSLER, ROBERT L. *Field Guide to the Orchids of Costa Rica and Panama,* Ithaca, NY: Comstock Publishing, 1993.

EDELMAN, MARC AND JOANNE KENEN, eds. *The Costa Rican Reader,* New York: Grove Weidenfeld, 1988.

EMMONS, LOUISE H. *Neotropical Rainforest Mammals — A Field Guide,* Chicago: University of Chicago Press, 1990.

HALL, CAROLYN. *Costa Rica: A Geographical Interpretation in Historical Perspective,* Boulder, CO: Westview Press, 1985.

HATCHWELL, EMILY AND SIMON CALDER. *Travellers Central America Survival Kit,* England: Vacation Work, 1991.

HERRERA, WILBERTH. *Costa Rica Nature Atlas Guidebook,* San José: Editorial Incafo, 1992.

HOWARD, CHRIS. *The Golden Door to Retirement and Living in Costa Rica* (8th ed.), San José: Costa Rica Books, 1997.

LARA, SILVIA AND TOM BARRY. *Inside Costa Rica,* Albuquerque, NM: Resource Center Press, 1995.

MAYFIELD, MICHAEL W. AND RAFAEL E. GALLO. *The Rivers of Costa Rica: A Canoeing, Kayaking and Rafting Guide,* Birmingham, AL: Mensha Ridge Press, 1988.

PALMER, PAULA. *What Happen: A Folk History of the Talamanca Coast,* San José: Editorama, 1993.

PALMER, PAULA, JUANITA SANCHEZ AND GLORIA MAYORGA. *Taking Care of Sibos Gifts,* San José: Editorama, 1991.

PEREZ-BRIGNOLI, HECTOR. *A Brief History of Central America,* University of California Press, 1989.

PERRY, DONALD. *Life Above the Jungle Floor,* New York: Simon & Schuster, 1986.

PRITCHARD, AUDREY AND RAYMOND PRITCHARD. *Driving the Pan-Am Highway to Mexico and Central America,* Heredia: Costa Rica Books, 1997.

RAS, BARBRA, ed. *Costa Rica: A Traveler's Literary Companion,* San Francisco, CA: Where-abouts Press, 1994.

STEPHEN, JOHN LLOYD. *Incidents of Travel in Central America, Chiapas & Yucatan,* Rutgers University Press, 1949.

SKUTCH, ALEXANDER. *Nature through Tropical Windows,* Gainesville: University of California Press, 1983.

STILES, F. GARY AND ALEXANDER SKUTCH. *A Guide to the Birds of Costa Rica,* Ithaca, NY: Cornell University Press, 1989.

THEROUX, PAUL. *The Old Patagonian Express: By Train Through the Americas,* U.S. Pocket Books.

WALLACE, DAVID R. *The Quetzal and the Macaw: The Story of Costa Rica's National Parks,* San Francisco: Sierra Club Books, 1992.

Photo Credits

All photographs are by Nik Wheeler with the exception of those listed below:

Buddy Mays: pages 3, 4, 5 *(left and right),* 6 *(left and right),* 7 *(right),* 10, 11, 12, 13, 15, 16, 17, 20 24, 26, 31 *(top and bottom),* 34, 37, 48, 51, 52, 53, 58, 59, 60, 61, 64, 69, 71, 76, 81, 84, 86, 89, 94, 99, 100, 102, 103, 117, 138, 161 *(right),* 170, 172, 182, 186, 189, 192, 193, 194, 195, 198, 200, 202, 203, 205, 206, 208, 209, 210, 211, 212, 213, 214, 215, 216, 217, 221, 223, 225, 227, 228, 229, 231, 233, 235, 236, 239, 254, 255, 257.

Joseph P. Yogerst: pages 18, 19, 22, 32, 33 *(top),* 118–119, 93, 124, 133, 144 *(left and right),* 148, 151, 156, 165.

Maribeth Mellin: pages 96, 97, 98, 224, 237 *(top and bottom).*

Quick Reference A–Z Guide
to Places and Topics of Interest with Listed Accommodation, Restaurants and Useful Telephone Numbers